Bureaucracy vs. Democracy in the Minds of Bureaucrats

Major Concepts in Politics and Political Theory

Garrett Ward Sheldon
General Editor

Vol. 7

PETER LANG
New York • Washington, D.C./Baltimore • Boston
Bern • Frankfurt am Main • Berlin • Vienna • Paris

Sung-Don Hwang

Bureaucracy vs. Democracy in the Minds of Bureaucrats

To What Extent Are These Ideologies Compatible with One Another?

PETER LANG
New York • Washington, D.C./Baltimore • Boston
Bern • Frankfurt am Main • Berlin • Vienna • Paris

Library of Congress Cataloging-in-Publication Data

Hwang, Sung-Don.
Bureaucracy vs. democracy in the minds of bureaucrats: to what extent are these ideologies compatible with one another?/ Sung-Don Hwang.
p. cm. — (Major concepts in politics and political theory; vol. 7)
Includes bibliographical references and index.
1. Bureaucracy. 2. Democracy. 3. Ideology. I. Title. II. Series.
JF1411.H9 302.3'5—DC20 93-47405
ISBN 0-8204-2437-4
ISSN 1059-3535

Die Deutsche Bibliothek-CIP-Einheitsaufnahme

Hwang, Sung-Don:
Bureaucracy vs. democracy in the minds of bureaucrats: to what extent are these ideologies compatible with one another? / Sung-Don Hwang.
–New York; Washington, D.C./Baltimore; Boston; Bern; Frankfurt am Main; Berlin; Vienna; Paris: Lang.
(Major concepts in politics and political theory; Vol. 7)
ISBN 0-8204-2437-4

The paper in this book meets the guidelines for permanence and durability of the Committee on Production Guidelines for Book Longevity of the Council of Library Resources.

Printed in the United States of America

To my wife, daughters, and son.

Contents

Acknowledgments

Strictly speaking, it is hard to say that this is all my own work. Rather, it is more appropriate to say that this book is the product of joint efforts; that of myself as the major writer and that of many contributors. I would like to express deep appreciation to my advisor, Professor John Sullivan in the Department of Political Science at the University of Minnesota. He, as an instructor of methodology courses and as my PhD dissertation advisor, sharpened and safely guided my methodological tools which were dull and might otherwise have been used in a dangerous way. I also would like to express special thanks to Professor Virginia Gray, whose comments were helpful in smoothing the logical flow of my arguments. The warm support that she provided for me while I was pursuing my PhD degree was a source of energy in completing the program. Professor Charles Walcott, who taught me organization theories and who is now at Virginia Polytech, showed me that vast array of organizational perspectives on politics and bureaucracy. His substantive comments on my manuscript helped me clarify its theoretical and practical relevance and enrich the content which would have otherwise been overlooked. I also owe my book to the outside readers at the Hubert H. Humphrey Institute of Public Affairs at the University of Minnesota. Professor John Bryson's comments helped make this book understandable to ordinary readers. The attention of my disseration to the issue of ideological tensions between bureaucracy and democracy is heavily influenced by Professor Richard Bolan's lecture on the philosophy of planning and his comments.

Writing a book in a foreign language is painstaking, challenging, and at the same time, rewarding. Professor John Turner will never be forgotten. He did a superb job for me not only in making significant comments, but also in correcting my writing style. Ron Seiner and Barbara Cruikshank read the first draft and suggested very useful conceptual and editorial comments. I appreciate Susan McAvoy's correction of my English translation of the questionnaire items. I am very proud of establishing close friendships with these former classmates.

I would also like to extend special thanks to the staff members at Peter Lang Publishing, Inc. for their constant patience and understanding in helping me publish this manuscript. Without Jacqueline Pavlovic's cordial assistance, this book would not have been a reality. Thanks also to Lillian Won and Jenny Chang at Hankuk University of Foreign Studies in Seoul for their assistance in editing and formatting my manuscript.

My family and relatives also played important supportive roles. My mother and parents-in-law provided continuous encouragement and support since I started my studies in the United States. I would also like to express thanks with love to my wife, Hyang-Woo, daughters, Yoon-Ju and Yoon-Mi, and son, Hyun-Chan for their patience and full support. It is my sincere hope that this book is a small token of reward to them.

Sung-Don Hwang
Seoul, Korea

Chapter 1

Introduction

One of the perplexing problems in modern societies is the tension between bureaucracy and democracy. Democracy is a "must" for all members of modern societies. Bureaucracy, as the most efficient and effective means to manage humans and other forms of resources, has become another "must" for maintaining modern societies. The history of modern societies, however, has witnessed anti-democratic consequences of bureaucracy like a loss of individual freedom, unequal treatment of people, secrecy, alienation, and a superiority of bureaucracy over its political masters. A complete democratic control over bureaucracy is not only uneasy because strong and effective resistance from bureaucracy is expected, but also undesirable because it may block the positive contributions of bureaucracy (i.e., efficiency and effectiveness).

The thesis highlighted by this tension is the compatibility between bureaucracy and democracy.[1] The major questions addressed by this thesis are: "To what extent are bureaucratic organizational principles an efficient and effective means for accomplishing democratic ends?" "To what extent are bureaucratic ideals compatible or incompatible with democratic ideals?" "How can we make bureaucracy compatible with democracy?" These questions are important because examinations of these questions provide a crucial basis for theoretical and practical evaluations of the current prevalence of bureaucracy, as well as the efficacy of institutional practices of democracy. For example, if, in fact, bureaucracy and democracy are not compatible with one another, the current prevalence of bureaucracy indicates the failure of democratic control over bureaucracy even for those modern states that claim to be democratic. If this is the case, then it may be said that remedial actions for redirecting the bureaucratization trend occurring within most contemporary states are of crucial necessity.

Bureaucratic Dominance and the Thesis of Compatibility Between Bureaucracy and Democracy

A logical starting point of the debates on the thesis of the compatibility between bureaucracy and democracy is the acknowledgement of the prevalence of the bureaucratic mode of social arrangement as a *de facto* trend. Once this is clarified, we can then ask, "To what extent and in what ways does strong bureaucracy pose threats to democracy?" Max Weber's insights into bureaucratic domination in modern societies, as Aberbach, *et al.* (1981:1) acknowledge, are remarkably prescient. Despite earlier predictions of the upcoming death of bureaucracy (e.g., Marx, 1932 and 1984; Bennis, 1970b; and Toffler, 1970), bureaucracy is still with us and has become even more powerful and pervasive (cf., Etzioni-Halevy, 1985). Substantive empirical evidence for such bureaucratic prevalence in modern times has been extensively documented (e.g., Etzioni-Halevy, 1985:99-224). The prevalence of bureaucracy is now so universal that it is found to be the dominant mode of societal arrangement both in capitalist and communist countries.[2]

Such prevalence of bureaucracy may be effectively demonstrated by the convergence between the two schools of thought (i.e., the Marxian school and the non-Marxian school) in their earlier predictions about the destiny of bureaucracy and their later modifications. That is, in the earlier arguments of each school on the destiny of bureaucracy, bureaucracy was commonly predicted to wither away. In their later versions of predictions, however, they acknowledge the prevalence of bureaucracy. This convergence is interesting in that the radical differences between the two schools of thought in epistemology, ontology, and primary research subjects and objects suggest more of a divergence than a convergence. Let me review the change of predictions in the non-Marxian literature first.

Some non-Marxians have argued that by now bureaucracy has passed its peak. An increasing rate of change and a more uncertain environment have made bureaucratic structures obsolete. They are therefore about to give way to other, more flexible types of organization. Bennis (1968), for example, predicted the coming death of bureaucracy.[3] Just two years later, however, in another article entitled, "A Funny Thing Happened on the Way to the Future" (1970b), he substantially revised his previous forecast. More recently, many other non-Marxian scholars have pointed out the *de facto* strengthening power of bureaucracy based upon their observations of various aspects of the recent development of bureaucracy (e.g., Beetham, 1987; Etzioni-Halevy, 1985; Rourke, 1978; Wynia, 1974; proponents and followers of "new public administration" like Frederickson, 1980, and the authors edited in Marini, 1971 and Waldo, 1971; Harmon and Mayer, 1986; Beckwith, 1972; Medeiros and Schmitt, 1977; the authors edited in Griffith, 1976; the authors who emphasize the significant role played by bureaucracy in policy processes like Ripley and Franklin, 1976, 1982;

Morris, 1985; Peters, 1984; Meier, 1987; Rourke, 1976; Pressman and Wildavsky, 1973; Radin, 1977; Bardach, 1977; Elmore. 9178; Aberbach. *et al.*, 1981; Fischer and Sirianni, 1984; Fainstein and Fainstein, 1980; and Dannhauser, 1980).[4]

The Marxian literature on state theory, which is based upon a different analytic framework focusing on different aspects of the phenomena than the non-Marxian literature, shows a similar change in predictions and modifications about the destiny of bureaucracy. In the classical Marxian literature on the state (Marx, 1984), bureaucracy was conceptualized as "a state apparatus," and the state was conceived of as an entity which was "necessarily" created to enhance the interests of the capitalist class. Classical Marxians predicted that capitalism will "incurably" collapse because of its "self-contradictions" which are intrinsic in the "capitalist mode of production" logic. The state, hence bureaucracy as part of the state, was predicted in the classical Marxian literature to wither away as capitalism comes to collapse. This prediction has two important consequences for the classical Marxian tradition. First, the state and bureaucracy cannot be said to have the status of a primary research subject. Second, even the "revolution by the working class" might be said to be not a mandatory, but merely a necessary action by which the working class can shorten the dying period of capitalism, the state, and bureaucracy, and thus accelerate the historical process toward realization of the classless communist society. Many neo-Marxians, however, have modified this classical Marxian prediction quite substantially.[5] Their modifications are based upon their acknowledgement of the significant role played by the state in the historical experiences of "late capitalism" and "post-revolutionary socialism." Therborn (1977:3), for example, argues that "the bitter experiences of fascism and Stalinism and the enduring legacy of the latter, have taught the firmest revolutionary opponents of capitalism that capitalism cannot be dismissed as a mere sham." One of the major reasons for the neo-Marxian modification of the classical Marxian prediction lies in neo-Marxists' notion of the "relative autonomy" of the state (Miliband, 1973; Offe, 1974, 1972; Poulantzas, 1989, 1975; Mandel, 1975; Carnoy, 1984; Therborn, 1978; Jessop, 1977, 1978, 1979, 1982; Heyderbrand, 1977; Althusser, 1970; Lukacs, 1971; Nordlinger, 1981; O'Connor, 1973). From this point of view, it can be said that the state and the bureaucracy are not merely a passive entity functioning as a means for the capitalist class, but a relatively autonomous entity having a "necessary symbiotic relationship" with the capitalist class. That is, bureaucracy promotes the interests of the capitalist class, while simultaneously promoting its own interests (e.g., materialistic power-building). It promotes capitalist interests on both political and economic sides. On the political side, it promotes the capitalist interest through the mechanism of the so-called "bourgeois democracy." On the economic side, it does so through varieties of economic policy interventions into the "capitalist mode of production."[6]

As this process of the state's promotion of the interests of capitalist class continues, capitalists are to be more dependent on the state, and the state thus can accumulate its relatively autonomous power to a substantial degree. Moreover, the fact that parliament's previous power over the bureaucracy has been curtailed and that its previous power of enacting rules and making political decisions has shifted to the bureaucracy have led the bureaucracy to be a *de facto* dominant state apparatus (Miliband, 1973; Offe, 1972; Poulantzas, 1978).

In sum, in spite of the well-known sharp differences in their ontology, epistemology, and primary research subjects and objects, the two schools of thought, Marxian and non-Marxian, are converging in such a way that their earlier predictions of bureaucracy's death are now commonly replaced by their acknowledgement of its prevalence. Indeed, this congruence between the two schools of thought is consistent with various empirical findings which tell us that bureaucracy is still very much with us, and that it has become even more pervasive in recent years.

Combined with the anti-democratic consequences of bureaucracy, this trend toward predominance of bureaucracy has signified the normative expectation that bureaucracy and bureaucrats ought to be compatible with democracy by being an efficient and effective means for accomplishing democratic ideals. Unfortunately, however, many empirical studies of the actual operation of bureaucracy and the behaviors of bureaucrats have suggested that this ideal is not met. In the field of Public Administration,[7] for example, a common criticism of the phenomenon of bureaucratization is that "the key decisions in modern nation-states are not made by the citizens or even by the officials they can sanction, but by bureaucrats who, as agents within a governmental institution are at least two or three steps removed from anyone the citizens elect" (Kranz, 1976:31). Given this fact, there is no *a priori* reason to believe that they are "accountable," "responsible," and "responsive" to their political masters.

Given the *de facto* predominance of bureaucracy, the important issue is not whether bureaucracy is really necessary. As Perrow (1979) emphasizes, bureaucracy is still the most efficient way to get society's business done. Nor is the issue, how to kill it. As Parkinson's Law (Parkinson, 1957) indicates, its immorality has already been widely accepted as a simple fact. Instead, the issue comes down to how to make bureaucracy conducive to democracy (i.e., its ability to get things done efficiently and effectively), or to put it in Strauss' (1961:284) terms, "how to tame (not kill) it effectively."

Objectivism vs. Subjectivism

The idea of objectivism has long been sustained for its pragmatic virtues since

Skinner attempted to apply it to the management of human beings.[8] The idea of objectivism constitutes the core of the so-called Durkheimian contention that the subjective aspects of social life are an "apparently manageable residue," and the justification of the Durkheimian position [i.e., "in order to avoid being misled by any non-objective 'preconceptions'" (Durkheim, 1964)]. It has been deeply embedded also in classical Marxist "historical materialism" where the elements of superstructure (such as religion, culture, ideology, symbols, ascetics, and individual's consciousness, values, and attitudes) are totally determined by the states of elements of the base structure (forces and relations of production); thus, the superstructural phenomena are the secondary subjects of study (e.g., Marx, 1932; Jakubouski, 1936, Lenin, 1975).

Objectivism, however, has been seriously challenged by the culturalist school of thought. The Skinnerian idea of objectivism (i.e., "operant conditioning"), especially the attempt to apply the idea to the management of human beings, has been challenged on normative and epistemological grounds. The major thrust of the criticism is that it is not only unethical, but also undemocratic. The freedom of individual human beings is denied when they are treated as the objects to be controlled. The core of the epistemological criticisms of the Skinnerian notion of "operant conditioning" is that humans are not passive before the external structural and institutional conditions as Skinner and his followers presume; rather, they are active agents who can determine the specific manifestations of the structural and institutional conditions in reality.

Regarding the Durkheimian contention and its justification, Levi-Strauss (1967:43) argues that "for fear of being misled," the objectivists are "compelled in advance to leave out of consideration all...nuances, details, and even values"; and thus the "overly subjective" aspects of social life are evaporated by the objectivists. The objectivist conception of the subjective aspects of social life as "apparently manageable residue" is dismissed by Turner (1983). According to him, "the appearance of manageability is deceiving since it is like excluding pieces of a child's puzzle: by giving the child only some of the pieces of the puzzle, we do not simplify his or her task, but make it impossible" (Turner, 1983:192). In a similar vein, White and McSwain (1983:304) argue that "a social science, especially one that puts its attention on the intimate world of organizational life, must be integrative in that it is a science that must comprehend and build on folk wisdom, religious and mystical knowledge, and immediate experience, as much as it does on the abstractions of [the structural entities]."

The classical Marxist contention has also been severely criticized and modified by such theorists as Pondy and Mitroff (1979), Berger and Luckmann (1966), Holzner (1968), Geertz (1964), Wuthnow, *et al.* (1984), Wuthnow (1985), D'Andrade (1984), Gramsci (1971),[9] Amariglio, *et al.* (1988), Hall (1988, 1982), Levine (1984), Spiro (1984), and Sahlins (1976). The core of these authors' arguments is the notion of "relative autonomy of the subjective dimension." That is, the subjective dimension is never a residue of secondary importance remaining after appreciating the objective structural dimension. It is not unidirectionally preselected by the structural dimension. Rather, the subjective and structural dimensions mutually limit each other's possible range of manifestation with an allowance of considerable autonomous variation. Regarding the relationship between structure and culture, a subjective phenomenon, Amariglio, *et al.* (1989), for example, argue:

> We cannot explain culture as the result of a single, determining social process. We cannot base our notion of culture on a single, discursively priveleged concept. [Culture] is the result of [overdeterminations] made both by political and economic forces, including class processes and the ordering of social behavior (p.487). [S]truggle over particular processes overdetermine class struggles. Likewise, struggles over the performance, appropriation, and distribution of surplus labor overdetermine these cultural processes. By not reducing culture to power or class, or reducing class to power or culture, we (can retain) the specificity of diverse social processes while showing that a more thorough understanding of one's specificity can be achieved by using a model of overdetermination to examine the intereffectivity of these processes (pp.498-499).

In a similar vein, Wuthnow (1985:3), who understands the cultural factors as "a behavioral phenomenon, or more precisely, as an analytic aspect of behavior," argues that "culture is neither reducible to more concrete forms of social structure nor comprised of subjective meanings." Similarly, Gramsci, who conceived of culture in his earlier writing as "disciplining of one's inner self," "appropriation of one's own personality," and "a superior consciousness whereby it becomes possible to understand one's own historical value, function in life, rights, and duties," argued in his later writings that the cultural dimension itself is "an arena of class struggle" (Adamson, 1980:31). Hall (1982:79-81) presents a similar viewpoint that contemporary class struggles are centered on the meanings and access the very means of "signification."

These criticisms of operant objectivism, as Swidler (1986) observes, have been followed by the recent resurgence of cultural studies in many fields. For example, since the late 1970s, the field of organization theory has witnessed a number of attempts to apply the cultural paradigm to the study of organizations (e.g., Donnellon, *et al.*, 1986; Morgan, 1986, 1984, 1983, 1980; Burrell and Morgan, 1979; Frost, *et al.*, 1985; Fine, 1984; Smircich, 1983a,b; Barley, 1983; Riley, 1983; Wilkins and Ouchi, 1983; Broms and Gahmberg, 1983; Gregory, 1983; Jelinek, *et al.*, 1983; White and McSwain,

1983; Heyderbrand, 1983; Forester, 1983; Turner, 1983; Ettlie and O'Keefe, 1982; Watson, 1982; Bhagat and McQuaid, 1982; Calder and Schurr, 1981; Pfeffer, 1981a, b; Bellone and Nigro, 1980; Sarbin and Scheibe, 1980; Pettigrew, 1979). This trend is also found in the field of business management where operant objectivism has been the most prevalent. Maclagan (1983), for example, argues that management theory, which defines employee responsibilities in purely objective and formal terms, must be replaced with subjectivist management theory which defines the responsibilities as a subjective belief held by employees regarding their role and obligations in relation to specific events.

The Study of the Subjective Dimension of the Compatibility Thesis: Major Research Questions and Significance

Many authors have examined the compatibility thesis from diverse angles, highlighting its normative and practical importance. Most intensively and extensively explored by most of these previous authors is the objective dimension of the compatibility thesis. Implicit in most of the previous studies of the compatibility thesis is the presumption of "objectivism." That is, they have put most of their energy into devising effective institutional structures which, they believe, make bureaucracy compatible with democracy. A tacit presumption underlying the focus of these authors is that whether bureaucracy can be compatible with democracy hinges on how the objective institutional structures are designed and arranged, and how effectively they are imposed on bureaucrats.[10] The major thrusts of objectivism in the debates about the compatibility thesis can be summarized as follows:

Institutional structures devised for making bureaucracy compatible with democracy exist outside of individual bureaucrats, and are thus presumed to be *externally* given to the individual bureaucrats. Individual bureaucrats are presumed to behave in a particular way, being conditioned, and thus manipulated, by the externally imposed institutional structures.

What is generally ignored in these attempts, however, is the possibility that the compatibility between bureaucracy and democracy at the institutional level (called hereafter "institutional compatibility") does not automatically guarantee actual democratization of bureaucracy. The literature of the subjective approach, reviewed in the previous section, has accumulated ample evidence supporting this possibility. The major intellectual heritage of this approach is that the compatibility between bureaucracy and democracy reflected within the minds of bureaucrats (called hereafter "subjective compatibility") might be significantly different from compatibility at the institutional level. If subjective compatibility is not fully attained, then institutional compatibility remains ineffective and unstable.

In line with this subjective approach, I decided to explore another dimension of the compatibility thesis which I shall call the subjective dimension. In contrast with this study of the compatibility thesis focusing on the objective dimension, my study stresses the subjective connotation of bureaucracy and democracy, stressed in three aspects. First, this stress is reflected in my understanding of the terms bureaucracy and democracy. They are understood not as *objective* forms of institutional structures themselves, but as forms of "ideologies." That is, bureaucracy and democracy are defined as coherent sets of ideals and instrumental principles that guide the operation of the *objective* structures of organizations, governmental institutions, and other forms of social institutions. For example, the major concern of my study is not the institutional structures of the administrative agencies within the executive branch of government. Rather, it is on such bureaucratic and democratic ideals as efficiency, effectiveness, instrumental rationalism, individual freedom, equality among people, openness to the public, etc. and such bureaucratic and democratic instrumental principles as hierarchical control, unity of command, self-directed task performance, participative decision-making, etc.[11]

Second, the emphasis upon the subjective connotations of bureaucracy and democracy is also reflected in my research questions themselves. That is, what I will examine are not the objective behaviors of bureaucrats, but their value orientations about bureaucratic and democratic ideologies. More specifically, the major research questions are such descriptive ones as "What do bureaucrats think of democratic ideology?" and "To what extent do these bureaucrats regard bureaucratic and democratic ideologies as compatible or incompatible with one another?" and such explanatory research themes as "Why do some bureaucrats more or less internalize these ideologies rather than others?" and "Why do individual bureaucrats perceive these ideologies as compatible or incompatible with one another?"

Third, the operational definition of the "compatibility between bureaucratic and democratic ideologies" to be used in my research also stresses subjectivity. As will be discussed in more detail in Chapter Five, it is defined in two ways depending on the methodological framework that I employ. On the one hand, it is defined as the extent to which one's internalization of bureaucratic ideology is associated with his/her internalization of democratic ideology. This definition is employed especially in the R-methodological analysis. On the other hand, it is defined as the extent to which one evaluates conceptual components of bureaucratic ideology as "democratic." This definition is employed especially in the Q-methodological analysis.[12]

The significance of studying the subjective dimension of the compatibility thesis can be established on many grounds. As reviewed earlier, the culturalists' critiques of objectivism suggest that inquiry into the objective dimension of the compatibility thesis is not sufficient for finding complete scientific "truths." What is at least equally important for this purpose is the exploration of the subjective dimension of the compatibility thesis. The importance of studying the subjective dimension of the compatibility thesis may also be demonstrated in the context of democratic reform of bureaucracy. It is a widely shared idea that both bureaucracy and democracy are not mono-faceted but multi-faceted concepts. Examinations of the subjective dimension of the compatibility thesis (especially the descriptive research questions) will clarify what kinds of conceptual components of democratic ideologies are salient to bureaucrats. It will also illuminate what are perceived as compatible or incompatible with one another, and how much variation exists among individuals or groups in the internalization of these ideologies. The result of this examination may be useful in determining what kinds of bureaucratic and democratic ideologies should be emphasized and who should be targeted by the reform.

Gruber's (1987) discussion of the costs associated with the attempt to control bureaucrats highlights another interesting contribution of the study. Her discussion suggests that examinations of the descriptive research themes will show what kinds of democratic ideologies are more or less agreeable to bureaucrats and more or less likely to attenuate bureaucratic ideology.[13] Studies of this type may thus provide useful strategic information to those who wish to develop a package of democratic reform with the least effectiveness and implementation costs.

One might argue against the study of the subjective dimension of the compatibility thesis on the ground that what bureaucrats think is one thing and how they behave is another. In general, the link between an individual's belief and behavior is inevitably problematic.[14] However, there is ample evidence of impressive consistency between them for professional elites like bureaucrats.[15] Consistency theory suggests that the study may have considerable *potential* to provide useful information by which to make the actual behavior of bureaucrats consistent with democratic ideology.

The other major research questions that I address as a way of exploring the subjective dimension of the compatibility thesis also highlights the study's practical significance. Examination of the explanatory themes will clarify which factors explain variation in the level of individual bureaucrats' internalization of bureaucratic and democratic ideologies, and in the degree to which they regard these ideologies as compatible with one another. The result of this analysis will enable the reformer to determine which means will be effective for democratic control of bureaucracy.

Finally, the significance of the study also lies in the fact that it can directly check the validity of the presumptions of existing debates about the compatibility thesis. Much of the debate about compatibility in the field of organization theory, for example, has been divergent due to different presumptions about work-related human nature (e.g., "Theory X"-type versus "Theory Y"-type).

State of Existing Research on the Subjective Dimension of the Compatibility Thesis and Research Tasks to be Undertaken

Thus far, I have addressed the major research questions highlighted in exploring the subjective dimension of the compatibility thesis. I have discussed their significance in relation with the objective approach to the compatibility thesis. In this section, I will discuss several research tasks that I will undertake as a way of overcoming several deficiencies of existing studies on the subjective dimension of the compatibility thesis.

Recently, several authors have explored the subjective dimension of the compatibility thesis. For example, based upon interviews with 39 public officials working in an American city, Gruber (1987) examines bureaucrats' own perspectives about democratic control of bureaucracy that are externally imposed on the bureaucrats, and their consequences on the cost of control. She found that bureaucrats have quite effective skills to resist democratic control whenever the control conflicts with their interests and value systems.

Aberach, *et al.* (1981) perform quite extensive and intensive inter-country comparative research on the attitudes of individual bureaucrats (and politicians) in several Western countries. They focus on attitudes towards roles (i.e., technocrats vs. politicians; governance vs. politics) in relation to several types of democratic ideologies (e.g., liberal vs. conservative; pluralist vs. populist vs. democrat). One of their major findings is that there are differences between bureaucrats and politicians in their ideological traits. Another important finding is that there are wide variations among countries in patterns of differences.

Hwang (1981) studied the attitudes of individual bureaucrats working in the Seoul city government in Korea toward "efficiency-effectiveness" and "democratic*ness*." A major finding of this study is that the attitudes of bureaucrats toward "efficiency-effectiveness" are negatively correlated with those toward "democratic*ness*." Another important finding of this study is that organizational traits of bureaucrats are significant determinants of their attitudes.

Rinehart and Bernick (1975) examined the attitudes of U.S. federal bureaucrats toward political participation. They focused on such issues as the extent to which individual bureaucrats participate in political activities beyond the limits prescribed by the law. The relevance of this study to my research is especially the independent variables that they found as significant determinants of bureaucrats' psychological commitment to political participation. The significant determinants they found include age, education, and types of agencies.

Presthus (1975) surveyed the attitudes of higher civil servants and legislators working in the federal and state levels of governments in the United States. He concentrated on their attitudes toward political and economic liberalism, and compared them with their Canadian counterparts. He found that there were significant differences between American and Canadian public officials in the extent to which they have favorable attitudes toward political and economic liberalism, and toward the relationship between political and economic liberalism. He ascribed the major reason for these differences to political and institutional public administrative differences between the U.S. and Canada.

Wynia (1974) examined American federal bureaucrats' attitudes toward democratic ideology as specified by McClosky (1964). He found wide variations among bureaucrats in the extent to which they had favorable attitudes toward democratic ideology. He also found that the variations result from age, educational level, years of service, and the types of agencies.[16]

These authors' research serve as a source for working hypotheses and provide useful insights for exploring the subjective dimension of the compatibility thesis. Most of their research, however, is incomplete in several aspects. My study is aimed at supplementing the following deficiencies of existing studies in the subjective dimension of the compatibility thesis.

First, most of these authors (except Hwang, 1981) investigate the individual bureaucrats' internalization of democratic ideology alone, without relating it to his or her internalization of bureaucratic ideology. Their implicit rationale is that if a large number of individual bureaucrats show a high level of internalization of democratic ideology, then this indicates the compatibility between bureaucracy and democracy, and *vice versa*. The problem of this rationale is that it is inappropriate for assessing the direct relationship between bureaucratic and democratic *ideologies*. As Hall's (1963) empirical findings suggest, there may be a substantial amount of variation among individual bureaucrats in their internalization of bureaucratic ideology. That is, his findings indicate that those who show a high level of internalization of democratic ideology might have a low level of internalization of bureaucratic ideology. If this is the case, then the existence of a large number of bureaucrats holding a high level of democratic belief does not necessarily indicate that bureaucratic ideology is regarded as compatible with democratic ideology within the minds of bureaucrats. Rather, it may indicate that a government operated by these bureaucrats would sacrifice the goal of effective and efficient management of governmental affairs. Hall's findings suggest that the relevance of these studies to the compatibility thesis is limited to a special case in which those with a high level of internalization of democratic ideology also have a high level of internalization of bureaucratic ideology. This is problematic, not only from a scientific viewpoint, but also from a practical concern. In order to supplement the deficiency of previous studies in this vein, I will investigate not only the extent to which bureaucrats internalize democratic ideology, but also how their internalization of bureaucratic ideology is interrelated with their internalization of democratic ideology.

Second, most of the previous studies of bureaucratics' beliefs about democratic ideology are also deficient from a methodological perspective. In measuring bureaucrats' attitudes toward democratic ideology, most of these authors follow the conventional measurement practice, which is often called "R-methodology." That is, before they measure individual bureaucrats' attitudes, they construct several conceptual components of democratic ideology which the researchers, not the respondents, regard as democratic. They develop certain forms of scales associated with their own conceptions of democratic ideologies, and then measure the degree of individual bureaucrats' internalization of this ideology. This is done by the extent to which the respondent accepts or rejects the scale items. Finally, they conclude that a respondent is highly democratic if his or her response score associated with a certain scale item(s) is high. A problem with this approach is that the respondents are not allowed to define democratic ideology. An unsatisfactory consequence is that, as the proponents of Q-methodology (e.g., Brown, 1980; McKeown and Thomas, 1988) maintain, their findings may be artifacts of the researcher's own conception of democratic ideology, which might be significantly different from that of the respondents' own understanding. The respondents may answer each ideology scale item without linking them to the particular conceptual components which the researchers think of as democratic. Instead, they may respond to the scale items by linking them to other things that are irrelevant to the researchers' notions of democratic ideology. If this is the case, then interpreting high (or low) response scores as a high (or low) level of the respondent's internalization of democratic ideology approaches the realm of arbitrary judgment. Another problematic consequence is that the R-methodological approach is only one perspective; that is a researcher's own conception of democratic ideology. Considering these pitfalls of R-methodology, I will examine bureaucrats' beliefs about democratic ideology using Q-methodology. In addition, I will examine the issue of subjective compatibility using both R- and Q-methodologies, and scrutinize the extent to which the methodological differences produce substantively different conclusions.

Finally, another unpersuasive point is found in the previous authors' explanations of the differences and similarities among the respondents in their internalization of the ideologies studied. Most of their explanations are partial and unsystematic. They are partial in that they explain the variations mostly in terms of "hard," objective factors[17] which are relatively easy to measure, while neglecting "soft," subjective factors. However, a vast literature, including culturalists' criticisms of objectivism, suggests that in explaining individual bureaucrats' internalization of bureaucratic and democratic ideologies, "soft," subjective factors are at least as important as these "hard," objective factors. For example, a careful examination of the basic reasoning behind existing theoretical and normative debates about the compatibility thesis (reviewed later) suggests that it is highly likely that the extent to which individual bureaucrats internalize bureaucratic and democratic ideologies would be significantly affected by such psychological traits of these bureaucrats as their own understandings of work-related human nature (e.g., "Theory X"-type vs. "Theory Y"-type). The literature of inter-country comparative studies has accumulated ample evidence suggesting that cultural factors like religion, perspectives on human nature, and other cultural categories are relevant to explaining people's internalization of bureaucratic and democratic ideologies.[18]

Most of the previous authors' explanations are also unsystematic in that they examine the explanatory variables mainly in a discrete fashion.[19] That is, they examine individual explanatory variables without relating them to each other. Methodologically, this means that they perform a series of simple bivariate analyses, their models suffer from specification error, and they fail to discern the direct impact of explanatory variables on dependent variables. Subsequently, this means that they do not provide strategically useful information in choosing more effective means by which to make bureaucracy compatible with democracy. This is because they cannot tell which variables are more or less powerful than others in explaining the variations of respondents' internalization of bureaucratic and democratic ideologies. In order to alleviate these deficiencies of previous explanations, my study will be constructed especially to discern the direct impact of the conventional objective independent variables and the subjective cultural variables. I will try to clarify the explanatory power of these variables.[20]

In sum, my research is aimed at exploring the subjective dimension of the compatibility thesis by examining (1) the extent to which the diverse conceptual components and types of democratic ideology that are discussed in the theoretical literature are actually regarded as democratic by bureaucrats, (2) the extent to which diverse conceptual components and types of bureaucratic ideology are conceived as compatible or incompatible with those of democratic ideology, and (3) what kinds of factors affect bureaucrats' internalization of bureaucratic and democratic ideologies and the degree of subjective compatibility.

NOTES

1 For brevity, I will hereafter call this thesis "the compatibility thesis."

2 For the prevalence of bureaucracy both in capitalist and communist countries, see Urban (1978), Hegedus (1976), Mullet (1970), and Mouzelis (1967, especially Chapter One). For the prevalence of bureaucracy at the systemic level, see Etzioni-Halevy (1985, especially Chapters Eight and Ten) and Bolan (1987); for the institutional level, see Waldo (1948, 1984), and Bolan (1987); for the organizational level, see Harmon and Mayer (1986) and Blau (1956); and for the individual level, see Chackerian and Abcarian (1984), and White (1956).

3 See also Bennis and Slator (1968) and Toffler (1970).

4 Some exceptions are found in recent sociological literature. Starbuck (1983:91) still makes a prediction which is quite similar to Bennis' earlier prediction. He argues that, "because organizations modify their behavior programs mainly in small increments that make sense to top managers, they change too little and inappropriately, and nearly all organizations disappear within a few years." The notions of "governmental overload" and "ungovernability" presented by the pluralists (e.g., Bell, 1975; Crozier, *et al.*, 1975; King, 1975; Rose, 1979; Wildavsky, 1973; Lindblom, 1979) are based upon similar presumptions about the power of bureaucracy. The major thrust of their presumptions is that an agency in the bureaucracy may be "still muddling, not yet through" because the power of bureaucracy is to be weakened due to a combination of increasing demands on governments from various interest groups whose interests are frequently conflicting with each other, governments' increasing ability to cope with such conflicting demands, and the civic indifference to and distrust of bureaucracy led by such inabilities of bureaucracy.

5 Some of the neo-Marxists still argue the declining power of bureaucracy quite similar to the pluralists' notions of "ungovernability" and "governmental overload." Wolfe (1977:270-271) for example, argues:

> The class struggle and the political process decided who got what. In later capitalism, the administration performs this function. But the formal ideology of bureaucracy is that it is non-political, conflict free and concerned only with administrative rationality. Caught between its politicized tasks and its depoliticized rationale, public adminstration in late capitalism searches

> for answers to its intractable task wherever it can find them, only to discover that each possible option causes as many problems as its solves. The public administration of late capitalism becomes weaker the stronger it appears to be, a contradiction ultimately caused by the gap between its political requirements and its administrative ideology.

6 For example, on the political side, the state promotes the interests of the capitalist class by setting the rules of the game, so-called "bourgeois democracy," which seems to be unconducive to the interest of the capitalist class, but is actually conducive to it. Offe (1974) argued that bourgeois democracy, which is represented by free elections and universal suffrage, has been managed to practice its class character and keep it concealed at the same time. Similarly, Therborn (1978) argues that bourgeois democracy is but the rule of the bourgeoisie through the instruments of free elections and universal suffrage in that the popular vote advances the bourgeoisie's central aims, integrating all social layers into the political framework of the state without giving up any of their actual power. On the economic side, the state also promotes the interests of the capitalist class by directly and indirectly intervening in the capitalist mode of economic production. The state's intervention seems to the classical Marxians quite unconducive to the logic of the capitalist mode of production-free market system. Some neo-Marxians, however, argue that it is in fact, quite conducive in that it can provide a strong material basis for the capitalist class through its economic policies for accumulating the "surplus value" of capital and labor (Jessop, 1982) and through those for preventing or delaying the "falling rate of return" which was assumed by classical Marxians to be an incurable tendency of capitalist mode of economic production (Harvey, 1982).

7 When I want to designate public administration as an academic field, I will use the term "Public Administration," while I will use the term "public administration" for designating public administration as a practice.

8 For Skinner's attempts to apply the idea of operant conditioning to the management of human beings, see Skinner (1975), Watts (1975), Stillman (1975), and Dowling (1977).

9 For Gramsci's conception of culture and a critique of the Marxian conception of culture, see also Adamson (1980), Nemeth (1980), and Clark (1977).

10 This kind of presumption is widely shared by previous authors regardless of

whether they accept or reject the compatibility between bureaucracy and democracy. In field of organization theory, for example, all of the prescriptions proposed by the proponents of the pro-compatibility argument (e.g., Taylor's "3 S's": simplification, standardization, and specialization of work procedures; Olson's selective economic incentive system and coercion; and Simon's hierarchical organizational decision-making structure) are focused upon the institutional structures within organizations. They believe that these prescriptions will make bureaucracy, defined as a large, complex organization, compatible with democratic ideals by preventing individuals from being trapped by intrinsic defects in human nature (e.g., "systematic soldiering" stemming from the individual's "natural laziness" for Taylor; difficulty in producing collective goods due to the "free-rider problem" inevitably resulting from the individual's rational self-interestedness for Olson; the inability to make rational decisions due to the intrinsic "boundedness of individual human rationality" for Simon). The "democratic" organizational principles proposed by the Human Relations School as counter arguments against the aforementioned classical organization theorists' prescriptions (e.g., McGregor's Theory Y managerial scheme; Herzberg's Two-Factor theory of motivation; and Likert's participative management) are all based upon the same belief that formal change in organizational structures is a precondition for the fulfillment of the democratic ethos they emphasize. Both the classical and neo-classical Public Administration theorists' ideas (e.g., "spoils system," "merit system," "economic incentive system," diverse principles of "scientific" administration, and internal and external control of bureaucracy) and the ideas of New Public Administration theorists (e.g., internal and external, "participative administration") are all based upon the presumption that changes in law, objective incentive schedules, the power structures among various governmental institutions, or organizational decision-making structures within public administrative agencies will result in the behavioral changes of public administrators. The same holds true for the many arguments presented in the state theory literature (e.g., the pluralist school's belief in the efficacy of plural composition of societal and governmental structures in taming the power of bureaucracy; the elitist school's emphasis upon the objective analysis of power structure; classical Marxists' emphasis on the changes in economic "base structures" prior to the changes in "super-structure;" and the corporatist school's belief that governmental laws should be enacted to enable the working class to participate in the governmental policy-making process.)

11 For more detailed definitions of bureaucratic and democratic ideologies used in my study, see Chapter Four.

12 For explanations of what R- and Q-methodologies are, see Chapter Five.

13 Gruber (1987:24, 149-190) stresses that "bureaucracies are not abstract administrative structures but agencies filled with real people with their own interests and with considerable resources to resist (outside control) when they do not mesh with those interests." She then convincingly shows, with firsthand empirical data, that a bureaucrat's subjective attitudes toward democratic controls operate as "perceptual filters," which determine the magnitude of costs associated with democratic controls. The costs she identifies are of two types: "effectiveness cost" and "enforcement cost." By effectiveness cost, she means the cost that is incurred when democratic control is accompanied by the demise of the very virtue of bureaucracy (i.e., efficiency and effectiveness in task performance). The enforcement cost, according to Gruber, is incurred when democratic control requires maintaining a monitoring system by which to check whether or not to punish the bureaucrat who seems not to behave as the controller desires. According to Gruber, the enforcement cost is highly likely to increase whenever democratic control is aimed at imposing constraints that are not agreeable to bureaucrats, since they, in most cases, possess adroit ability and ample resources to resist such constraints.

14 For an overview of the controversy about this link, see LaPier (1935) and Rokeach (1966-1967).

15 See, for example, Searing (1978) and Aberbach, *et al.* (1981:especially 30-32). For a general overview of consistency theory, see Fishbein (1967: especially Part Three).

16 Witte's (1980) research on the attitudes of workers and managers in a private firm toward participation provides many suggestive hypotheses to those who wish to study the compatibility thesis focusing especially on government officials.

17 The objective factors which have received most of these previous authors' attention are, for example, (1) individual bureaucrats' socio-economic status, such as age, income, sex, educational level, etc.; (2) such organizational traits of the individual bureaucrat as functional characteristics of their tasks (e.g., "client-oriented" vs. "organization-oriented," "programmed" vs. "non-programmed," and "line" vs. "staff"), their hierarchical positions, etc.; (3) such organizational and institutional characteristics of the agencies to which the individual bureaucrats belong as types of major policies that the agency deals with and hierarchical position of the agency

in relation to other agencies; and (4) early-childhood as well as in-career socialization factors like "democratic" vs. "authoritarian" family relationships, characteristics of major residential areas (e.g., urban vs. rural), characteristics of the job possessed by the person who most influenced the subject (e.g., entrepreneurial vs. managerial vs. working class), the length of their bureaucratic careers, etc.

18 For the cross-cultural analysis of bureaucratic ideologies, see Riggs (1968, 1970). For the cross-cultural analysis of democratic ideologies, see Lipset (1963), Almond and Verba (1962, 1980), and Szalay and Kelly (1982).

19 A prototypical example is Wynia (1974).

20 See Chapter Five for a detailed description of the independent variables to be considered.

Part I

The Debates

A review of previous debates about the compatibility thesis reveals that different authors arrive at different conclusions about the relationship between bureaucratic and democratic ideologies by juxtaposing different aspects of bureaucracy within different kinds of democratic ideologies. This is found both within and across many fields (e.g., sociology of organization, management science, Public Administration, political science, etc.). This suggests that there are many kinds of bureaucratic and democratic ideologies, and accordingly, many sub-relationships between these ideologies that are relevant to the study of the subjective dimension of the compatibility thesis. Given the limited resources available, however, all kinds of bureaucratic and democratic ideologies addressed in all fields cannot be studied. A choice must be made. The choice is inevitably difficult and potentially arbitrary, as it is with most social scientific research. A precaution must be kept in mind, however. The choice directly determines the range of substantive issues to be dealt with. Accordingly, the practical utility and theoretical relevance of the study will be determined by this choice. If the number and kinds of ideologies chosen are too small and narrow, the theoretical and practical relevance of the study will be too low. In sum, the number and kinds of bureaucratic and democratic ideologies to be chosen as objects of study should be manageably small, but at the same time, not too narrow as to produce results that have theoretical relevance and practical utility.

In the chapters that follow, I will first review major debates about the compatibility thesis posed especially in the fields of organization theory and Public Administration and then review the conceptual components of bureaucratic and democratic ideologies. The focus of the review will be vested on the major themes debated, the conclusions reached, and the reasoning behind the conclusion. I will then draw from the literature review the specific substance of, and modes of relationships between, bureaucratic and democratic ideologies which I examine.

Chapter

2

Debates about the Compatibility Thesis in the Field of Organization Theory

In the field of organization theory,[1] bureaucracy has been conceived of as "a large-scale complex organization" and a mode of managerial principles for organizing human and other resources. Debates about the compatibility thesis posed in this field highlight bureaucratic and democratic ideologies, and the relationship between these ideologies, that are especially relevant to the internal operation of public administrative agencies. The debates revolve around such themes as to what extent bureaucratic ideals (e.g., organizational efficiency and effectiveness) and bureaucratic managerial principles (e.g., hierarchy, unity of command, external control, economic incentive system, etc.) are conducive to the ideals of "organizational democracy." Organizational democracy includes such liberal democratic ideals as individual freedom, "self-actualization," individual economic well-being, and psychological satisfaction, as well as equality among particular groups of people, popular sovereignty, and openness to others within organizations. Also debated is the extent to which the "democratic" managerial principles proposed by the proponents of the Human Relations School [e.g., McGregor's (1960) "Theory Y"-type managerial scheme, Argyris' (1973a) and Likert's (1967) "participative" managerial scheme, etc.] are, and can be indeed, conducive to both the ideals of organizational democracy and bureaucracy.[2]

The field has witnessed heated controversies about these themes. Two points are suggested by the work of classical and neo-classical organization theorists (e.g., Taylor, 1947; Fayol, 1949; Simon, 1985, 1982, 1981, 1976, 1973, 1957, 1955; March and Simon, 1958), Preston (1987) and, by implication, a rational choice theorist (Olson, 1965), the proponents of "Management By Objectives" (e.g., Odiorne, 1979, 1965; McConkie, 1979; Mali, 1972; Carroll and Tosi, 1970) and the cybernetic theorists (e.g., Lundgren, 1974;

McCorduck, 1979). The first is that bureaucratic managerial principles are intrinsically compatible not only with bureaucratic ideals, but also with the ideals of organizational democracy. The second is that the "democratic" managerial principles proposed by the proponents of the Human Relations School are incompatible with the bureaucratic ideals as well as with the ideals of organizational democracy.[3]

The basic reasoning behind these pro-compatibility arguments are as follows:

(1) In order to fulfill the welfare of individuals within bureaucracy, there should be a sufficient amount of resources.[4] For example, Simon (1973) argues:

> To state the matter more concretely, the United States is today the prime example of a society that has solved the problem of scarcity - although not fully the problem of distributing its plenty to all its members. It has solved the problem of scarcity that makes lavish use of organizations, and considerable use of authority in their operation. *If now, in search of self-actualization, we eliminate those organizational forms, or redesign them to de-emphasize the use of formal authority, will the society remain sufficiently productive to allow opportunity for self-actualization? My own answer to this question is pessimistic* (p.350, emphasis added).

Similarly, Preston (1987) argues:

> Quite simply, those who criticize bureaucracy in the name of freedom have failed to realize that, *if we are to choose freely, we must have the resources which form the basis for choice.* In any imaginable rendering of present and future society, *it is clear that the resources needed for individuals to make free choices must be provided within a bureaucratic context* (p.775, emphasis added).

(2) Under ordinary circumstances, production of these resources is severely limited by the problematic human nature of the individuals within organizations. Taylor (1947) and Olson (1965) argue that the major limiting factor is the individual's natural tendency toward "systematic soldiering" (Taylor) or "free riding" (Olson), both of which result from a "Benthamite" view of human nature: pursuit of pleasure (i.e., economic self-interest for Taylor; benefit for Olson) and avoidance of pain (i.e., work for Taylor; cost for Olson). While Taylor and Olson ascribe the difficulty of producing resources to

the rational nature of individuals, Simon (1985, 1982, 1981, 1976, 1957) ascribes it to the "boundedly rational" nature of individuals. According to Simon, individuals intend to be rational in making decisions; in practice, however, they cannot be perfectly rational; rather, they can only be "boundedly" rational. Their capacity to make perfectly rational decisions is, in practice, significantly constrained by the limited availability of necessary resources and their psychological limit for gathering and processing information.

(3) These difficulties can be overcome *only* by relying on carefully designed *organizational* measures, which are essentially in line with the Weberian conception of bureaucratic organizational principles. Taylor, for example, maintains that such a problematic feature of human nature can be warded off by the principles of scientific management which are in essence the bureaucratization of work procedures. Similarly, Olson maintains that the negative effects of human nature can be restrained by using "selective incentive systems" and "coercive measures." These measures are basically Weberian in that external motivation of individuals with economic rewards and punishments (or their surrogate, promotion) are emphasized. The "bounded rational model of organizational decision-making" proposed by Simon is also Weberian in that the model presumes the hierarchical organizational structure of formal authority as a key to solving the problem of bounded-rationality on the part of individuals within organizations. Proposed in a similar vein are "Management By Objectives" in which the organizational, rather than individual goals are highlighted as the most important standard for evaluating task performance; and the "cybernetics of organization" in which the centralized decision-making structure is emphasized.

The exclusiveness of their arguments (noted above by the term "*only*") is implicit in Taylor's (1947:9) view that his scientific management is *the best* way to ensure "maximum prosperity for [all members of organizations regardless of employers or employees]" and "to liberate them out of their misbelief that their welfare can be maximized by the pursuit of their [ill]-conceived self-interest." In his response to Argyris' (1973a) "humanistic" approach to organizations, Simon (1973) argues that the bureaucratic managerial principles are superior to the "democratic" managerial principles proposed by the Human Relations School. Says Simon (1973):

> In Argyris' Dionysian world, reason is one of the shackles of freedom. The rational man is cold, constrained, incapable of self-actualization and 'peak experiences.' Man must throw over his reason, must respond to impulse in order to release the swaddled Real Person within. In my Apollonian world, *reason is the handmaiden of freedom and of creativity. It is the instrument that enables me to have peak experiences*

> *unimaginable to my cat or my dog. It is the instrument that enables me to dream and design. It is the instrument that enables me and my fellow men to create environments and societies that can satisfy our basic needs, so that all of us, and not just a few, can experience some of the deeper pleasures of sense and mind.* And because we depend so heavily upon reason to create and maintain a humane world, we see the need to understand reason better; to construct a tested theory of reasoning man (p.352, emphasis added).

Note that the aforementioned reasoning for the compatibility between bureaucracy and organizational democracy is indirect. That is, most authors do not support their pro-compatibility arguments by pointing out the direct logical consistency between the bureaucratic managerial principles and the ideals of organizational democracy. Rather, they argue for the bureaucratic managerial principles' *indirect* contributions to democratic ideals. For example, they claim that producing resources is a necessary, but not sufficient, condition for enhancing the ideals of internal democracy. Preston (1987) is an exception in that he presents a pro-compatibility argument by articulating the direct logical consistency between bureaucratic managerial principles and the ideals of organizational democracy. The bureaucratic managerial principles include technical division of labor, decision-making on the basis of fixed jurisdictional areas and established rules, and hierarchical distribution of authority. The ideals of organizational democracy include three forms of free choices: "technical choice" as a means to achieve selected purposes; "substantive choices" determining the goals to be pursued; and "formal choices" encompassing the repetoire of established rules or procedures that provide a predictable decision framework within which both technical and substantive choices are made.[5]

The pro-compatibility arguments thus far reviewed have long been seriously challenged by numerous scholars in the field of organizational theory on normative as well as empirical grounds.[6] The proponents of the Human Relations School are some of these scholars. Their theoretical and empirical studies suggest that the bureaucratic managerial principles are incompatible not only with the ideals of organizational democracy, but also even with bureaucratic ideals. They argue that only the alternative managerial principles they propose (i.e., "democratic" managerial principles) are compatible both with the ideals of organizational democracy and with the bureaucratic ideals. The major thrust of their reasoning can be summarized this way:

(1) The nature of the individual human being is fundamentally different from the one that legitimates the bureaucratic management of organization. For example, McGregor (1960), in his characterization of the "Theory Y"-type managerial scheme juxtaposed to the "Theory X"-type managerial scheme,

views human nature as follows:

> The average human being does not inherently dislike work. Depending upon controllable conditions, work may be a source of satisfaction (and will be voluntarily performed) or a source of punishment (and will be avoided if possible)...The average human being learns, under proper conditions, not only to accept but to seek responsibility. Avoidance of responsibility, lack of ambition, and emphasis on security are generally consequence of experience, not inherent human characteristics (pp.47-48).

Similarly, Argyris (1973a), in his critique of the rational-man view, argues:

> Man [is] a person who feels, experiences chaos; manifests spontaneity; becomes turned-on without planning it or being able to explain it in terms of consistency of conscious purpose; thinks divergently; and who may strive, at times, to separate himself from his past[.] [This kind of man] is not the primary concern of the intendedly-rational man organization theorists (p.261).

Thus, the bureaucratic managerial principles which emphasize strict control and close supervision are not appropriate for management of these ordinary individuals.

(2) The range of welfare that is meaningful to ordinary individual human beings within organizations is wider than the proponents of the bureaucratic mode of organization presume. It includes not only the satisfaction of such lower needs as economic and other physiological needs emphasized by the bureaucratic managerial principles, but also that of such higher needs as individual freedom, self-actualization, imagination, ingenuity, and creativity (cf., Maslow, 1970, 1965, 1962, 1954; McGregor, 1960; Argyris, 1973a, 1973b). Under ordinary circumstances, the lower needs are usually met to a substantial degree, and the higher needs are thus more meaningful and important to individual human beings (cf., Maslow, 1970). Within the managerial scheme guided by bureaucratic managerial principles, however, these higher needs are de-emphasized, if not totally denied, in most cases. In this sense, bureaucratic managerial principles are not, and cannot be, compatible with the ideals of organizational democracy.

(3) The bureaucratic managerial principles do not maximize organizational efficiency and effectiveness. This is because, as McGregor (1960:48) and Argyris (1973a:261) commonly maintain, the intellectual potential of the average human being (i.e., imagination, ingenuity, and creativity) are critical resour-

ces for maximizing organizational efficiency and effectiveness. But, under the bureaucratic mode of organizational management, these potentials can only be partially utilized.[7] This is because the bureaucratic managerial principles do not effectively motivate individuals. That is, the economic incentive system emphasized by the bureaucratic managerial principles focuses exclusively on such lower needs of individuals as economic security and other physiological needs. These lower needs are already satisfied to a substantial degree under ordinary circumstances. Thus, the incentive systems which focus on these needs do not effectively attract individuals to higher levels of work-performance. Herzberg (1966, 1968), for example, distinguished between the factors that alleviate or remove individuals' dissatisfaction (what he calls the "hygiene factors") and those that produce satisfaction (what he calls the "motivational factors"). According to him, alleviation or removal of individuals' dissatisfaction does not necessarily lead to a higher level of work-performance; rather, it leads at best to maintenance of current levels of work-performance. A higher level of work-performance results only when the hygiene factors are utilized. Hertzberg takes bureaucratic managerial principles as a prototypical example of a hygiene factor. Thus, Hertzberg's scheme suggests that bureaucratic managerial principles are not necessarily conducive to bureaucratic ideals.

(4) The ideals of organizational democracy and the resources necessary for attaining them are best attained *only* by "democratic" managerial principles. The substance of "democratic" managerial principles has been characterized in various ways.[8] McGregor's (1960) "Theory Y"-type managerial scheme has often been taken as a prime example. The core principles of this managerial scheme are "individuals' self-direction and self-control in the service of objectives to which they are committed" (McGregor, 1960:46). He proposes this managerial scheme as an alternative to the bureaucratic managerial principles which he calls the "Theory X"-type managerial scheme.[9] Similar points are emphasized in the "participative" managerial scheme proposed both by Argyris (1973a) and by Likert (1967). Argyris (1973a), for example, characterizes the substance of "democratic" managerial principles as a managerial scheme in which "individuals become more of a master of its own fate and a designer of its own future," (p.254) "having more personal choices, being proactive and taking initiative" (p.265). According to Bennis and Slater (1968:4), the "democratic" managerial principles emphasize:

1. Full and free communication, regardless of rank and power.
2. A reliance on consensus, rather than the more customary forms of coercion or compromise to manage conflict.
3. The idea that influence is based on technical competence and knowledge rather than on the vagaries of personal whims or prerogatives of power.
4. An atmosphere that permits and even encourages emotional expres-

sion as well as task-oriented acts.

5. A basically human bias, one that accepts the inevitability of conflict between the organization and the individual, but that is willing to cope with and mediate this conflict on rational grounds.[10]

Similar to the classical and neo-classical organization theorists, the proponents of the Human Relations School take an exclusive position in their argument of the superiority of their alternative managerial principles over others. However, the content of their argument is opposite to that of the classical and neo-classical organization theorists. That is, they argue that the "democratic" managerial principles they propose are superior to the traditional bureaucratic ones in attaining *both* bureaucratic and democratic ideals. Argyris (1973b), for example, in his response to Simon's (1973) critique,[11] states:

> I believe that if organizational designs and management theories are not enlarged to include my view of man [and the democratic mode of organization], *the organizations will not be able to continue their remarkable accomplishments. True, [the bureaucratic] organizations have produced high economic standards, but they have also (unintentionally) produced, for many of their participants, a low quality of life, and this has effects upon the outputs* (p.355, emphasis added).

Note that there are similarities between these proponents of the "democratic" managerial principles and the proponents of the bureaucratic ones. As Harmon and Mayer (1986:282-283) point out, theorists reviewed thus far commonly believe that the basic interests of organizations and the interests of individuals may ultimately be made congruent with one another. In other words, the proponents of the "democratic" managerial principles and those of the bureaucratic ones believe that, in principle, there is no fundamental and irreconcilable conflict between organizational and individual interests. The only difference between these two groups of organization theorists lies in their prescriptions of how to achieve it. They are similar to each other also in that they commonly handle the issue of organizational democracy from the perspective of popular democracy. Important to both of these two groups of organizational theorists is the realization of organizational democracy for the majority of, if not *all*, organizational members.

Many other scholars in the field of organization theory, however, have been suspicious of the congruence between organizations and individuals. Morrow and Thayer (1978), for example, ascribe the core of organizational democracy to the idea of "humanism," (i.e., that work should meet individual needs for fulfillment). They ascribe bureaucratic organizational principles to the idea of "materialism" (i.e., that work should meet needs for personal income and organizational productivity). They then argue that materialism and humanism are not natural partners but only an "odd couple" that cannot be pronounced husband and wife. They believe that there are fundamental contradictions between the organizational imperatives and the welfare of individual human beings. Similarly, Scott (1974), a systems theorist, argues:

> [P]ersonal satisfaction and organizational efficiency are compatible only at a most superficial level. The kinds of satisfaction sought for by true humanists are nonmaterialistic. Hence, any attempt to mold humanism to the goals of organizations either will pervert the humanistic values or erode organizational rationality. *We cannot have it both ways* (p.248, emphasis added).

This presumption of *de facto* existence of fundamental contradictions within organizations has been the basis for many authors' anti-compatibility arguments in which an egalitarian democratic ethos is stressed. The major thrusts of these anti-compatibility arguments and the reasoning behind them can be summarized as follows:

(1) Organizations are basically composed of two classes or groups: those who rule and those who are ruled. The rulers are usually owners of the organization, male, on the top of organizational hierarchies, possess critical resources, etc. Those who are ruled are respectively employees, female, at the bottom of organizational hierarchies, do not possess critical resources, etc. Their interests are fundamentally contradictory with one another.

(2) Viewed from the perspective of the ruled, the basic nature of organizations, regardless of whether they are guided by bureaucratic managerial principles or by the Human Relations School's "democratic" ones (especially when they are used as a means for fulfilling organizational imperatives) is a "psychic prison," or a means for domination and repression of the ruled by the rulers. For example, Marxian organization scholars (e.g., Buroway, 1985; DiTomaso, 1984; Heyderbrand, 1977, 1983; Burris and Heyderbrand, 1981; Edwards, 1978; Rachleff, 1982; Harring, 1981; Whyte and Blasi, 1982; Clegg and Dunkerly, 1980; Hodges, 1970; Merkle, 1968) argue that any organizational mode aimed at maximizing organizational efficiency, whether it is bureaucratically or "democratically" designed, is a form of domination by the capitalist class over the labor class, which will result in "alienation" on the part of the latter. Those who see organizations as "psychic prisons" argue that excessive concerns with productivity, planning, and control are an expression of "sublimated anal eroticism" or an illusory attempt to preserve and tie down life in the face of death (cf., Morgan, 1986:199-232). To those who study organizations from the feminist perspective (e.g., Kanter, 1977; Rustad, 1984, 1984;

Mansbridge, 1984), bureaucratic managerial principles, especially the principle of hierarchy, are obsolete extensions of the "patriarchal" family structure, by which male domination is maximized.

(3) Any conception of organizational democracy must be class-specific. It must be made especially from the perspective of the ruled. The major ideals of organizational democracy highlighted from this perspective are "emancipating," "liberating," and "transcending" the ruled by the rulers out of organizational domination and repression, and "psychic prison"; also important is equality between the rulers and the ruled in the distribution of power to make organizational decisions and the welfare of the ruled.

Several authors have presented general prescriptive guidelines for attaining these egalitarian democratic ideals within the organizational context. They include abandonment of the paradigm of materialism and separation of work from worker's income (Morrow and Thayer, 1978), "social praxis of inter-subjectivity based upon genuine open communications" (cf., Habermas, 1981, 1979), "action frame of reference" (Silverman, 1971), and "disaggregated decision rules oriented toward mutuality and consensus" (Harmon, 1981, 1980; Hummel, 1977).[12]

NOTES

1 My attention is given to the particular debates posed in these fields for two reasons. First, the subjects of my research, public administrative agencies and public administrators that are modal examples of bureaucracy and bureaucrats, respectively, have traditionally been the major subjects of these fields. Second, I think that the debates about the compatibility thesis addressed in these fields cover fairly comprehensively those issues that are addressed in other relevant fields. The second reason needs a reservation, however. Focusing on these fields precludes examination of the relationship between bureaucracy and democracy highlighted particularly at the macro-societal level. That is, my study does not directly incorporate such issues addressed mostly in state theory literature as: "To what extent does bureaucracy (conceived as an arm of the state) 'rule' the society beyond 'governing' it?" "To what extent does it have autonomous power against the influence of particular components of the macro-societal environments (e.g., classes, elites and non-elites, organized interest group as a whole and non-organized mass) in its ruling and governing activities?" and "In whose interests does it rule and govern?"

2 For the operational definition of "bureaucracy" and "democracy" used in my study, see Chapter Five.

3 I distinguish those arguments that hold bureaucracy to be compatible with *organizational* democracy from those who hold bureaucracy to be compatible with democracy in a broader *society*. The literature of organization theory is related to the former, while the literature of Public Administration is related to the latter.

4 Diverse terms are used for designating these resources. For example, to the classical and neo-classical organization theorists, these resources are called "organizational surplus." Olson's (1965) understanding of the term 'collective good' generally coincides with the meaning of these resources. For Preston (1987), these resources are specified into skills, time, information, funds, and stability.

5 However, it should be noted that tautological error is deeply involved in Preston's reasoning of his pro-compatibility argument. As a defense of bureaucracy against those who criticize it in the name of freedom, Preston (1987:775) argues that "a substantial degree of freedom is possible within the context of bureaucracy" (p.773, emphasis added) and that "the resources needed for individuals to make free choices *must* be provided *within* a bureaucratic context." A problematic feature of his argument is that tautological error is deeply embedded in his reasoning. Preston commits two types of tautological errors. First, he criticizes other authors' arguments about the compatibility thesis based upon his own definitions of bureaucracy and democracy that are different from those of the authors. For example, Preston states, "the presumed conflict between freedom and bureaucracy exists because we have used an inadequate *conception* of freedom and adopted an excessively rigid *view* of bureaucracy" (p.773, emphasis added). By framing the problem as a matter of definition, Preston is already prone to make a tautological error at the very initial stage of his analysis. Indeed, he tries to show the compatibility between bureaucracy and freedom by *redefining* the concept of freedom. His definition of freedom is: "the conscious deliberation of those who make them and are not adequately accounted for by forces that can be neither recognized nor controlled" (p.777). This definition is, as Preston himself notes (pp.774, 776-777), the one that is deliberately made different from those definitions of freedom which are prevalent in the anti-compatibility arguments (i.e., "positive vs. negative conceptions of freedom"). Thus, his conclusion that is markedly different from others' becomes driven by his own definition of freedom that is also markedly different from others.

Another type of tautology is found in Preston's supplementary explanation of his own definition of freedom. "Bureaucracy" and "democracy" are not defined independently from one another; thus, they are already mutually dependent by the definition itself. For example, Preston argues that a man is free if, and only if, he is responsible for his actions and that the degree of responsibility and free choice can be determined "by examining whether a person possesses, before acting, the capacities and conditions that make it possible to deliberate about the decision to be made" (p.778). What makes this tautologous is that he specifies the "capacities" and "conditions" with those that are not independent of the conception of bureaucracy. "Skills" and "established ideas and practices," which he lists as major elements of the capacities (p.781, 787), and the conditions he specified (e.g., "free choice is not possible in an unpredictable, chaotic environment" (p.788) are all the very central features of Max Weber's ideal type bureaucracy. Thus, his conclusion of pro-compatibility becomes directly driven by his already *bureaucratized* definition of freedom.

This type of tautology is also found in his conception of bureaucracy. Regarding the often criticized propensity of bureaucracy to threaten individual freedom, he argues that it is an extrinsic, rather than intrinsic, characteristic of bureaucracy which "results from rapid social or political change...beyond the requirements of bureaucratic organization" (p.789). Thus, in his analytic framework, bureaucracy becomes, by definition, innocent of the anti-democratic phenomena within bureaucracy.

Another good example of the tautological problem is Friedreich's (1976) justification of his and his associate's earlier argument (Friedreich and Cole, 1932; cited from Friedreich, 1976:41-42) that "bureaucracy and democracy are not antithetical, but they belong to each other as structural aspects of a fully organized living community" (i.e., compatibility between bureaucracy as a governmental institution and external democracy, especially responsibility to the citizens). Quite similar to Preston (1987), Friedreich (1976:42) maintains that "the argument that democracy and democratization are a substitute for bureaucracy depends upon certain misunderstandings about legitimacy and authority [, which] in turn are the result of a mistaken view of power as necessarily to be understood in terms of command and obedience - a widespread view of power since Hobbes" (p.42). By redefining the concepts of power, legitimacy, and authority to be conducive to the basic nature of bureaucracy, Friedreich (1976) maintains that "[d]emocratization and bureaucracy go hand in hand" (p.47) and that "bureaucracy...will strive for responsibility as well as efficiency" (p.51).

6 The antithetical tendency of bureaucracy to internal democracy is an old issue which can be traced back even to the time when the concept of bureaucracy was intiated as an analytic concept. For example, Max Weber, who originated "bureaucracy" as an analytic concept, recognized this anti-democratic feature of bureaucracy. According to him, bureaucracy creates a person (bureaucrat) who is nothing but a little cog in a big machine, who clings to his position while desperately hoping to become a bigger cog: "specialists without spirit, sensualists without heart" (Weber, 1958:182). In a somewhat different context, though Karl Marx, too, in his analysis of alienation, pointed out the antithetical tendency of bureaucracy to internal democracy. According to him, the strict hierarchy and discipline and the bureaucrat's veneration of authority make the individual bureaucrat unaware of the parasitic and oppressive nature of his/her job (cf., Mouzelis, 1967:10). Michels (1915) empirically found the anti-democratic nature of bureaucracy (i.e., the "iron law of oligarchy") in the intra-organizational context.

7 A group of scholars who are often called "pathologists of bureaucracy" (e.g., Selznick, 1949; Gouldner, 1957; Merton, 1957; Blau, 1955; Thompson, 1977) deny the classical and neo-classical organization theorists' justification of bureaucracy as the best efficiency-maximizer.

8 For more detailed compilation of these scholars' conceptions of humanitarian managerial principles, see Hwang (1981:29-42).

9 According to McGregor, the core principles of the "Theory X"-type managerial scheme are external control and threat of punishment.

10 Note that the last three points suggest that Bennis and Slater presume that the bureaucratic managerial principles can be combined with the democratic managerial principles. In this case, it may be said that Bennis and Slater do not deny the logical compatibility between bureaucracy and organizational democracy.

11 A part of Argyris' argument, especially that the humanitarian managerial principles are better than the bureaucratic ones in enhancing efficiency and productivity, has been empirically tested by many scholars. The results are inconclusive, however. For example, Lippit and White (1964) and Price (1973) support the argument, while Witte (1980), Ronan (1970), Vroom (1964), Fleischman and Peters (1962), Brayfield and Crockett (1955) present evidence against it.

12 Note, however, that these prescriptions have been proposed, or criticized, mostly on normative and speculative grounds. Empirical evidence indicating that applications of these prescriptions does or does not actually result in enhancement of the egalitarian democratic ideals has not been well documented yet.

Chapter 3

Debates about the Compatibility Thesis in the Field of Public Administration

The debates of organization theorists about the compatibility thesis are focused on the substance of, and the relationship between, bureaucratic and democratic ideologies that are relevant to the internal operation of public administrative agencies. In contrast, the debates posed in the field of Public Administration highlight those that are relevant especially to the external context of public administrative agencies.[1] That is, they have conceived bureaucracy as a governmental institution, especially the public administrative agencies within the executive branch of government, and as a mode of principles guiding their external relationships with other surrounding institutions (e.g., the legislature, the judiciary, political parties, citizen groups, etc.).[2]

The major theme around which the debates about the compatibility thesis in this field have centered is to what extent bureaucracy is conducive to the ideals of popular democracy. It includes such a passive ideal as bureaucracy's accountability to elected politicians, and such active ideals as openness, responsiveness, and responsibility to the citizens. Bureaucracy is juxtaposed with liberal democracy which emphasizes individual citizens' freedom of choice, and the egalitarian democracy which stresses equality, especially for underprivileged citizens.

As in the case of the debates in the field of organization theory, the debates about the compatibility thesis in the field of Public Administration are characterized by controversy and diversity in their conclusions and reasoning. An anti-compatibility argument is implied in an old, but sill active[3] tradition of American public administration which is often called "Jacksonianism" or "Jacksonian Democracy."[4] The major thrust of the anti-compatibility argument implied in Jacksonianism is that public administration, especially if it is bureaucratically managed, sets up an obstacle to the fulfillment of democratic ideals, especially constitutional and popular democratic ideals. The major reasoning behind this anti-compatibility argument is that bureaucratic public administration will become a seedbed for domination by an elite class of government officialdom.

By understanding government officers' jobs as "so plain and simple that men of intelligence may readily qualify themselves for performance," President Andrew Jackson presented, and put into practice, a "democratic" principle for public administration which is often called the "spoils system." According to this prescription, public administrative professions should be filled with ordinary citizens who are appointed by the political parties that win elections and replaced with new ones whenever there is a change of party after an election.[5]

During the Progressive era, the efficacy of the Jacksonian formulation of "democratic" public administration was fundamentally criticized for having the negative consequences of inefficiency in the patronized civil service system, corruption, and lavish use of public resources. Classical Public Administration theory emerged as a reaction to these negative consequences of Jacksonian democracy and as a support for Progressive movements.[6] Implied in the classical theorists' prescriptions and understandings (e.g., Wilson, 1887; Goodnow, 1900; Willoughby, 1927; Gulick and Urwick, 1937) is the belief that the Jacksonian "democratic" principles for public administration are incompatible with bureaucratic ideals, efficiency, and with democratic ideals (especially constitutional democracy and popular democracy). Following are the major thrusts of the arguments of the classical theorists which are relevant to the compatibility thesis.

(1) "The basic 'good' is efficiency...and efficiency is *axiom number one* in the value scale of administration" (Gulick 1937:193, emphasis added).

(2) The Jacksonian "democratic" principles are incompatible with the ideal of efficiency in that, as historical experience proves, they resulted in patronization of civil service systems, corruption, and lavish use of public resources. In order to ensure efficiency, public administrative agencies should be administered with bureaucratic principles. They should be separated from politics" (Wilson, 1887); the major tasks for public administrators should be those apolitical ones that can be summarized as "POSDCORB" (Gulick, 1937); the appointment of public administrators and their task performance should be politically neutral; public administration should be structured and managed according to the Taylorian "scientific" principles (which are the very bureaucratic ones in Max Weber's terms). These include division of labor: departmentalization, specialization, hierarchy of authority, unity of command, principle of span of

control, and coordination, that is, the principle of "homogeneity."

(3) Public administration by these bureaucratic managerial principles is congruent with the ideals of constitutional democracy and popular democracy. It provides a majority of citizens with public goods and services of better quality and in the most efficient and economical way. The principle of hierarchical control within public administrative agencies can be matched with the principle of external control of bureaucracy by elected politicians. That is, through the successive and hierarchical chains of command and subordination, the elected politicians can effectively enforce their will even down to the rank-and-file public administrators, thus ensuring the accountability of public administrators to the elected politicians.[7]

The widespread societal turbulence and distrust of government during the 1960s and 1970s in the United States provided momentum for a group of scholars in the field of Public Administration to challenge the fundamentals of traditional public administration both as an academic field and as a practice. They are the so-called proponents of New Public Administration.[8]

Quite explicit in the work of the proponents of New Public Administration is the anti-compatibility argument that public administration, if guided by bureaucratic principles of public administration like those proposed by classical and neo-classical theorists of public administration, is far from all of the democratic ideals mentioned above. The major thrusts of their arguments are as follows:

(1) The Wilsonian dichotomy is more fiction than reality. Public administrators not only are affected by political actors in numerous ways, but also are involved in making *political* decisions beyond their traditional role of *technical* decision-maker. Public administrative agencies are basically a "policy battlefield," in which numerous policy interests are concentrated and realized.

(2) Given the *de facto* political nature of public administrators and public administrative agencies, "efficiency," "economy," and "accountability" are not sufficient justifications for compatibility. Important normative requirements for public administration that must be *added* to the list of traditional ones are "responsibility" and "responsiveness" directly to the citizens and "social equity" for the underpriveleged citizens in distributing public goods and services.[9]

(3) In order to meet these normative requirements, the traditional public administration guided by bureaucratic principles should be fundamentally reformed. More specifically, the power of bureaucracy should be strengthened and its traditional role (i.e., neutral policy-arbitrator or policy-implementor) must be replaced with a new proactive role (i.e., policy advocate). In addition, the bureau-

cratic principles of public administration should be replaced with "participative public administration" which emphasizes internal participation (i.e., decentralization of decision-making structures so that those in the lower hierarchies can influence the crucial decision-making within the agencies) and external participation (i.e., citizens' participation in crucial decision-making and administration of bureaucracy).

(4) Regarding the relationship between "participatory" reforms and bureaucratic ideals (i.e., efficiency and economy), the proponents of New Public Administration, quite similar to the organization theorists of the Human Relations School, presume that their reforms enhance not only "democratic" ideals but also bureaucratic ideals, in the long run (cf., Frederickson, 1971).

Following the American tradition of liberal democracy, the public choice theorists of public administration (e.g., Ostrom, 1974; Niskanen, 1971) argue that traditional bureaucracy as a mode of producing public goods and services is not compatible with democracy. Using the "market" metaphor, they understand the relationship between public administrative institutions and citizens basically as an economic relationship between producers and consumers in the marketplace. Based upon this understanding, they pose the anti-compatibility argument in these terms:

(1) The most important democratic ethos is the enhancement of the freedom of individual citizens to choose the kinds and quantity of public goods and services they want to purchase.

(2) The bureaucratic mode of production of public goods and services in which production is hierarchically and unilaterally arranged is basically the monopolistic, or oligopolic, mode of production. Thus, it does not, and cannot accomplish both bureaucratic ideals (i.e., efficient production of public goods and services) and the liberal democratic ideal (i.e., individual citizens' freedom of choice).

(3) The democratic ethos can be successfully achieved *only* by replacing the traditional bureaucratic principles with the principle of competition among public administrative agencies and between governmental agencies and private corporations in producing public goods and services.

(4) Such competition enhances not only the democratic ideal, but also the bureaucratic ideal. That is, the public goods and services are produced in the most efficient and economical ways under the competitive scheme of public administration.

Note that there is a crucial difference between New Public Administration theorists and public choice theorists of public administration. The New Public

Administration theorists believe that one of the means to attain their democratic ideals is by strengthening the political power of public administrative agencies and public administrators. In contrast, the public choice theorists of Public Administration suggest that any strengthening of bureaucracy's power means governmental monopoly over the production of public goods and services, and thus is antithetical to their democratic ideal.

The critical theorists of public administration (e.g., Denhardt and Denhardt, 1979; Denhardt, 1981; Dunn and Fozouni, 1976) understand the bureaucratic principles of public administration as a means of institutional domination by public adminstrators in their relations with citizens. Their work commonly suggests that the bureaucratic principles of public administration are intrinsically incompatible with the ideals of popular democracy. The focal point of their reasoning can be summarized as follows:[10]

(1) The pervasive distrust or even hostility toward public administrators by citizens indicates the lack of congruence between the interests of public administrators and those of the public, and the existence of systematic distortions in communications between various parties.

(2) Because of bureaucracy's hegemony over the machinery of public authority, its "technical interests" in efficiency and control leave little if any room for citizen participation in the "public sphere."

(3) In addition to restricting citizen participation in the public sphere, this dominance of technical rationality results in alienation both within and from public administrative agencies.

(4) Only through the democratization of social relations of public administrators and the public (i.e., "open communications" based upon relentless criticism of practices and constructions of meaning associated with public administrative agencies) can the pathologies be brought to light, questioned, and contested.

(5) Regarding the relationship between their "democratic" prescriptions and bureaucratic ideals, the critical theorists of public administration, unlike the proponents of the New Public Administration, argue that the democratization of social relationships should take precedence over the technical concerns of effectiveness and efficiency. Thus Denhardt argues:

> The central question is no longer how the individual may contribute to the efficient operation of the system, but how the individual may transcend that system (Denhardt, 1981:131; cited from Harmon and Mayer, 1986:329).

NOTES

1 Note, however, that this is an analytic distinction. In the field of Public Administration, many authors have been taking the perspective of organization theory and examining the compatibility thesis especially in terms of the internal context of the public administrative agencies (e.g., Harmon and Mayer, 1985; Fischer and Sirianni, 1984; Thayer, 1980, 1981). I have reviewed these authors' works under the category of organization theory literature.

2 Those who have examined bureaucracy from the perspective of organization theory have conceived bureaucracy mainly as a mode of organizational principles for managing the internal affairs of the public administrative offices.

3 The philosophy of Jacksonianism is still implicit in the justification of the contemporary practice of appointment of "outsiders" as government officials. Sharkansky (1978), for example, argues:

> By now, a series of administrative reforms has all but eliminated the spoils systems in the federal civil service and has curtailed it sharply in most state and local governments. Yet several features still testify to the remaining strength of this element in administrative organizations. Senior positions in many public agencies are filled by the chief executives' appointment of 'outsiders' brought in from private life, rather than by people who have devoted their careers to the agency. In this way, administration is thought to remain responsive to the wishes of the 'people'; either because the elected chief executive makes the top appointment or because the appointees are citizens rather than professional bureaucrats (p.106).

4 For a useful overview of the practice of Jacksonianism in public administration, see White (1956) and Knott and Miller (1987, especially Chapter Two).

5 The core of Jacksonian philosophy is well expressed in Jackson's following statement:

> Office is considered as a species of property and government rather as a means of promoting individual interests than as an instrument created solely by/for the service of the people.

> Corruption in some and in others a perversion of correct feelings and principles divert government from its legitimate ends and make it an engine for the support of the few at the expense of the many. The duties of all public officers are, or at least admit of being made, so plain and simple that men of intelligence may readily qualify themselves for their performance; and I cannot but believe that more is lost by the long continuance of men in office than is generally to be gained by their experience. In a country where offices are created solely for the benefit of the people, no one man has any more intrinsic right to official station than another. Offices were not established to give support to particular men at the public expense. No individual wrong is, therefore, done by removal, since neither appointment to nor continuance in office is a matter of right...The proposed limitation would destroy the idea of property now so generally connected with official station, and although individual distress may be sometimes produced, it would, by promoting that rotation which constitutes a leading principle in the republican creed, give healthful action to the system (Van Riper, 1958:36-37, cited from Sharkansky, 1978:105-106).

6 For an historical review of public administration as practiced as an academic field in the United States, see Mosher (1975), Allensworth (1973), Golembiewsky (1977), and Knott and Miller (1987).

7 This point has been emphasized in the early work of Simon, Thompson, and Smithburgh (1956), who might be called, in this and other senses, "the neo-classical theorists of public administration," especially in their arguments about the relationship between internal and external controls of bureaucracy.

8 For a useful overview of New Public Administration provided by its proponents, see Waldo (1971), Marini (1971), Frederickson (1980), and Bellone (1980). For a useful critical review of New Public Administration, see Golembiewsky (1977:Chapter Four), and Wamsley (1976).

9 The meaning of "responsibility" emphasized by the proponents of New Public Administration is one that is conceptually differentiated from "accountability." Presthus (1975) summarizes the conceptual differentiation as follows:

> 'Responsibility' and 'accountability' should be differentiated.

Accountability refers to the hierarchical or legal locus of responsibility. Responsibility, on the other hand, has personal, moral connotations and is not necessarily related to formal role, status, or power, although it is probably true that greater power brings greater responsibility. Thus, a department head is *accountable* for the actions of all his subordinates, although in actual fact, he is not *responsible* for their use of power which he must delegate to them...On the other hand, in exercising discretion every official is morally responsible for his decisions, although he is not often legally accountable. In practice, responsibility must be shared; it percolates throughout the entire administrative apparatus. Accountability, which concerns the formal relationships, can never be shared. The bureaucracy is regarded as being accountable to elected representatives and to the courts who apply the rule-of-law doctrine. Within the executive branch, accountability is sought through a hierarchy of offices and duties that seem to make possible a 'line of command' from the top to bottom...Responsibility is also bound up with discretion. When an official has no power to choose among alternatives, he cannot be held personally responsible because he has exercised no choice. In modern administration, however, it is clear that officials do have considerable discretion. Responsibility is now diffused throughout the bureaucracy and traditional measures of popular control suffer accordingly. The resulting necessity of relying on the moral and professional ethics of the official is complicated by the fact that he is often not only legally unaccountable, but anonymous. In practice, this means that his legally accountable chief must often assume a burden of moral responsibility that properly belongs to his subordinates (pp.411-412, emphasis original).

10 This summary relies heavily upon Harmon and Mayer (1986:326-329).

Chapter 4

Specification of the Conceptual Components of, and the Relationships Between, Bureaucratic and Democratic Ideologies

As reviewed thus far, most previous debates about the compatibility thesis in the fields of organization theory and Public Administration have centered around the compatibility between bureaucracy and democracy at the institutional level. Of primary concern in my study, however, is "subjective compatibility" by which I mean the compatibility between bureaucratic and democratic ideologies construed in bureaucrats' minds. Behind my focus upon subjective compatibility, there is an acceptance of the notion that subjectivity is not a passive entity which is determined unidirectionally by the objective structure; rather, it is more an active entity which *co-exists* with the objective structure not only being affected by the objective structure, but also affecting it by substantiating the specific mode of its existence in reality (cf., Berger and Luckmann, 1967; Hall, 1988, 1982; Brown, 1980). The core reasons are not the institutional structures themselves which exist outside the individuals, but more essentially their meanings which are intersubjectively constructed by the individuals and exist within the inner selves of these individuals and which may be different among individuals.

The subjectivist notion provides two important justifications for studying the compatibility thesis. First, bureaucrats' own subjective perpectives on, and internalizations of, bureaucratic and democratic ideologies may affect the actual operation of bureaucratic and democratic institutional devices to a significant degree. In other words, if the same bureaucratic and democratic ideals are operated by those who have different understandings and internalization of the ideologies embedded in these institutional devices, different results are likely.[1] Second, in a similar vein, the compatibility between bureaucracy and democracy at an institutional level does not necessarily indicate subjective compatibility.

Unless subjective compatibility is accomplished, institutional compatiblity is not yet real. Rather, it constitutes an element of formalism. In other words, bureaucracy is more likely to be compatible with democracy when bureaucracy is operated by key bureaucrats who possess a higher level of subjective compatibility than when it is operated by those who possess a lower level of subjective compatibility. In sum, the subjectivist notion suggests that studying subjective compatibility focusing upon the patterns of key bureaucrats' understandings and internalizations of bureaucratic and democratic ideologies will provide useful insights on the limit of the compatibility between bureaucracy and democracy at an institutional level and the strategies to overcome this limit.

Based upon these speculations, I will abstact in this section the major conceptual elements of bureaucratic and democratic institutional devices addressed in the fields of organization theory and Public Administration thus far reviewed.[2] The literature reviewed thus far reveals that there is a schematic similarity and a substantive difference between the debates about the compatibility thesis posed in the field of organization theory and those posed in the field of Public Administration. The schematic similarity is that authors in both fields address the compatibility thesis within the same framework of a means-and-ends relationship. That is, the debates posed in these fields commonly revolve around such issues as: To what extent can, and do, bureaucratic (or democratic) instrumental principles enhance democratic (or bureaucratic) ideals?[3] The substantive difference between these fields is related to a contextual factor. Authors in the field of organization theory have addressed these issues focusing mostly upon the internal context of bureaucratic institutions. This contextual difference of focus has led authors to construe the conceptual elements of bureaucracy and types of democratic ideologies in substantively different ways, and accordingly, to address substantively different sub-issues of the compatibility thesis.

In order to deal with the theoretical debates posed in these fields in a relevant way, I focus my exploration of the subjective dimension of the compatibility thesis on the conceptual components of, and the sub-relationships between, bureaucratic and democratic ideologies that are schematized by the same factors that produce the similarity and differences between the two fields. Taking the means-and-ends framework into consideration, I construe bureaucratic ideology as being composed of bureaucratic ideals and bureaucratic instrumental principles. The substantive content of bureaucratic ideals and instrumental principles is construed especially with those conceptual components which have received primary concern in both fields. They can be summarized as follows:

Bureaucratic Ideals:

A. Instrumental Rationalism

1. i.e., efficient performance of tasks and effective attainment

of goals

B. Maintenance of Order

2. i.e., a state of affairs which is stable and predictable

Bureaucratic Instrumental Principles:

A. Hierarchy of Authority and Control
B. Unity of Command
C. Division of Labor
D. Simplification, Standardization, and Specialization of Task
E. Technical Competence as a Primary Criterion for Evaluating People
F. Impersonal Relationships Among People
G. Task Performance Based Upon Formal Rules and Regulations
H. Separation Between Administration and Private Ownership
I. Reliance on and Use of Written Documents

I construe democratic ideology in a similar fashion. It is treated as being composed of democratic ideals and democratic instrumental principles. Note here that the literature review indicates that in both fields, a substantive difference in the debates about the compatibility thesis has been brought about from the juxtaposition of bureaucracy with different categories of democratic ideology (i.e., liberal, egalitarian, and popular). This suggests that, in order to examine the subjective dimension of the compatibility thesis with a specific relevance to these fields, the conceptual components of democratic ideals and instrumental principles should be specified within each of these categories of democratic ideology. The following is a summary of the major conceptual components of democratic ideology specified in this way:

Democratic Ideals

A. Liberal Democratic Ideal
    1. Individual Freedom
B. Egalitarian Democratic Ideal
    1. Equality Among Particular Groups of People
C. Popular Democratic Ideal
    1. Popular Sovereignty
    2. Openness to Others

Democratic Instrumental Principles

A. Liberal Democratic Instrumental Principle
    1. Self-Directed Task Performance

B. Egalitarian Democratic Instrumental Principle
  1. Participative Decision-Making by Disadvantaged Minority
C. Popular Democratic Instrumental Principle
  1. Consensus-Based Decision-Making

The source for the differences between the two fields (i.e., the contextual difference bringing about the difference in substantive issues) suggests that these conceptual components of bureaucratic and democratic ideologies can be further differentiated by each of the internal and external contexts in which bureaucratic institutions and bureaucrats are situated. For the sake of research managability, however, I will construe the conceptual components of bureaucratic and democratic instrumental principles only in terms of the internal context. In sum, the contour of the conceptual components of bureaucratic and democratic ideologies framed in these ways can be summarized as Figure 4-1.

Construing the conceptual components of bureaucratic and democratic ideologies in these ways indicates that there are a number of sub-relationships which can be examined in studying the subjective dimension of the compatibility thesis. Theoretically, more than 100 dyads can be drawn to depict the relationships between the conceptual components of bureaucratic ideology and those of democratic ideology. As schematically summarized in Figure 4-2, I will examine only those dyads of relationship which are, in my opinion, directly relevant to the normative and theoretical debates posed in the two fields. One set of relationships which I will examine is depicted by Set I. Set I includes the relationship between bureaucratic ideology and democratic ideology as a whole (i.e., BURO vs. DEMO) and the more specific relationships between bureaucratic ideology as a whole and each category of democratic ideology (i.e., BURO vs. LIBDEMO; BURO vs. EQDEMO; and BURO vs. POPDEMO).

The relationships specified in Set I do not reflect the substantive difference caused by the contextual factor and the scheme of means-and-ends relations. The second set of relationships that I will examine is included in Set II. Although these are the same as those included in Set I, the conceptual components of bureaucratic and democratic ideologies related with one another in Set II are specified in terms of the internal context of bureaucratic institutions and bureaucrats. I will also examine the relationships between bureaucratic and democratic ideologies which are, as depicted in Sets III and IV, construed in terms of the internal and external contexts of bureaucratic institutions and bureaucrats, and the scheme of means-and-ends relations. Presented in Set III are the relationships among conceptual components of bureaucratic and democratic ideologies which do not reflect the substantive difference among the liberal, egalitarian, and popular democratic ideologies. The relationships presented in Set IV are composed of three subsets of relationships which are the same as those in Set III, except that the relationships are differentiated by each of the

Figure 4 - 1 **A Conceptual Scheme of Bureaucratic and Democratic Ideologies To Be Examined**

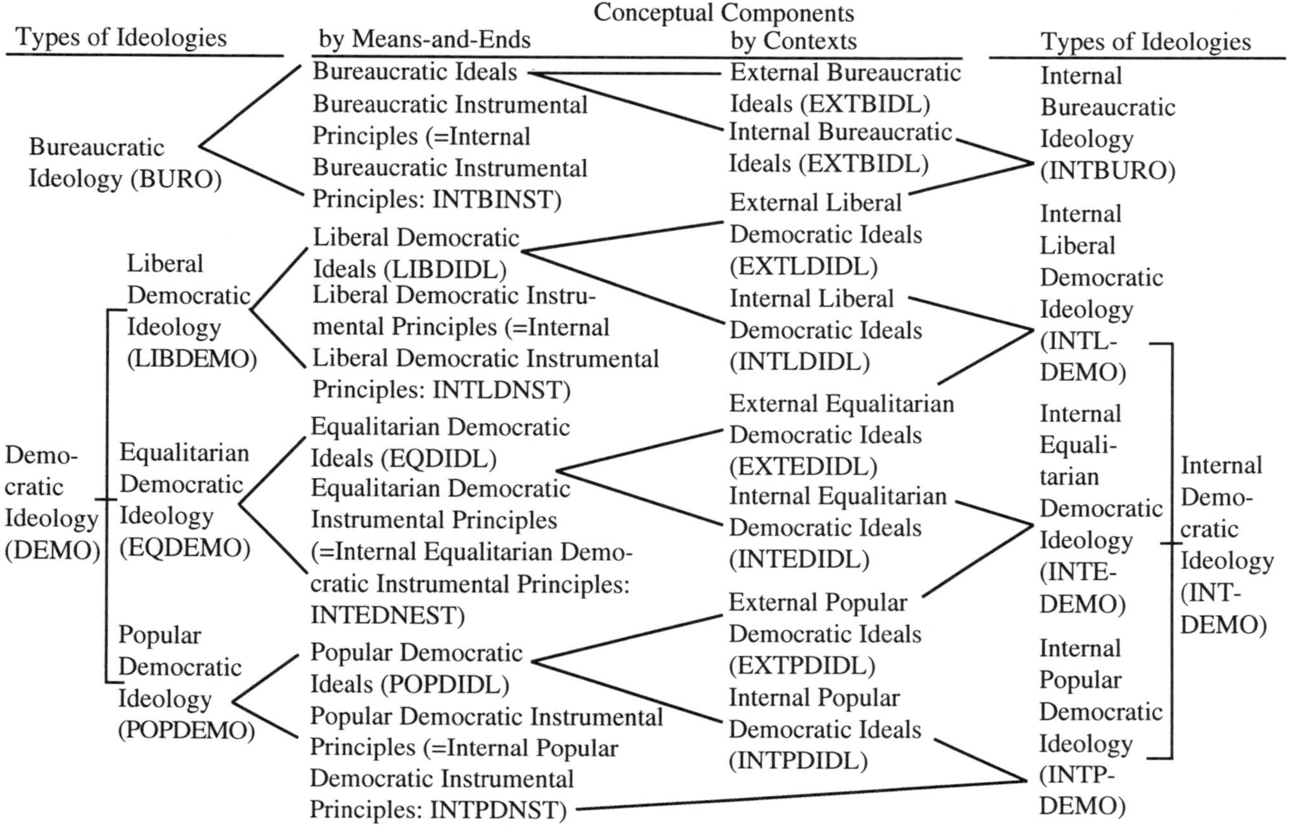

Figure 4 - 2 **Types of Relationships Between Bureaucratic and Democratic Ideologies**

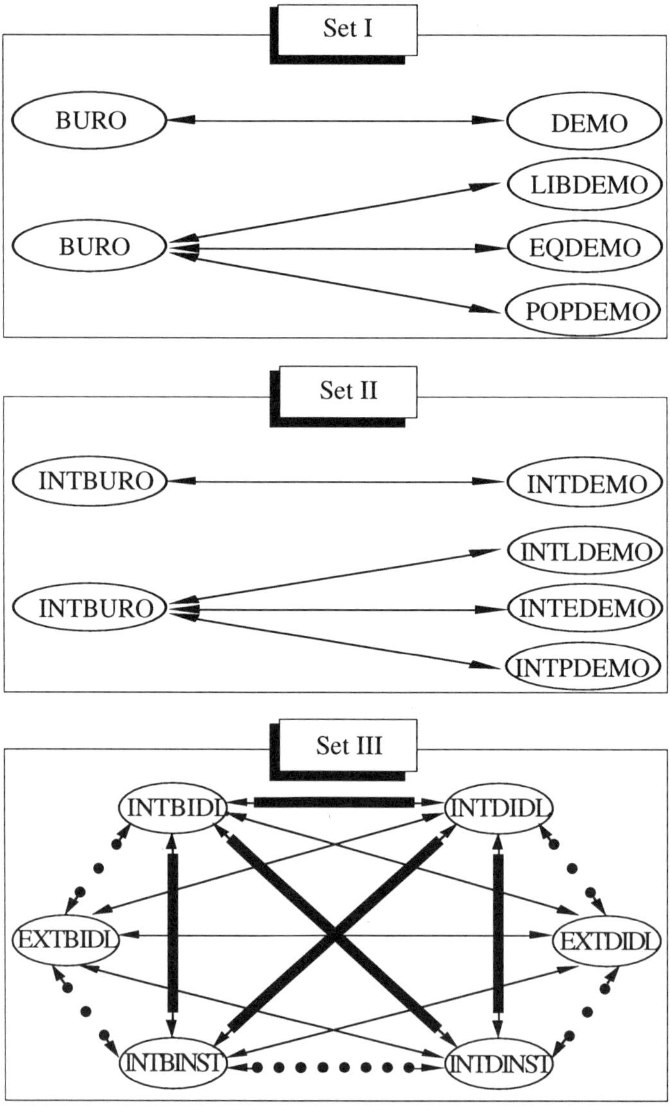

(continued on next page)

Figure 4 - 2 (continued) **Types of Relationships Between Bureaucratic and Democratic Ideologies**

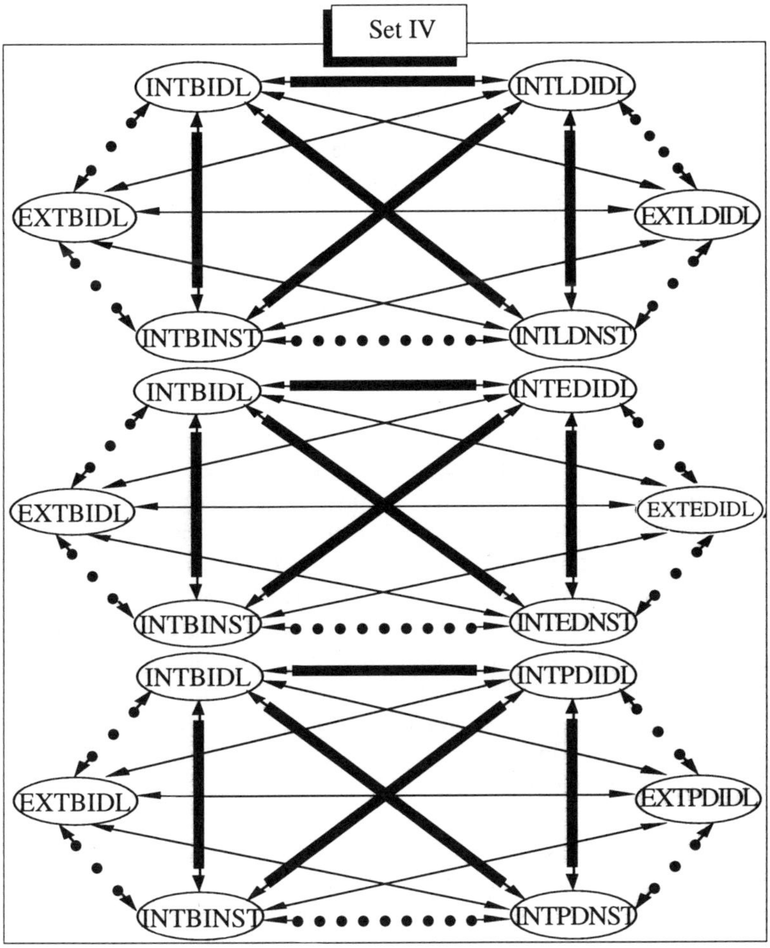

Note: *Notations are equivalent to those explained in Figure 4-1.

* Relationships depicted with thick solid arrows are relevant to debates about compatibility thesis posed in field of organization theory.

*Inter-contextual relationships depicted with thin solid arrows are relevant to debates about compatibility thesis posed in field of Public Administration.

*Relationships depicted with dotted arrows are not directly relevant to debates about compatibility thesis posed in field of Public Administration.

three categories of democratic ideology.

Note that in studying the relationships presented in Sets III and IV, the relationships depicted with thick lines are those relevant specifically to the debates about the compatibility thesis posed in the field of organization theory. The relationships that are relevant to the debates posed in the field of Public Administration are depicted with thin lines. These relationships will be examined with the framework of hypothesis testing. That is, the directions of these relationships will be hypothesized with specific references to the relevant debates posed in these fields in Chapter Five. The empirical validity of each hypothesis will then be tesed in Chapter Six.

The relationships which are not directly relevant to the debates posed in these fields are depicted with dotted lines. Of the relationships depicted with dotted lines in Sets III and IV, the inter-contextual relationships among the conceptual components of democratic ideology are included in my list of research themes, in order to examine Mosher's (1968) notion of logical contradiction between the requirement of internal democracy and that of external democracy. Mosher (1968) convincingly states:

> [D]emocracy within administration, if carried to the full, raises a logical dilemma in its relation to political democracy. All public organizations are presumed to have been established and to operate for public purposes (i.e., purposes of the people). They are authorized, legitimized, empowered, and usually supported by authorities outside of themselves. To what extent, then, should 'insiders,' the officers and employees, be enabled to modify their purposes, their organizational arrangements, and their means of support? It is entirely possible that internal administrative democracy might run counter to the principles and objectives of political democracy in which the organizations of government are viewed as instruments of public purpose (p.18).

As such, Mosher's argument inflicts a pessimistic idea on the neo-classical organization theorist's pro-compatibility argument. Other relationships depicted with dashed lines will be examined merely for heuristic purposes.

NOTES

1 In Korea, for example, where the same bureaucratic and democratic insti-

tutional devices that are found in Western countries have been applied to Korean public administration, it is widely pointed out that the actual operations of these institutional devices are different from what they are in Western countries. One of the major reasons frequently pointed out by a number of Korean scholars of Public Administration is that the institutional devices have been operated by key bureaucrats whose understandings and internalization of the ideologies embedded in these institutional devices are quite different from those of Western bureaucrats (e.g., Ahn, 1984:129-150).

2 Throughout my study, these conceptual elements are used as bureaucratic and democratic ideologies embedded in the institutional devices.

3 Implicitly though, the debates about the compatibility thesis have also revolved around the relationship between bureaucratic and democratic ideals.

Part II

The Evidence

This part of the book is aimed at checking the empirical validities of the debates about the compatibility thesis. In what follows, I will first describe the strategy of empirical inquiry focusing on the theoretical objects of study, the characteristics of South Korean bureaucrats chosen as the population for this inquiry, the sampling methods, the questionnaire and data collection, and finally, the methodological framework for analyzing the data collected.

Part II is composed of two chapters: Chapter Five reviews the methodology used to check the validity of the debates on the compatibility thesis and Chapter Six presents the results and discussions of data analyses I collected to test the empirical validity of the debates.

Chapter

5

Strategy of Empirical Inquiry

Choosing the Theoretical Objects of Study

The major political, economic, and social functions in contemporary societies are performed mostly by institutions (and people within them) which are large in size and complex in structure and functions. If by "bureaucracy" we mean a large, complex organization, and "bureaucrats" are therefore the individuals within these organizations, then it would not be an exaggeration to say that virtually all major institutions (and people within these institutions) in public and private sectors of modern society can be characterized as "bureaucratic." The major theoretical objects of my study are limited to public bureaucratic institutions and public bureaucrats. The substantive focus will be on public administrative agencies (and public administrators) which are often classified collectively as the executive branch of government. The significance of public administrative agencies and public administrators in their impact on society has been convincingly demonstrated in the policy study literature. They have been frequently characterized as among the crucial actors, since they determine not only the menus of policy agenda and policy options to be chosen by political decision-makers in other institutions,[1] but also, through the process of policy-implementation, the specific outcome of the policy is chosen.[2]

There are many kinds of public administrators and public administrative agencies within the executive branch of government. Most authors who have examined the subjective dimension of the compatibility thesis have focused on bureaucrats at the national or state level of government. Local bureaucrats have usually been left out.[3] This is understandable in that the services they deliver may not be the most important in a global sense. Local bureaucrats, however, as Gruber (1987:90) maintains, are "the frontline troops in the battle for democratic control, having an immediacy to people's daily lives that often leaves citizens to care passionately about what an agency does, and to feel close enough to the agency to make their concerns known." In fact, as Stone and Stone (1975) and Mosher (1975) observe, the history of public administration both in the United States and in European countries shows that, for this reason, cities have been the focal point of public administration as practice, as a field of study, and as self-conscious profession. In addition, the fact that cities, as Mosher (1975:8) maintains, are where "the services of public administrators have most demonstrably been made more effective and less costly" suggests that a study of the subjective dimension that focuses on local bureaucrats would have a high level of practical utility. All of these points indicate that there is a significant lacuna in previous authors' explorations of the subjective dimension of the compatibility thesis. For these reasons, I chose to study local bureaucrats, particularly public administrators working in public administrative agencies at the city level of government.

Another factor I considered in choosing the theoretical objects of study was the hierarchical level of bureaucrats. People within public administrative agencies range from rank-and-file employees located at the bottom of the hierarchy to executive officials located at the top. Choosing those best suited to be the objects of this study requires determining which of them best approximates the pure definition of a "bureaucrat." Of many characteristic components of "bureaucrat" on a theoretical level,[4] I particularly considered such analytic characteristics as (1) full-time career service, (2) continuous job-training, and (3) insulation of recruitment of officials and their career promotion from political changes and pressures outside the agencies. The first two characteristics prompted me to exclude the rank-and-file staff within public administrative agencies. The last characteristic led me to exclude the senior officials located at the top of public administrative agencies. Therefore, the objects of my study became the mid-level public bureaucrats. There is also a substantive reason for this choice. Although they have weaker formal authority to make decisions than senior public officials, they can, and do, supercede their senior officials in many cases. For example, the quality of decisions made and the effectiveness of implementing the decisions are frequently determined by the type of information that is available to decision-makers and implementors. In most cases, the hierarchy of formal authority is affected by one's location in the channel of communication. Located in the middle of communication channels, the mid-level bureaucrats can, and do, filter the substance and quantity of information that flows up and down within an agency as well as in and out of the agencies. Thus, they can, and do, impose effective constraints on decision-making of senior officials and on the implementation of decisions by the rank-and-file.

Korean Bureaucrats as an Empirical Population

I selected my sample subjects from the population of 3,031 mid-level public officials working at the main and regional offices of the Seoul Metropolitan Government in South Korea (called hereafter Seoul city government, or simply the government).[5] Based on consultations with specialists on personnel management of the government, I empirically defined "mid-level bureaucrats" to be officials in the main office whose ranks ranged from the 2nd to the 6th grades, as well as officials in regional offices whose ranks ranged from the 4th to the 6th grades.[6]

I chose this population because the issue of democratization in Korea is important, and the role of local bureaucrats in the process is also crucial. A series of democratic events, often called "democratization movements," occurred in Korea during the 1980s. As well documented by Lee (1990), the sudden death of President Park in 1979 ignited an explosion of diverse demands from almost all sectors of Korean society. These demands were matched by the establishment of diverse groups and institutions, and were molded into forceful movements for the democratization of the Korean government. The demands for political democratization met with severe resistance from Chun's regime which was as authoritarian as that of President Park. The harsh repressions under Chun's regime, however, did not dampen political democratization movements. Instead, they resulted in diversification of groups participating in the movements, strengthening the organizational solidarity of the groups and widening citizen support for the movements. The dynamism was evidenced by massive protests in the center of Seoul city during June 1987. The protests were led by diverse and fairly well-organized groups of people including religious figures, intellectuals, journalists, students, workers, farmers, opposition political parties and ordinary citizens. The number of participants in these protests was so large that it was described as "the largest since the April 19 uprising in 1960." A series of these political democratization movements became a primary force ending Chun's regime and enabling direct national presidential election to be held for the first time in nearly 20 years.

At least two consequences of these movements are apparent, and highlight the appropriateness of Korean bureaucrats and bureaucracy for study of the subjective dimension of the compatibility thesis. First, these movements have led Korean officials to be exposed to diverse conceptions of democratic ideologies, including those that I wish to examine. They came to witness quite vividly many clashes between authoritarianism and diverse demands for "democrac*ies*," and the immediate consequences of these clashes. Second, government officials, whether they liked it or not, were now forced to be a part of these democratization movements. As a matter of fact, a substantial portion of the efforts toward democratization has been channelled into exerting pressure on government officials for democratization of public administration. A prime example of this pressure is the demand for implementation of local self-government which was written into the constitution but not implemented for nearly 30 years. Since one of President Roh's electoral promises was to bring local self-government into being during his term, the issue of local self-government received top priority by both the opposition and the ruling parties.[7]

At least in Korea, the issue of local self-government must be interpreted as the issue of institutional revolution. This is because it involves a fundamental rearrangement of the structural bases of virtually all political and economic institutions which have been established under the centralization principle of government. For example, Seoul city government emerged as one of the major centers of the movement toward local self-government. As a result, the government is independent of the central government's control, the city mayor is elected directly by the residents of the city, and the government thus has to be more responsive to its citizens. Internally, the movement toward local self-government means that the regional offices are no longer under the direct control of the main office. As such, the demands for local self-government mean the politicization of city government and a fundamental breakdown of entrenched hierarchical, bureaucratic structures.[8]

All of these developments suggest it is likely that the officials included in my empirical population will have quite contrasting attitudes and beliefs about bureaucratic and democratic ideologies. Thus, they provide a sufficiently diverse pool of potential subjects that should maximize my chances to examine the variety of perspectives that are pertinent to the compatibility thesis. In addition, because implementation of local self-government is imminent in Seoul city government, this situation provides a good opportunity for me to establish a baseline for a future quasi-experimental study of another important theme. That is, by studying the subjective dimension of the compatibility thesis before and after the transition took place in Seoul city government, I can eventually examine the extent to which institutional change affects individuals' subjective beliefs and attitudinal systems.

Viewed from a methodological standpoint, the population selected for study is appropriate in that it has characteristics that closely approximate the previously mentioned theoretical definition of "bureaucracy" and "bureaucrats" especially in four respects: individual, organizational, institutional, and cultural. The individual officials included in this population have all three characteristics of "bureaucrats." That is, they are all career civil servants who were recruited through highly competitive written and oral examinations. They are highly motivated to be trained not only at training institutions owned by their city governments, but also at other educational institutions, including ordinary colleges and universities. Except for a few cases, their career promotions have been insulated fairly well from political pressures.

In addition, the Seoul city government included in this empirical population is located within an organizational and institutional setting which is quite bureaucratic. As of 1990, Seoul was composed of more than 10 million citizens (3 million households), about one-fourth of South Korea's total population. The demands pressing the Seoul city government are huge and diverse, leading the government to increase its budget and manpower. In 1990, the budget was over $6 billion (compared to about $600 million in 1980). As of 1989, the total number of employees in the Seoul city government topped 50,000, compared to 40,000 employees in 1980.[9]

The variety of demands was matched by the structural and functional complexity of Seoul city government as an organization. Seoul government is run by one main office called *Bon-Chong* and 22 regional offices called *Gu-Chong*. The organizational functions of these main and regional offices are diversified by the types of demands. The main office is organized mainly into 15 bureaus called *Guk*, which are collectively divided into 85 divisions and 285 subsections. All of these organizational components of Seoul city government are molded into a hierarchical, bureaucratic structure. A brief look at the organizational chart of the government suggests that all regional offices are hierarchically controlled by the main office. Although much discretion to make autonomous decisions in performing tasks has been recently delegated to the regional offices, all major resources for regional offices (budget and manpower) are distributed and controlled by the main office. The hierarchical structure is found not only between the main and regional offices as such, but also within each office. As commonly depicted in each office's organizational chart, the organizational components of each office are hierarchically interconnected within each functional category.

Bureaucratic nature is found not only in the organizational setting of the city government, but also in its political, institutional setting. That is, the city mayor is not elected, but is appointed by the president. The city government as a whole has been under the supervision of the prime minister's office. The Korean officials included in my empirical population are also located within a cultural setting which is generally amenable to bureaucratic ideology. As most of the scholars who study the cultural background of Korean public administrators argue, the traditional value systems in Korea are composed of many elements which are fairly consistent with bureaucratic ideology.[10] "Authoritarianism," "formalism," "order-oriented view of nature" and "emphasis upon loyalty to the three equivalents (king, father, and teacher)" are merely some of the many examples of Korean traditional values and beliefs cited as evidence for this argument.

Sample Subjects and Sampling Procedures

I selected 300 sample subjects from this population, using the stratified random sampling method. In accordance with the relative ratio of the total number of mid-level officials between the main office and the 22 regional offices (i.e., 1:2.8), I decided to choose 79 sample subjects from the main office and 221 subjects from the regional offices.

In determining who would be chosen as the actual respondents among the 79 sample subjects assigned to the main office, I first considered the functional characteristics of the departments to which the respondents belonged. I decided to select respondents working in those departments dealing with economic and industrial policy, environmental policy, welfare policy, maintenance of internal and social order and security, and those dealing with public relations.[11] For efficiency, I chose five departments from the main office, each of which were recommended by experts on Seoul city government's organizational structures and functions, as best representative of each functional category. Based upon the personnel data provided by the experts, I stratified the 79 respondents in accordance to the ratio of the total number of mid-level officials among these five departments and the between-rank ratio embedded in the population of the main office.

Similar procedures were used in sampling respondents from the regional offices. All regional offices have quite similar organizational characteristics (e.g., hierarchical structures, functional arrangements of tasks, size of work force, etc.) and provided the same public services. This suggested that the selection of these regional offices for the survey would not inject a serious bias into sampling procedures and interpretations of data gathered from the survey. Considering these characteristics of the regional offices, I chose three regional offices which were the most typical and easily accessible.[12] I then stratified the 221 samples assigned to the regional offices in accordance with the relative ratio of total mid-level officials among these three regional offices (i.e., 75, 73, and 73 for Office A, Office B, and Office C, respectively) and the between-rank ratio embedded in the population of all regional offices.

Once the size of each elementary sampling unit was determined in this way, I randomly chose the predetermined number of actual respondents among all relevant officials, using the organizational charts of the main office and the three regional offices. The structure of my stratified sample as explained, is presented in Table 5-1.

Table 5 - 1 **Composition of Empirical Population and Stratified Sample**

Office & Bureaus		Rank: 2nd Grade	3rd Grade	4th Grade	5th Grade	6th Grade	Total
Empirical Population	Main Office	14	7	79	240	456	796
	Regional Office	-	-	132	528	1575	2235
	Total	14	7	211	768	2031	3031
Stratified Sample — Main Office	Bureau of Industrial & Economic Affairs	-	-	1	6	12	19
	Bureau of Parks & Environment	1	-	1	5	8 (7)	15 (14)
	Bureau of Health and Social Affairs	1	-	1	4	6	12
	Bureau of Internal Affairs	-	1	5	8	15	29
	Office of Public Relations	-	-	-	1	3	4
	Sub-Total	2	1	8	24	44 (43)	79 (78)
Stratified Sample — Local Office	Office A	-	-	5	18	52 (51)	75 (74)
	Office B	-	-	4	17	52	73
	Office C	-	-	4	17	52	73
	Sub-Total	-	-	13	52	156 (155)	221 (220)
Stratified Sample	Total	2	1	21	76	200 (198)	300 (298)

Note : Two respondents provided incomplete and useless responses. They were thus dropped out. Numbers in parentheses are those adjusted for these respondents.

Questionnaire and Data Collection

I used two sets of questionnaires to collect data: one for R-methodological analysis and the other for Q-methodological analysis.[13] The questionnaire for R-methodological analysis was composed of 72 items which were organized into two parts. The first part contains 24 items to identify the respondents' traits which will be used as independent variables (see Part I of the questionnaire presented in Appendix I). The second part was composed of 48 statements reflecting the conceptual components and types of bureaucratic and democratic ideologies specified in Chapter Four (see Part II of questionnaire). The questionnaire for the Q-methodological analysis, which is called, "Q-sample" by the proponents of Q-methodology, was composed of the same 48 statements; however, each statement was printed on a separate card.[14]

My survey research was done during the first three weeks of August 1990. Each of the 300 respondents chosen was marked on the organizational chart of each office sampled. After getting approvals from chief officials of the five departments within the main office and chief officials of the three regional offices, I distributed the questionnaire to each of the pre-selected respondents. Of the pre-selected 300 respondents, 270 were asked to answer only the questionnaire constructed for R-methodological analysis. The respondents were asked to rate the questionnaire items on a Likert-type seven-point scale reflecting the degree of their agreement or disagreement. The questionnaires completed by these respondents were collected three to four days after giving the questionnaires to them. The responses of only two respondents were unusable. Some missing data in the remaining 268 responses were replaced with average scores. According to the respondents, it took an average of 30 to 40 minutes for them to complete the questionnaire.

The remaining 30 respondents were selected randomly from Office C. The survey of these respondents was performed by face-to-face contact. Each respondent was invited into a room provided by the chief of a particular office, and asked to perform three tasks in a consecutive manner. First, the respondent was asked do the same thing as the other 270 respondents. Upon completing this task, the respondent was asked to perform another task. The respondent was asked to deal with 48 items in the second part of the questionnaire. The content of the items and response scales were the same as those used for the first task. In the second task, however, the items and the Likert-type seven-point response scale were arranged in a different format. Similar to the 48 questionnaire items, each of the seven response categories was also written on individual cards. The respondent was then asked to place each questionnaire item on one of the seven response cards which fit best with his/her response.[15]

After completing the second task, the respondent was asked to perform a final task, called "Q-sorting" by the proponents of Q-methodology. Each subject was asked to place the 48 cards of Q-samples on a Q-sorting scale chart (see Figure 5-1) according to the extent to which he/she evaluated the statement written on each card as "democratic." More specfically, each subject was instructed first to sort the cards into three groups (i.e., democratic statements, undemocratic statements, and those hard to judge). The subject was then instructed to select two statements which he/she thought were the most democratic out of the group of statements he/she sorted as democratic, and then to place them on any of the two cells located on the far-right side of the chart. Similarly, the subject was instructed to select the most undemocratic statements out of the group of statements he/she sorted as undemocratic, and then to place them on any of the two cells located on the far-left side of the chart. The subject was then instructed to shuffle all the remaining 44 cards and to sort these cards into the same three groups. Then the respondent was asked to select three cards of statements which he/she thought were the most democratic among the secondly-sorted group of democratic statements and then to place them on the three cells rated as "+4." The subject was then asked to proceed performing a similar sorting procedure for the second-most undemocratic statements. For these statements, the respondent was asked to place them on any of the three cells rated as "-4." The subject was then asked to deal with the remaining 38 statements following the same procedures until all cards were placed on the chart. The respondent was encouraged to modify his/her previous sorting whenever a modification seemed necessary.[16]

The responses provided by these 30 respondents were all usable. There were no missing responses. On average, it took about 30 to 40 minutes for each of these 30 respondents to complete the first task, about 15 to 20 minutes to complete the second task, and about 45 minutes to complete the Q-sorting session.

Methodological Frameworks for Data Analyses

The data were analyzed differently by the two types of research questions mentioned in Chapter One (i.e., descriptive and explanatory research questions). In the following sections, I will describe the basic methodological frameworks of my data analysis for each type of research question.

The Methodological Framework for Descriptive Data Analyses

As mentioned in Chapter One, one of the major descriptive questions I wish to examine is: "To what extent are bureaucratic and democratic ideologies com-

Figure 5 - 1 **Response Scale Chart for Q-Sorting**

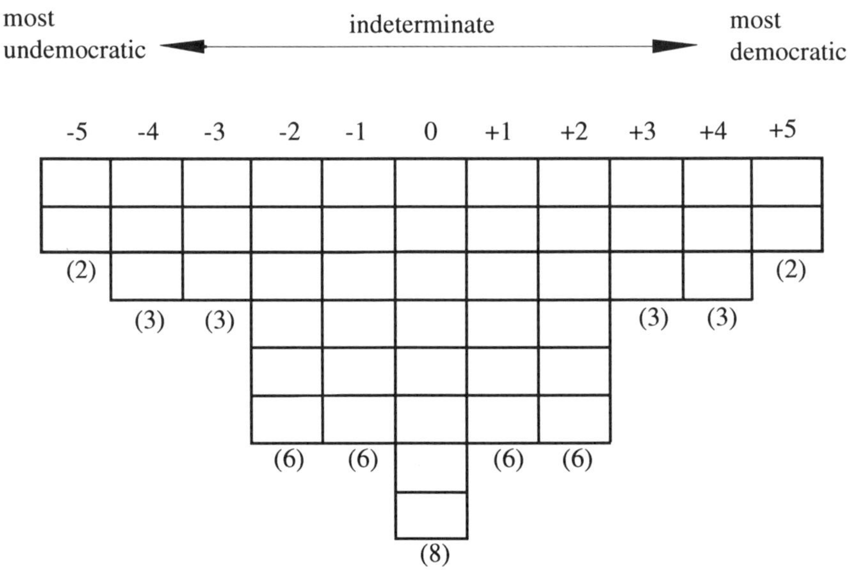

patible or incompatible with one another within individual bureaucrats' own minds?" I first examined this question within the conventional R-methodological framework. Following the assumption underlying classical measurement theory, I assumed that each of the theoretically-construed conceptual components was a latent variable which could not be directly observed; rather it could be measured only indirectly through a medium of empirical indicators. The 48 statements in the R-methodological questionnaire mentioned above served as these indicators. Response scores on these questionnaire statements were analyzed within the framework of conventional factor analysis. That is, the "compatibility" was examined in terms of the correlation coefficients among the factors identified. As in typical R-methodological factor analyses, factors were interpreted as abstract concepts. These concepts were assumed to be observed collectively by the individual indicators loaded on that factor. In my case, factors correspond particularly to the theoretically-construed conceptual components of bureaucratic and democratic ideologies. Accordingly, the relationships among these conceptual components were analyzed in terms of the magnitudes and directions of correlations among these factors. If the coefficient was positive and significantly greater than zero, then this was interpreted as an indication of compatibility (if negative and significantly smaller than zero, then it is evidence of incompatibility) among the conceptual components represented by the factors.

Note that compatibility among several conceptual components were excluded from the R-methodological descriptive analyses because the multiple indicators of these conceptual components were found to have low reliability (see Appendix II). They are particularly the egalitarian democratic ideology (EQDEMO) and all of its conceptual components (INTEDEMO, EXTEDIDL, and INTEDNST); the internal liberal democratic ideology (INTLDEMO); the internal liberal and popular democratic instrumental principles (INTLDNST and INTPDNST), and those pertaining to the external liberal and popular democratic ideals (EXTLDIDL and EXTPDIDL). Accordingly, the relationships among these conceptual components had to be excluded from my R-methodological descriptive analyses. These relationships were examined only within the Q-methodological framework in which, as Brown (1980) maintains, the empirical validity and reliability of the questionnaire are nowhere at issue. In sum, my R-methodological descriptive analyses dealt with all relationships depicted in Set III, all but the relationship between BURO and EQDEMO in Set I, and all but the relationships between INTBURO and INTEDEMO, and between INTBURO and INTLDEMO in Set II.

This R-methodological analysis was followed by Q-methodological analysis. Q-methodological analysis was performed on the data collected from the third task mentioned above. The major reason for examining the theme of subjective compatibility within the Q-methodological framework was to deal with omissions from the R-methodological analysis. In the R-methodological analysis, democratic ideology was predefined in terms of the conceptual components that I abstracted from the theoretical literature. The degree of a respondent's internalization of democratic ideology was then measured by the extent to which the respondent agreed or disagreed with the statements that were supposed to collectively express the theoretical version of democratic ideology. What this R-methodological measurement scheme enabled me to accomplish was the relationship of bureaucratic ideology with only one version of democratic ideology (i.e., theoretical version). Bureaucrats, however, may have diverse perspectives on democratic ideology. For example, some bureaucrats may view certain conceptual components of the theoretical version of democratic ideology as democratic, while others view the same components as undemocratic or irrelevant to democratic ideology. Accordingly, it is likely that the content of subjective compatibility may be more diverse than I can describe with the R-methodological analysis. Q-methodology enabled me to supplement this deficiency of R-methodological analysis as follows:[17]

The perspective of individual subjects on democratic ideology are represented by the raw data itself. That is, the location of statements on each of the completed Q-sorting scale charts (i.e., the magnitude and sign of the statements) represents the extent to which each subject evaluates the conceptual components expressed by the statements as democratic. Therefore, each Q-sorting scale chart makes it possible to analyze each subject's own perspective particularly in terms of which conceptual components constitute his or her own conception of democratic ideology.

In order to get a parsimonious understanding of the diverse perspectives of individual subjects, I performed a Q-factor analysis using the p.c.q. computer program.[18] The core of this Q-factor analysis was to identify "Q-factors," where each Q-factor represents essentially a group of subjects who share a common perspective, and where the number of Q-factors are smaller than the number of subjects. Therefore, identification of Q-factors enabled me to summarize the diverse individual perspectives with a smaller number of group perspectives. In the analysis, this appeared as a reduction of the original 30 Q-sorting scale charts into a smaller number of new Q-sorting scale charts (the number of these charts is equal to the number of Q-factors identified). The new Q-sorting scale charts were obtained through a series of conversion processes in which an array of factor scores associated with each Q-factor were converted into rounded factor scores so that their scaling scheme conformed to the original one (i.e., -5, -4, -3, -2, -1, 0, +1, +2, +3, +4, +5). The data arranged in these new Q-sorting scale charts was used as a primary basis of my Q-methodological analysis.[19]

I scrutinized the content of each group's perspective on democratic ideology by analyzing the magnitudes and directions of the rounded Q-factor scores of the 22 statements that I thought expressed the conceptual components of democratic ideology (i.e., D1 through D22). Note that a rounded factor score of a certain statement on a new Q-sorting scale chart represents the extent to which the subjects associated with a Q-factor *collectively* view the conceptual component expressed by the statement is evaluated as democratic.[20] That is, Q-factor scores of statements are essentially measures of the degree to which certain conceptual components reflected in the statements are salient to a group of respondents represented by a Q-factor. In other words, they are the measures of the extent to which certain conceptual components are significant in constituting a perspective shared by a group of bureaucrats.[21]

Following the conventional practice of Q-methodology, I interpreted a conceptual component expressed by a statement as a highly salient ingredient of a group perspective on democratic ideology, particularly if the statement's rounded Q-factor score was equal to or greater than three. Otherwise, it was interpreted as indicating that the corresponding conceptual components do not significantly constitute the group perspective. Note that a number of conceptual components of democratic ideology were expressed by negatively-worded statements (i.e., D4, D7, D8, D9, D10, D14, D18, and D19). For these cases, the interpretation was reversed. That is, if the rounded factor scores of these statements were equal to or less than -3, the conceptual components expressed by these statements in a positive way were interpreted as highly salient ingredients of a group perspective. Otherwise, they were interpreted as insiginificant in constituting it.

After examining each group's perspective on democratic ideology in a separate fashion, I compared the group perspectives focusing on the uniqueness of each perspective and the commonality among them. The unique characteristics of each group perspective were described particularly in terms of the content of the statements that distinguished a Q-factor from other Q-factors. Similarly, the commonality among the perspectives was described in terms of the content of the statements that did not distinguish the corresponding Q-factor from other Q-factors. I judged whether or not a statement distinguished a certain Q-factor from other Q-factors by examining the extent to which the statement's rounded factor scores associated with other Q-factors. Employing a 1% significance level, I judged that the two rounded factor scores were significantly different from one another if they differed by an amount in excess of 2.56 units of standard error of differences. The statement was then interpreted as distinguishing the perspective represented by the Q-factor from other perspectives represented by other Q-factors. Otherwise, the statement was interpreted as constituting a commonality among the perspectives.

After scrutinizing bureaucrats' own perspectives on democratic ideology, I then examined the theme of subjective compatibility in two ways. First, I examined it by investigating the locations of individual statements that I thought expressed the conceptual components of bureaucratic ideology on the Q-sorting charts obtained as a result of the Q-factor analysis explained above. Note that the subjects were asked to sort out these statements in accordance with the extent to which they thought of them as democratic. The rounded Q-factor scores of these statements thus can be directly used as a measure of the extent to which a group of subjects associated with a Q-factor understand the bureaucratic conceptual components expressed by these statements as compatible with the democratic ideology presumed in their own minds. More specifically, if the rounded Q-factor score of a bureaucratic statement was equal to or greater than three, it was interpreted as indicating that the subjects associated with a Q-factor collectively view the bureaucratic conceptual component expressed by the statement as highly compatible with their own conception of democratic ideology. If equal to or less than -3, it was interpreted as indicating that they view the bureaucratic conceptual component as highly incompatible with their own conception of democratic ideology. Note that which conceptual components are particularly salient to each group's conception of democratic ideology has already been clarified by the above-mentioned analysis. Therefore, it was possible to clarify particularly which conceptual components of bureaucratic ideology are understood by each group of subjects as compatible or incompatible with which conceptual components of democratic ideology.

Second, the Q-methodological examination of subjective compatibility was also made on the diverse sets of the relationships between the conceptual components of bureaucratic ideology and those of democratic ideology specified in Figure 4-2. The conceptual components were expressed by a multiple number of statements. Therefore, I examined the subjective compatibility by analyzing the extent to which the average Q-factor score of a group of bureaucratic statements collectively expressing the conceptual components of bureaucratic ideology is different from or similar to that of a group of democratic statements that collectively express the conceptual components of democratic ideology. If the average rounded Q-factor score of a certain group of bureaucratic statements was greater or smaller than that of a group of democratic statements, then this was interpreted as evidence of incompatibility between the bureaucratic and democratic conceptual components that the corresponding statements collectively express (if not significantly greater or smaller, then evidence of compatibility). In statistical terms, this was an analysis of the difference between two means. The test statistic used for this analysis is:

$$t = \frac{\overline{X} - \overline{Y}}{\sqrt{\dfrac{\dfrac{(X_i - \overline{X})^2 + (Y_j - \overline{Y})^2}{n_x + n_y - 2} \times (n_x - n_y)}{n_x \times n_y}}}$$

, where

t = t-value;
$\overline{X}$ = average rounded Q-factor scores of the statements associated with a bureaucratic conceptual component, X;
$\overline{Y}$ = average rounded Q-factor scores of the statements associated with a democratic conceptual component, Y;
X_i = rounded Q-factor score of ith statement associated with X;
Y_j = rounded Q-factor score of jth statement associated with Y;
n_x = number of statements associated with X;
n_y = number of statements associated with Y;
i = 1,2,3,...,26;
j = 1,2,3,...,22.

The comparison between the result of this second analysis and that of the R-methodological analysis enabled me to investigate the extent to which the methodological difference may produce substantively different conclusions about the subjective compatibility. Note that a different number of statements were used for these two types of analyses. Only those statements that passed the reliability test were taken into account in the R-methodological analysis, whereas all statements were considered in the Q-methodological analysis. Thus, in order to make the comparison fair, I performed a second Q-methodological analysis with the statements that were used for the R-methodological analysis, and compared its result with that of the R-methodological analysis.

The Methodological Framework for Explanatory Data Analyses

My explanatory analysis is, as pointed out in Chapter One, aimed at finding major factors that affect bureaucrats' internalization of bureaucratic and democratic ideologies and the degree of subjective compatibility. I attempted to find them within the R-methodological framework, especially through multiple regression analysis.[22] That is, the attitudinal variations found in the descriptive analyses (especially the R-methodological descriptive analyses) were treated as dependent variables. Of diverse traits possessed by individual bureaucrats, a number that are relevant to the theoretical interests of this study or expected to have significant explanatory power were selected as independent variables. Of primary concern in my explanatory analyses were the magnitudes and directions of the regression coefficients of these independent variables.

Dependent Variables. As summarized in Table 5-2, two sets of dependent variables were of primary concern in my explanatory analyses. The first set of dependent variables are those representing the variations of individual bureaucrats' attitudes and beliefs about each of the theoretically-construed conceptual

Table 5 - 2 **Categories and Measures of Dependent Variables**

Categories	Variable Name	Measures
Set I: Variables Representing Attitudes Toward Individual Components of Bureaucratic and Democratic Ideologies	**BURO**	SUM (B1, B3, B4, B5, B8, B9, B10, B11, B13, B14, B15, B16, B17, B18, B19, B20, B21, B22, B23, B25, B26)
	DEMO	SUM (D1, D2, D3, D6, D11, D12, D15, D16, D17, D20, D21, D22)
	LIBDEMO	SUM (D1, D2, D3, D6, D17)
	POPDEMO	SUM (D12, D15, D16, D21, D22)
	INTBURO	SUM (B3, B4, B10, B11, B13, B14, B15, B16, B17, B18, B19, B20, B21, B22, B23, B25, B26)
	INTDEMO	SUM (D3, D12, D15, D17, D20, D21, D22)
	INTPDEMO	SUM (D12, D15, D21, D22)
	INTBIDL	SUM (B3, B4, B10, B11, B13, B14, B15)
	EXTBIDL	SUM (B1, B5, B8, B9, B13)
	INTBINST	SUM (B16, B17, B18, B19, B20, B21, B22, B23, B25, B26)
	INTDIDL	SUM (D3, D12, D15)
	EXTDIDL	SUM (D1, D2, D6, D11, D16)
	INTDINST	SUM (D17, D20, D21, D22)

(continued on next page)

Table 5 - 2 (continued) **Categories and Measures of Dependent Variables**

Categories	Variable Name	Measures
Set II: Variables Representing Congruity Between Attitudes Toward Components of Bureaucratic & Democratic Ideologies	**BURO-DEMO**	$\sqrt{(\text{ZBURO} - \text{ZDEMO})^2 / 2}$
	BURO-LIBDEMO	$\sqrt{(\text{ZBURO} - \text{ZLIBDEMO})^2 / 2}$
	BURO-POPDEMO	$\sqrt{(\text{ZBURO} - \text{ZPOPDEMO})^2 / 2}$
	INTBURO-INTDEMO	$\sqrt{(\text{ZINTBURO} - \text{ZINTDEMO})^2 / 2}$
	INTBURO-INTPDEMO	$\sqrt{(\text{ZINTBURO} - \text{ZINTPDEMO})^2 / 2}$
	INTBIDL-INTDIDL	$\sqrt{(\text{ZINTBIDL} - \text{ZINTDIDL})^2 / 2}$
	INTBIDL-EXTDIDL	$\sqrt{(\text{ZINTBIDL} - \text{ZEXTDIDL})^2 / 2}$
	INTBIDL-INTDINST	$\sqrt{(\text{ZINTBIDL} - \text{ZINTDINST})^2 / 2}$
	EXTBIDL-INTDIDL	$\sqrt{(\text{ZEXTBIDL} - \text{ZINTDIDL})^2 / 2}$
	EXTBIDL-EXTDIDL	$\sqrt{(\text{ZEXTBIDL} - \text{ZEXTDIDL})^2 / 2}$

(continued on next page)

Table 5 - 2 (continued) **Categories and Measures of Dependent Variables**

Categories	Variable Name	Measures
Set II: Variables Representing Congruity Between Attitudes Toward Components of Bureaucratic Ideology and Those Toward Components of Democratic Ideology	**EXTBIDL-INTDINST**	$\sqrt{(\text{ZEXTBIDL} - \text{ZINTDINST})^2 / 2}$
	INTBINST-INTDIDL	$\sqrt{(\text{ZINTBINST} - \text{ZINTDIDL})^2 / 2}$
	INTBINST-EXTDIDL	$\sqrt{(\text{ZINTBINST} - \text{ZEXTDIDL})^2 / 2}$
	INTBINST-INTDINST	$\sqrt{(\text{ZINTBINST} - \text{ZINTDINST})^2 / 2}$
	INTDIDL-EXTDIDL	$\sqrt{(\text{ZINTDIDL} - \text{ZEXTDIDL})^2 / 2}$
	INTDINST-EXTDIDL	$\sqrt{(\text{ZINTDINST} - \text{ZEXTDIDL})^2 / 2}$

Note: a. Standardized variables are notated by placing "Z" in front of variable name (e.g., ZBURO, ZDEMO, etc.)
b. Notation meanings are as follows:

BURO : Attitudes toward bureaucratic ideology
DEMO : Attitudes toward democratic ideology
LIBDEMO : Attitudes toward liberal democratic ideology
POPDEMO : Attitudes toward popular democratic ideology
INTBURO : Attitudes toward internal bureaucratic ideology
INTDEMO : Attitudes toward internal democratic ideology
INTPDEMO : Attitudes toward internal popular democratic ideology

(continued on next page)

Table 5 - 2 (continued) **Categories and Measures of Dependent Variables**

INTBIDL :	Attitudes toward internal bureaucratic ideals
EXTBIDL :	Attitudes toward external bureaucratic ideals
INTBINST :	Attitudes toward internal bureaucratic instrumental principles
INTDIDL :	Attitudes toward internal democratic ideals
EXTDIDL :	Attitudes toward external democratic ideals
INTDINST :	Attitudes toward internal democratic instrumental principles
BURO-DEMO :	Congruity between attitudes toward bureaucratic ideology and those toward democratic ideology
BURO-LIBDEMO :	Congruity between attitudes toward bureaucratic ideology and those toward liberal democratic ideology
BURO-POPDEMO :	Congruity between attitudes toward bureaucratic ideology and those toward popular democratic ideology
INTBURO-INTDEMO:	Congruity between attitudes toward internal bureaucratic ideology and those toward internal democratic ideology
INTBURO-INTPDEMO:	Congruity between attitudes towards internal bureaucratic ideology and those toward internal popular democratic ideology
INTBIDL-INTDIDL :	Congruity between attitudes toward internal bureaucratic ideals and those toward internal democratic ideals
INTBIDL-EXTDIDL :	Congruity between attitudes toward internal bureaucratic ideals and those toward external democratic ideals
INTBIDL-INTDINST :	Congruity between attitudes toward internal bureaucratic ideals and those toward internal democratic instrumental principles

(continued on next page)

Table 5 - 2 (continued) **Categories and Measures of Dependent Variables**

Variable	Description
EXTBIDL-INTDIDL :	Congruity between attitudes toward external bureaucratic ideals and those toward internal democratic ideals
EXTBIDL-EXTDIDL :	Congruity between attitudes toward external bureaucratic ideals and those toward external democratic ideals
EXTBIDL-INTDINST :	Congruity between attitudes toward external bureaucratic ideals and those toward internal democratic instrumental principles
INTBINST-INTDIDL :	Congruity between attitudes toward internal bureaucratic instrumental principles and those toward internal democratic ideals
INTBINST-EXTDIDL :	Congruity between attitudes toward internal bureaucratic instrumental principles and those toward external democratic ideals
INTBINST-INTDINST :	Congruity between attitudes toward internal bureaucratic instrumental principles and those toward internal democratic instrumental principles
INTDIDL-EXTDIDL :	Congruity between attitudes toward internal democratic ideals and those toward external democratic ideals
EXTBIDL-INTDINST :	Congruity between attitudes toward internal democratic instrumental principles and those toward external democratic ideals

components.[23] Just as the theoretically-construed conceptual components were treated in the descriptive analyses as latent factors being indirectly measured with several empirical indicators, so was each of these dependent variables treated as a composite of several empirical indicators. That is, each of these dependent variables was measured by the sum of individual bureaucrats' scores on the indicators having significant and positive loadings on a factor that corresponds to the dependent variable.

The second set of dependent variables was considered in order to explain the variations of compatibility between bureaucratic and democratic ideologies reflected within the minds of individual bureaucrats. The dependent variables included in the second set are essentially the measures of "attitudinal congruity"; that is, the extent to which individual bureaucrats accept or reject to the same degree, the two conceptual components or types, of bureaucratic and democratic ideologies juxtaposed with one another (Figure 4-2). Operationally, the attitudinal congruity was measured by the distance between the point representing individual bureaucrats' standardized attitudinal scores on the two conceptual components and the 45° line which represents a perfect congruity (see Figure 5-2). The geometric formula for calculating this distance is:

$$XY_i = \sqrt{\frac{(X_i - Y_i)^2}{2}}$$, where

XY_i = an individual bureaucrat i's score of attitudinal congruity pertaining to the two conceptual components or types of bureaucratic and democratic ideology (say, X and Y) under consideration;

X_i = an individual bureaucrat i's standardized score of attitudinal favorableness regarding one of two conceptual components, X;

Y_i = an individual bureaucrat i's standardized score of attitudinal favorableness regarding the other conceptual component, Y.

Independent Variables. The independent variables examined in my explanatory analyses are summarized in Table 5-3. Note that they are classified into three categories in accordance with the level of their specificity. Category I includes the most inclusive independent variables which represent basically the four types of individual bureaucrats' traits mentioned in Chapter One. That is, included in this category are the three objective types of traits (i.e., "organizational traits," "socio-economic traits," and "socialization backgrounds"), and the subjective type of traits (i.e., "cultural traits," "religious traits," and "the trait pertaining to perspectives on work-related human nature"). As indicated in Chapter One, most previous authors have taken the objective types of traits as

Figure 5 - 2 **Measure of "Attitudinal Congruity"**

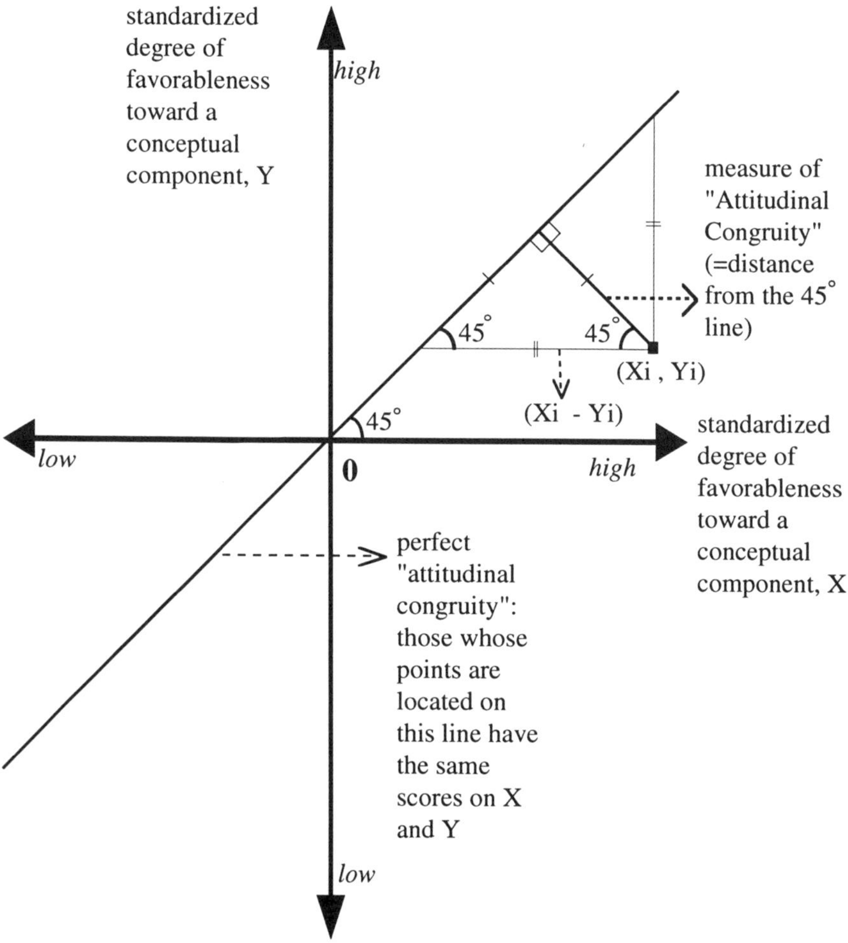

Table 5 - 3 **Categories and Measures of Independent Variables**

Independent Variables			Meaning of Variables Under Category III and Measurement Scheme
Categ. I	Categ. II	Categ. III	
Organizational Traits	Types of Office (3-1)	OFFICE	Dichotomous Discrete Measure: If respondent works at main office, OFFICE = 1; otherwise (i.e.,regional offices) 0.
	Types of Major Policy Dealt with by the Bureau (3-1)	INDECON ENV WELF INTORD PUBREL	6-Categorical Discrete Measure: If respondent belongs to bureau in charge of industrial and economic policies, INDECON = 1; otherwise 0. If respondent belongs to bureau in charge of environmental policies , ENV = 1; otherwise 0. If respondent belongs to bureau in charge of social welfare policies, WELF = 1; otherwise 0. If respondent belongs to bureau in charge of management of internal affairs, INTORD = 1; otherwise 0. If respondent belongs to bureau in charge of public relations, PUBREL = 1; otherwise 0. Category excluded represents those who belong to bureau in charge of other types of policies.
	Years of Service (3-2)	YRSERVE	Continuous Measure
	Official Ranking (3-3)	HIRANK MIDRANK	3-categorical Discrete Measure: If respondent's ranking is higher than 5th grade, HIRANK = 1; otherwise 0. If respondent is a 5th grader, MIDRANK = 1; otherwise 0. Category excluded represents 6th graders.
	Job Classification (3-3)	JOBCLAS	Dichotomous Discrete Measure: If respondent is classified as general administrative career, JOBCLAS = 1; otherwise (i.e., technical career) 0.
	Degree of Routinization of Performing Tasks (3-4)	ROUTINE MID-ROUTN	3-categorical Discrete Measure: If respondent notes his/her job is "slightly routinized," "routinized," or "very routinized," ROUTINE = 1, otherwise 0. If "middle," MIDROUTN = 1; otherwise 0. Category excluded represents those who checked "slightly unroutinized," "unroutinized," or "very unroutinized."

(continued on next page)

Table 5 - 3 (continued) **Categories and Measures of Independent Variables**

Independent Variables			Meaning of Variables Under Category III and Measurement Scheme
Categ. I	Categ. II	Categ. III	
Organ-iza-tional Traits	Number of Superiors (3-5)	SUPERIOR	Continuous Measure
	Number of Subordinates (3-6)	SUB-ORDNT	Continuous Measure
Socio-Econo-mic Traits	Age (1-1)	AGE	Continuous Measure
	Annual Family Income (1-2)	INCOME	Continuous Measure
	Level of Education (1-3)	PREUNIV	3-categorical Discrete Measure: If respondent did not attend college, PREUNIV = 1; otherwise 0. If respondent attended college, UNIV = 1; otherwise 0. Category excluded represents those whose educational level is higher than college.
		UNIV	
	Gender (1-4)	SEX	Dichotomous Discrete Measure: If respondent is male, SEX = 1; otherwise 0
Sociali-zation Back-grounds	Region Where Grown-up (2-1)	RURAL	3-categorical Discrete Measure: If respondent grew up mostly in rural area during middle and high school, RURAL = 1; otherwise 0. If respondent grew up mostly in mid-size urban area, MIDURBAN = 1; otherwise 0. Category excluded represents those who grew up mostly in large, metropolitan area.
		MID-URBAN	
	Family Economic Condition (2-2)	POOR	3-categorical Discrete Measure: If respondent reports family was "slightly poor," "poor," or "very poor" during middle and high school, POOR = 1; otherwise 0. If "middle," AVECON = 1; otherwise 0. Cateogry excluded represents those who report "slightly rich," "rich," or "very rich."
		AVECON	

(continued on next page)

Table 5 - 3 (continued) **Categories and Measures of Independent Variables**

Independent Variables			Meaning of Variables Under Category III and Measurement Scheme
Categ. I	Categ. II	Categ. III	
Socialization Backgrounds	Early Loss of Parents (2-3)	PARNTDIE	Dichotomous Discrete Measure: If at least one of respondent's parents were dead when he/she was in middle and high school, PARNTDIE = 1; otherwise (i.e., both were all alive) 0.
	Experience of Parental Divorce (2-4)	DIVORCE	Dichotomous Discrete Measure: If respondent reports that his/her parents divorced when he/she was in middle and high school, DIVORCE = 1; otherwise 0.
	The Most Influential Person's Job (2-6)	PUBURO PVBURO FARMER SELFEMP	5-categorical Discrete Measure: If respondent reports that most significant influence was from person whose job was public bureaucrat, PUBURO = 1; otherwise 0. If private bureaucrat (e.g., private company managerial employee), PVBURO = 1; otherwise 0. If farmer, FARMER = 1; otherwise 0. If self-employed, SELFEMP = 1; otherwise 0. Category excluded represents those who report that most significant influence was from person whose job was other than above-mentioned job categories.
	Atmosphere of Communication within Family (2-6)	AUTH-FMLY AVEFMLY	3-categorical Discrete Measure: If respondent reports family atmosphere during socialization period was "slightly strict," "strict," or "very strict" so that it was not easy to express himself or herself, AUTHFMLY = 1; otherwise 0. If respondent checked mid-point, AVEFMLY = 1; otherwise AVEFMLY = 0. Category excluded represents those who report that atmosphere was "slightly free," "free," or "very free."

(continued on next page)

Table 5 - 3 (continued) **Categories and Measures of Independent Variables**

Independent Variables			Meaning of Variables Under Category III and Measurement Scheme
Categ. I	Categ. II	Categ. III	
Cultural Traits	Religious Culture (4-1)	PROTEST CATHOLIC BUDDHIST NONE	5-categorical Discrete Measure: If respondent reports he/she believes in Protestantism, PROTEST = 1; otherwise 0. If Catholicism, CATHOLIC = 1; otherwise 0. If Buddhism, BUDDHIST = 1 ; otherwise 0. If no religion, NONE = 1; otherwise, 0. Category excluded represents those who report they believe in confucianism.
	Societal Culture (4-2)	MATERIAL MIXCULT	3-categorical Discrete Measure: If 2 most important societal goals chosen by respondent belong to Inglehart's category of "materialistic culture" (A, C, E, F, I and J) and at same time, if least important goal chosen belongs to Inglehart's category of "post-materialistic culture" (B, D, G, H, K, and L) MATERIAL = 1; otherwise 0. If 2 most important goals chosen are both matrialistic and post-materialistic, or if goal chosen as least important is opposite to 2 goals chosen as most important, MIXCULT = 1; otherwise 0. Category excluded represents those who have post-materialistic culture (i.e., those who choose two post-materialistic goals as most important and at same time, one materialistic goal as least important).

(continued on next page)

Table 5 - 3 (continued) **Categories and Measures of Independent Variables**

Independent Variables			Meaning of Variables Under Category III and Measurement Scheme
Categ. I	Categ. II	Categ. III	
Cultural Traits	Perspectives on Work-related Human Nature (4-3)	THEOX	3-categorical Discrete Measures: If respondent agrees with statement expressing the Theory X-type perspective while disagreeing with, or taking mid-position about, the statement expressing the Theory Y-type perspective, THEOX = 1; otherwise 0. If respondent agrees or disagrees with both statements, or if respondent takes mid-position about both statements, XYMIXED = 1; otherwise 0. Category excluded represents those who are interpreted as having the Theory Y-type perspective (i.e., those who agree with statement expressing the Theory Y-type perspective while disagreeing with, or taking mid-position about, statement expressing the Theory X-type perspective).
		XYMIXED	

Note : Numbers in parentheses designate questionnaire items that correspond to each variable. For specific content of each questionnaire item, see Appendix I, especially Part I.

major independent variables. However, I additionally include the subjective type of traits in my list of independent variables, viewing the subjectivist notion that culture is not a passive, but an active entity. That is, following the subjectivist line of logic discussed in Chapter One, I assume that subjective entities are not merely determined by objective entities in a unidirectional fashion; but they also influence the objective entity by determining how individuals understand the symbolic meanings of the objective entities. Insofar as the compatibility thesis is concerned, this culturalist proposition suggests that what kind of subjective traits an individual bureaucrat possesses would make a significant difference in the extent to which he/she internalizes bureaucratic and democratic ideologies, and the extent to which his/her attitudes and beliefs toward one ideology are congruent with those toward the other ideology.

As represented by those in Category II, each of these individual variables is differentiated into more specific forms of independent variables which I will call the "sub-independent variables." Diverse sub-independent variables can be selected legitimately as representing each of the four types of individual traits. The sub-independent variables listed in the table are those that have been frequently chosen as independent variables by previous authors who conducted similar studies and/or those related to my theoretical interests.[24]

Category III includes notations designating the most specific forms of independent variables. These variables are those into which the independent variables in Categories I and II are "operationalized" at the empirical level. I will call the independent variables included in Category III the "measured variables." Except for those that can be reasonably operationalized as an interval measure (i.e., age, annual family income, years of service, and number of superiors and subordinates), all measured variables are operationalized into several discrete categories in accordance with my theoretical interests.[25]

I measured individual bureaucrats' traits pertaining to these independent variables by directly asking them. The specific questionnaire items I used for this purpose are presented in Appendix I (especially Part I).

Models and Methods of Explanatory Analyses. My explanatory analyses are composed of two different sets of examinations. First, I examine the extent to which the dependent variables vary by the measured independent variables in Category III. Given the lack of established theories informing specifically what dependent variables should be regressed on what independent variables in exploring the subjective dimension of the compatibility thesis, I regressed each of the dependent variables specified in Table 5-1 on all of the measured independent variables specified in Table 5-2. I then empirically discerned which of these independent variables had a significant impact on which dependent variables and which did not. I analyzed the extent to which the traits of individual bureaucrats represented by each dependent variable differ by each category of these independent variables. For those operationalized as interval measures, of primary concern was the extent to which the dependent variables change with a unit change of each of these measured independent variables.[26]

Standard t-tests procedures were used. Those variables operationalized as categorical measures were analyzed following standard procedures for the use of dummy variables in a regression model.[27] In order to avoid the problem of "perfect multicollinearity," one of the discrete categories for each variable was excluded from the regression model. If the coefficient of a certain category of an independent variable included in the model was found to be statistically significant, then it was interpreted as indicating a significant difference between the included and excluded categories in the traits represented by the dependent variable included in the model. If statistically insignificant, then it was concluded that there was no difference between these categories.[28]

Second, I analyzed the explanatory power of the independent variables on a group basis. The independent variables in Categories I and II were of primary concern in this analysis. This analysis was done within the framework of an F-test for examining the joint impact of a group of several independent variables on dependent variables. As indicated by the following formula, the core of this analysis was the comparison between the R^2 of an "unrestricted regression model" and that of a "restricted regression model":

$$F_{(q,\, N\text{-}k)} = \frac{(R^2_{UR} - R^2_{R})/q}{(1 - R^2_{UR})/(N\text{-}k)} \quad \text{, where}$$

$F_{(q,\, N\text{-}K)}$ = F-value with (q, N-k) degrees of freedom;
R^2_{UR} = R^2 of unrestricted model,
R^2_{R} = R^2 of restricted model;
k = number of coefficients in the unrestricted model;
q = number of variables excluded from the unrestricted model;
N = number of cases.

The unrestricted regression model is one in which all measured independent variables are included. The restricted model is the same as the unrestricted model except that the independent variables or the most inclusive variables under consideration are excluded. If the R^2-difference between these two models was statistically significant, then it was interpreted as indicating that the independent variables in Categories I or II associated with the excluded measured independent variables explained to a significant degree the variations of dependent variables included in the regression model.[29]

The results of all of these descriptive and explanatory analyses and substantive interpretations of them are presented in the next chapter.

NOTES

1 See, for example, Allison's (1971) "bureaucratic decision-making model."

2 See, for example, Mazmanian and Sabatier (1981 and 1983), Ripley and Franklin (1982), Bardach (1977), and Pressman and Wildavsky (1973).

3 Obvious exceptions are Gruber (1987) and Hwang (1981).

4 For more detailed discussion of the analytic definition of bureaucrats, see Gerth and Mills (1946:196-244).

5 A practical reason for this choice is that, for myself as a native Korean, Korean officials were the most researchable. The accessibility to key informants and respondents in Korea was greater than in other countries. More importantly, by taking Korean officials as my research subjects, I was able to resolve most effectively the problem of language, which is one of the important factors in determining the researchability of the subjective dimension of the compatibility thesis.

6 The career civil servants in Seoul city government are hierarchically ranked following a nine-grade system with the ninth grade being the lowest. While the second and third grades occur at both the main and regional offices, those at the regional offices were not treated as "mid-level bureaucrats." The reason for this is that they, as the chief and vice-chief officials for the regional offices, have more command and control functions which are more consistent with high-level bureaucrats. Rather, the fourth, fifth, and sixth grades in the regional offices were selected as the mid-level bureaucrats. For more detailed descriptions of the ranking systems of Seoul city government see *Seoul Statistical Year Book* (1989:400-413).

7 The issue of democratic reform is salient also within Korean public administration agencies. The origin of the authoritarian bureaucratic nature of Korean public administrative agencies is traced back to the era of colonial government of Korea by Japan. This nature was deeply imprinted into the Korean administrative systems as the government came under the control of the military sector since the early 1960s. During this period, key posts of the major public administrative agencies were staffed by those who had military backgrounds and who were the first generation trained for managing organizations in a bureaucratic way. This authoritarian, bureaucratic nature of public administrative agencies has continued until

now. However, since the early 1980s, a number of reforms have been made. This special recruitment for mid-ranking officials, which favored military retirees, was cancelled. Substantial authority to make final decisions was delegated to the field agencies that are hierarchically lower. The unionization of public officials, which had been prohibited by the constitution, was selectively allowed. As such, the issue of democratic reform is no longer confined to academic debates; rather, it has become a real issue. For a more detailed description of the Korean public administrative system, see Park (1991), Yu (1991), and Cho (1991).

8 President Roh's promise is being realized. Nationwide elections for constituting two levels of local legislatures were held in March and June 1991, respectively. The mayoral election for Seoul city government and other major city governments were also held.

9 The demographic, financial, and organizational data of Seoul city government are cited from *Shi Jung* (1981, 1990, 1991).

10 See, for example, Ahn (1984), Paik (1982), and Kim (1981).

11 The extent to which bureaucrats' attitudes toward bureaucratic and democratic ideologies vary in accordance with these functional categories is one of the major research themes for my explanatory analysis.

12 For purposes of maintaining anonymity, I will refer to each of these offices as Office A, Office B, and Office C.

13 The questionnaire items used are those which passed a pretest which was aimed at checking the appropriateness of the original questionnaire items to the context of Korean public administration and administrators. The participants in this test were ten Korean public officials of Seoul city government, three Korean scholars, and five Korean graduate students majoring in Public Administration. As a result of this test, items that were identified as "hard to understand," "unclear," "inappropriate," or "irrelevant" were eliminated.

14 In many instances of Q-methodological research, Q-samples are often selected from generic sources of communication materials used by the subjects themselves. My Q-samples, however, were chosen from the theoretical literature as such. The major reason for this choice is that a primary concern of my study is to examine how bureaucrats subjectively understand the theoretically-construed concepts of bureaucratic and democratic

ideologies. The Q-samples selected in this way are called "structured Q-samples." For a more detailed discussion of selecting Q-samples, see Brown (1980:28-29 and 1970).

15 I asked the respondents to perform the second task in addition to the first task in order to accomplish three things. First, it was designed to fit my validity of my multiple indicators in a rigorous way. That is, it was designed to fit my validity test particularly to Campbell and Fiske's (1959) multitrait-multimethod matrix method. By having the respondents answer the same questionnaire items in two different ways, I created a situation in which the same traits were measured by two different methods. This design enabled me to compare the correlations among the same traits measured by two different methods with the correlations among the different traits measured by the same method and those among the different traits measured by two different methods. As a result, I was able to examine two important types of validities: concurrent and discriminant validities. That is, I was able to test the ability of my multiple indicators to discern similarities and differences among the traits I wanted to deal with in the study (see Appendix II for detailed procedures and results of this validity test). Second, it was designed to test the reliability of the individual questionnaire items. Since the respondents came to answer the same questionnaire items twice by performing the two tasks, the result of the second task, combined with that of the first task, enabled me to test the reliability particularly by the test-retest method (see Appendix II for detailed procedures and results of this reliability test). Finally, I designed the second task in order to have the respondents well-prepared for the third task. In order for the third task to be successfully performed, the respondent must be well-acquainted with the content of the questionnaire items. The content used for the third task is the same as that used for the first and second tasks. Thus, by having the respondents perform the second task in addition to the first task, I created a situation in which the respondents came to read and think about the questionnaire items at least twice.

16 The Q-sorting scale chart completed by each subject provides two types of information. First, it summarizes the subject's own understandings of democratic ideology. That is, the location of democratic statements on the chart clarifies which of the conceptual components expressed by the democratic statements are particularly salient or insalient to the subject's own conception of democratic ideology. Second, the congruence between bureaucratic and democratic statements in their locations on the chart summarizes which conceptual components of bureaucratic ideology are understood as compatible or incompatible with the conceptual components that

are thought of as democratic by the subject. For specific analyses of this information, see the next section.

17 Given this pitfall of R-methodological analysis, and the strength of Q-methodological analysis, one might ask why Q-methodological analysis does not serve as the only means of investigation. The reason is that an important thing that is difficult to accomplish in the Q-methodological analysis can be accomplished in the R-methodological analysis. That is, because the subjects studied for Q-methodological analysis are small in number (i.e., 30) and confined to a particular portion of the population (those working in a regional office), the findings obtained from the Q-methodological analysis cannot be generalized to the whole population that I wish to examine. In contrast, the subjects studied for R-methodological analysis are fairly large in number and sufficiently diverse. Thus, the result of the R-methodological analysis can be generalized to the population under consideration in this study.

18 For a detailed discussion of Q-factor analysis, see Brown (1980).

19 For more detailed explanations of the conversion procedures and the interpretation of the rounded factor scores, see Chapter Six.

20 For more detailed discussion of treatment of factor scores in Q-methodology, see Brown (1980:239-247).

21 Viewed from the R-methodological standpoint this Q-methodological analysis deals with the issue of the extent to which the theoretical version of democratic ideology coincides with bureaucrats' own conceptions of democratic ideology. This is because, as described in Chapter Four, the statements used for my Q-methodological analysis were constructed by referring to the theoretical literature. As will be presented in Chapter Six, I incorporated this issue in interpreting the results of Q-methodological analysis.

22 I did not employ Q-methodology for this explanatory analysis because Q-methodology is useful for explanatory analysis when a researcher is concerned with a fairly small number of independent variables. If, however, the number of the independent variables is large, as in my case, Q-methodology becomes useless because, as in the case of simple bivariate regression method, the confounding effects among independent variables are not controlled in an explanatory analysis based upon Q-methodology.

23 The dependent variables that belong to the first set represent individual bureaucrats' attitudes and beliefs about the conceptual components of bureaucratic and democratic ideologies, not the conceptual components themselves. For the sake of convenience, however, the same notations used in Figures 4-1 and 4-2 to designate the conceptual components and types are used in my explanatory analyses to designate the first set of dependent variables. For example, BURO and DEMO, which are used in Figures 4-1 and 4-2 to designate the "bureaucratic" and "democratic" ideologies are used in my explanatory analyses to designate the dependent variables representing individual bureaucrats' attitudes and beliefs about these ideologies.

24 I selected the sub-independent variables representing the organizational traits of individual bureaucrats by referring to Berger and Cummings (1979), Rinehart and Bernick (1975), and Wynia (1974). For those representing the socio-economic traits, I referred to Moskos and Bell (1964), Rinehart and Bernick (1975), and Wynia (1974). For socialization backgrounds, I referred to Chackerian and Abcarian (1984) and Dennis, *et al.* (1968). For those sub-independent variables pertaining to "subjective traits," I referred Inglehart (1977), Aberbach, *et al.* (1981), and Almond and Verba (1980, 1963). "Perspectives on work-related human nature," as I discussed in Chapter One, was selected for my own theoretical interests. Note that, although the independent variables selected by these authors were related to the dependent variables that are not exactly the same as mine, I used these variables as independent variables for explaining my dependent variables based upon a presumption that they would be generally applicable to my study.

25 In addition to the theoretical concern, in specifying the categorical variables, I considered the appropriateness of the categories to the context of my population of Korean public administrators. I did so, for example, in determining the period of the socialization process. "Young age," which is the core of socialization theory, was operationally defined as the period when one attends middle and high schools. The major reason for this operationalization was that, at least in Korea, it is widely pointed out that this period is one in which people are the most sensitive and susceptible to external stimuli, and that people's experiences during this period have the most significant impact on the attitudinal frameworks and belief systems which endure for the rest of their lives.

26 My explanatory analysis is more explanatory and speculative than confirmatory or theory-driven. Note, however, that, as presented in the next chap-

ter, relationships between several dependent and independent variables were examined in a confirmatory fashion. For example, I performed formal statistical tests to check the empirical validity of the two competing lines of thoughts about work-related human nature posed in the field of organization theory (i.e., "Theory X"-type perspective vs. "Theory Y"-type perspective). I thought that the implications of the debates about work-related human nature posed in the field of organization theory were as follows: all other things being equal, those who have the "Theory X"-type perspective on human nature (i.e., dislike to work) are more likely than those who have the "Theory Y"-type perspective (i.e., like to work) to be susceptible to the internal bureaucratic ideals and instrumental principles. Similarly, other things being equal, those who have the "Theory Y"-type perspective on human nature are more likely than those who have the "Theory X"-type perspective to be susceptible to the internal democratic ideals and instrumental principles. In my explanatory analysis, the first implication was equated with a hypothesis that particularly for INTBURO, INTBINST, and the regression coefficient of the dummy variable, THEOX, would be positive and significantly greater than zero. The second implication was equated with a hypothesis that particularly for INTDEMO, INTPDEMO, and the regression coefficient for THEOX, would be negative and significantly smaller than zero.

27 See, for example, Pindyck and Rubinfeld (1981:111-116).

28 For those independent variables operationalized into more than three categories, the excluded category served as a criterion category for comparing the other categories included in the model. Suppose, for example, that a certain independent variable is operationalized into three catgories, say A, B, and C, and that A and B are the categories included in a regression model while C was the excluded category. If the coefficient of A is significant and positive, and if B's coefficient is insignificant, then it is concluded that those who belong to A have, to a greater degree, the trait represented by the dependent included in the model than those who belong to B and C. If the coefficients of both A and B are statistically significant in the same direction, then the comparison between A and B in their explanatory power is made following the standard procedures for testing the difference between two regression coeffients. For more detailed discussion of statistical analysis with dummy variables, see Pindyck and Rubinfeld (1981:123-126).

29 For more detailed discussion of this F-test for joint impact of multiple independent variables, see Pindyck and Rubenfeld (1981:117-119).

Chapter 6

Empirical Findings and Discussions

R-Methodological Analysis of the Compatibility Between Bureaucratic and Democratic Ideologies in the Minds of Bureaucrats

Recall that, of the relationships among the conceptual components of bureaucratic and democratic ideologies depicted in Figure 4-2, my R-methodological analysis deals with all relationships depicted in Set III; all but the relationship between bureaucratic ideology conceived as a general concept and egalitarian democratic ideology in Set I; and all but the relationships between internal bureaucratic ideology and internal egalitarian democratic ideology and internal liberal democratic ideology in Set II. Also recall that in the R-methodological analysis, the compatibility among the conceptual components of bureaucratic and democratic ideologies is operationally defined as the correlation between respondents' internalization of one conceptual component and those of another conceptual component.

Figure 6-1 summarizes a result of the LISREL analysis especially pertaining to the relationship between bureaucratic ideology (BURO) and democratic ideology (DEMO), each of which is conceived as a general concept.[1] As presented in the figure, it is found that the factor correlation between BURO and DEMO is positive and statistically significant (i.e., $r = .685$, $p < .001$). This indicates that Seoul city government officials regard the general concepts of bureaucratic and democratic ideologies as compatible with one another.

Note that, as found in the review of the theoretical debates about the compatibility thesis, different conclusions about the compatibility between bureaucratic and democratic ideologies may be made, depending on what kinds of bureaucratic and democratic ideologies are juxtaposed with each other. Considering this, I have additionally performed a series of LISREL analyses by de-

Figure 6 - 1 **LISREL Analysis of Relationships Between Bureaucratic and Democratic Ideologies**

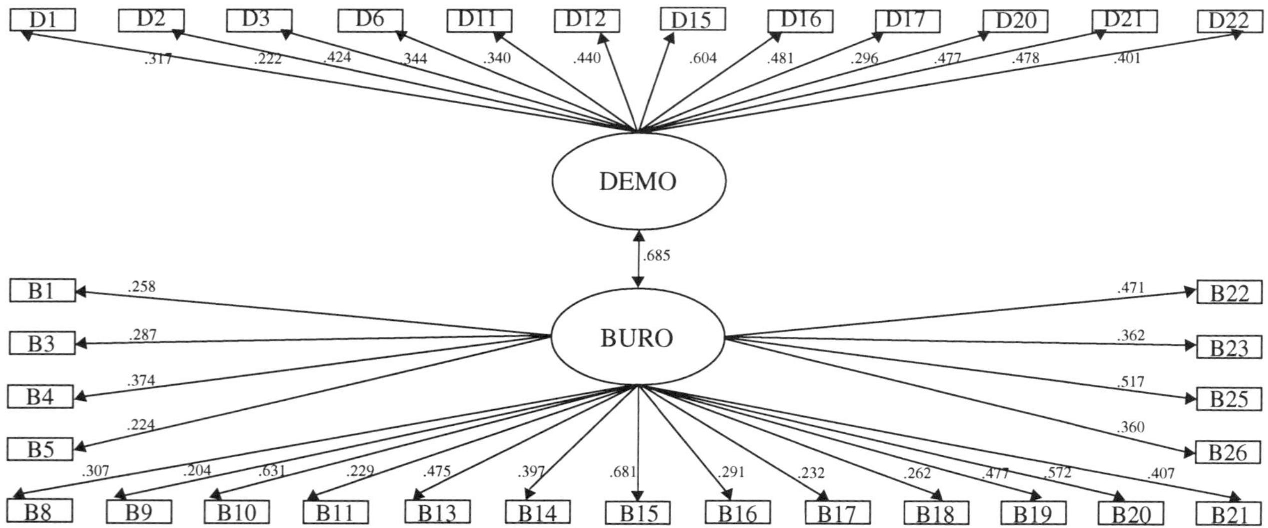

Note: Factors are circled and measures are boxed. See Fig. 4-1 for factor notation meanings. See Appen. I for specific measure contents. Coefficients estimated by maximum likelihood estimation method. All coefficient estimates at 0.1% significance level. Chi-square with 488 degrees of freedom = 1059.40 (chi-square/degrees of freedom = 2.17); goodness of fit index = .816; adjusted goodness of fit index = .789; root mean square residual = .074. Error of measures modeled as correlated with each other if they are associated with same factor and adjacent in questionnaire. For brevity, error terms and relationships among them are not depicted in figure. Correlated with each other are errors of B3 and B18, of B4 and B17, of B10 and B25, of B15 and B23, of D1 and D2, of D6 and D11, of D15 and D20, and of D17 and D22. Estimates of covariances between these erors are all statistically significant at 0.5% significance level.

composing the general concepts of bureaucratic and democratic ideologies into more specific conceptual components. The overall conclusions from these analyses is that Seoul city government officials regard most of the more specific conceptual components of bureaucratic and democratic ideologies as compatible with each other.

Figures 6-2 and 6-3 summarize the results of LISREL analyses in which the general concept of bureaucratic ideology (BURO) is juxtaposed with two types of democratic ideologies [i.e., liberal democratic ideology (LIBDEMO) and popular democratic ideology (POPDEMO)]. As presented in Figure 6-2, the factor correlation between BURO and LIBDEMO is positive and statistically significant (i.e., $r = .602$, $p < .001$). The factor correlation between BURO and POPDEMO, as presented in Figure 6-3, is also positive and statistically significant (i.e., $r = .728$, $p < .001$). These findings indicate that in the minds of Korean bureaucrats, bureaucratic ideology as a general concept is conceived as being compatible with both liberal and popular democratic ideologies.

Figures 6-4 and 6-5 summarize the results of LISREL analyses in which bureaucratic and democratic ideologies are conceptualized, particularly in terms of the intra-organizational aspect of government agencies. As presented in Figure 6-4, it is found that the factor correlation between internal bureaucratic ideology (INTBURO) and internal democratic ideology (INTDEMO) is positive and significantly different from zero (i.e., $r = .662$, $p < .001$). Similarly, as presented in Figure 6-5, the factor correlation between internal bureaucratic ideology (INTBURO) and internal popular democratic ideology (INTPDEMO) is positive and significantly different from zero (i.e., $r = .739$, $p < .001$). These findings suggest that Korean bureaucrats regard these ideologies as being compatible with one another.

Figure 6-6 summarizes the result of LISREL analysis in which the concepts of bureaucratic and democratic ideologies are decomposed into specific conceptual components in two ways. First, the concepts are specified according to whether they are related to the ideals or to the instrumental principles for attaining the ideals. Second, they are also specified according to whether they are related to the intra-organizational aspect of government agencies or to the external relationships of bureaucrats with citizens, legislators, or society in a general sense. A number of interesting findings are summarized in this figure.

First, it is found that Seoul city government officials regard internal bureaucratic ideals (INTBIDL) and internal bureaucratic instrumental principles (INTBINST) as compatible with all of the specific conceptual components of democratic ideology [i.e., internal democratic ideals (INTDIDL), external democratic ideals (EXTDIDL), and internal democratic instrumental principles (INTDINST)]. This is indicated particularly by the positive factor correlations between INTBIDL and each of the three conceptual components of democratic ideology, and those between INTBINST and each of the three conceptual com-

Figure 6 - 2 **LISREL Analysis of Relationship Between Bureaucratic and Liberal Democratic Ideology**

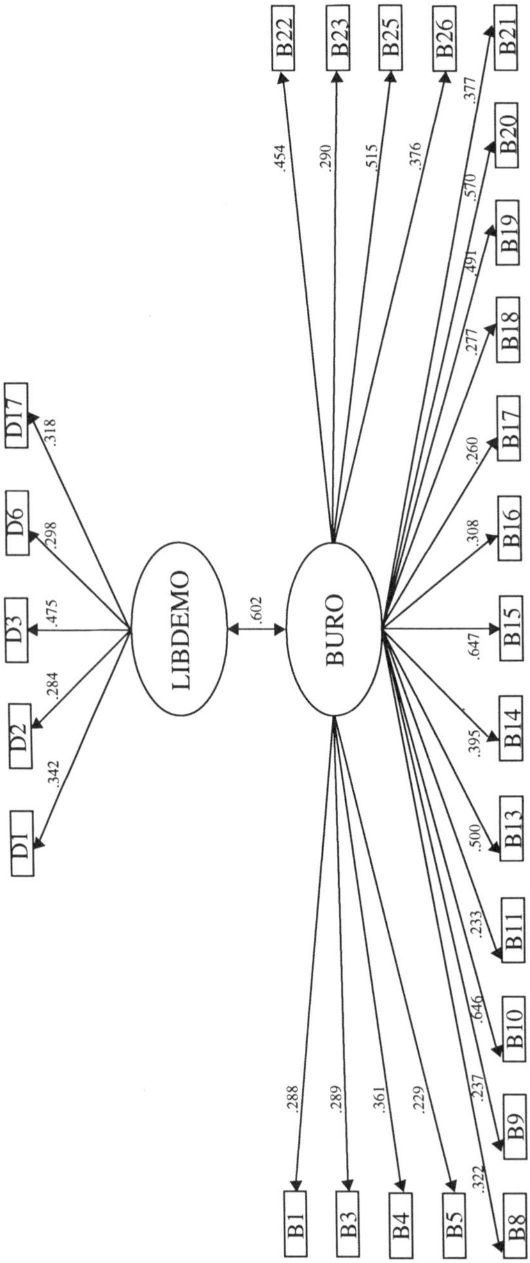

Note: Factors are circled and measures are boxed. See Fig. 4-1 for factor notation meanings. See Appen. I for specific content of measures. Coefficients estimated by maximum likelihood method. All coefficient estimates at 0.1% significance level. Chi-square with 293 degrees of freedom = 666.05 (chi-square/degrees of freedom = 2.27); goodness of fit index = .847; adjusted goodness of fit index = .817; root mean square residual = .073. Errors of measures are modeled as correlated with each other if measures are associated with same factor and adjacent in questionnaire. For brevity, error terms and relationships among them are not depicted in figure. Correlated with each other are errors of B3 and B18, of B4 and B17, of B10 and B25, of B15 and B23, and of D1 and D2. Estimates of covariances between errors are all statistically significant at 0.5% significance level.

Figure 6 - 3 **LISREL Analysis of Relationship Between Bureaucratic and Popular Democratic Ideology**

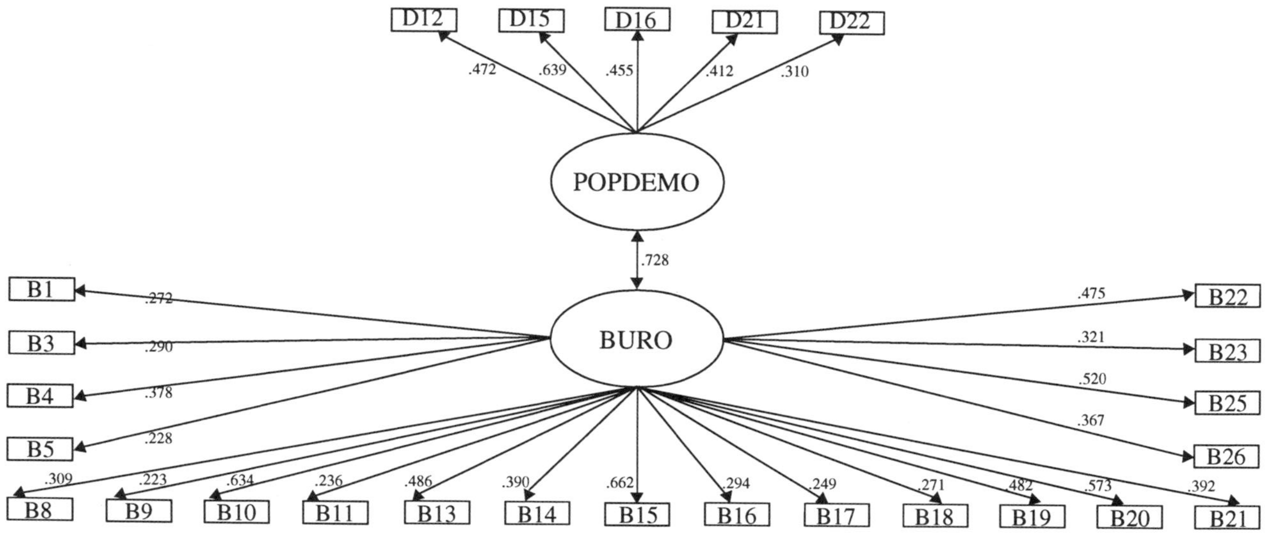

Note: Factors are circled and measures are boxed. See Fig. 4-1 for factor notation meanings. See Appen. I for specific content of measures. Coefficients estimated by maximum likelihood method. All estimates of coefficients are at 0.1% significance level. Chi-square with 294 degrees of freedom = 624.20 (chi-square/degrees of freedom = 2.12); goodness of fit index = .855; adjusted goodness of fit index = .827; root mean square residual = .070. Errors of measures are modeled as correlated with each other if measures are associated with same factor and adjacent in questionnaire. For brevity, error terms and relationships among them are not depicted infigure. Correlated with each other are errors of B3 and B18, of B4 and B17, of B10 and B25, and of B15 and B23. Estimates of covariances between errors are all statistically significant at 0.5% significance level.

Figure 6 - 4 **LISREL Analysis of Relationship Between Internal Bureaucratic and Internal Democratic Ideology**

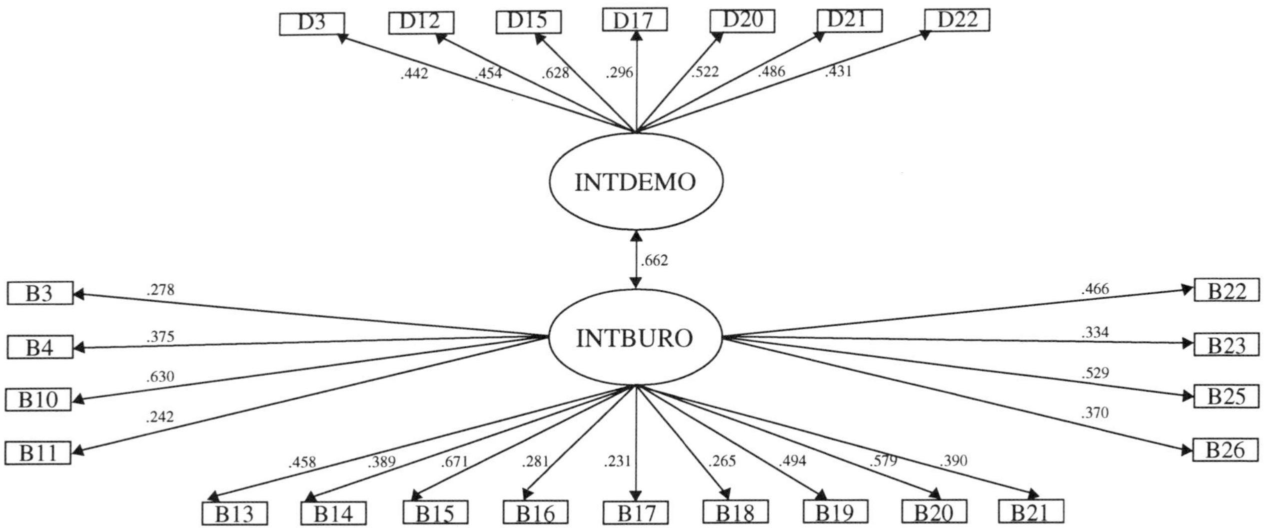

Note: Factors are circled and measures are boxed. See Fig. 4-1 for factor notation meanings. See Appen. I for specific measures. Coefficients estimated by maximum likelihood estimation method. All coefficient estimates are at 0.1% significance level. Chi-square with 246 degrees of freedom = 575.43 (chi-square/degrees of freedom = 2.34); goodness of fit index = .856; adjusted goodness of fit index = .825; root mean square residual = .073. Errors of measures modeled as being correlated with each other if measures are associated with same factor and adjacent in questionnaire. For brevity, error terms and relationships among them are not depicted in figure. Correlated are errors of B3 and B18, of B4 and B17, of B10 and B25, of B15 and B23, of D15 and D20, and of D17 and D22 . Estimates of covariances between these errors are all statistically significant at 0.5% significance level.

Figure 6 - 5 **LISREL Analysis of Relationship Between Internal Bureaucratic and Internal Popular Democratic Ideology**

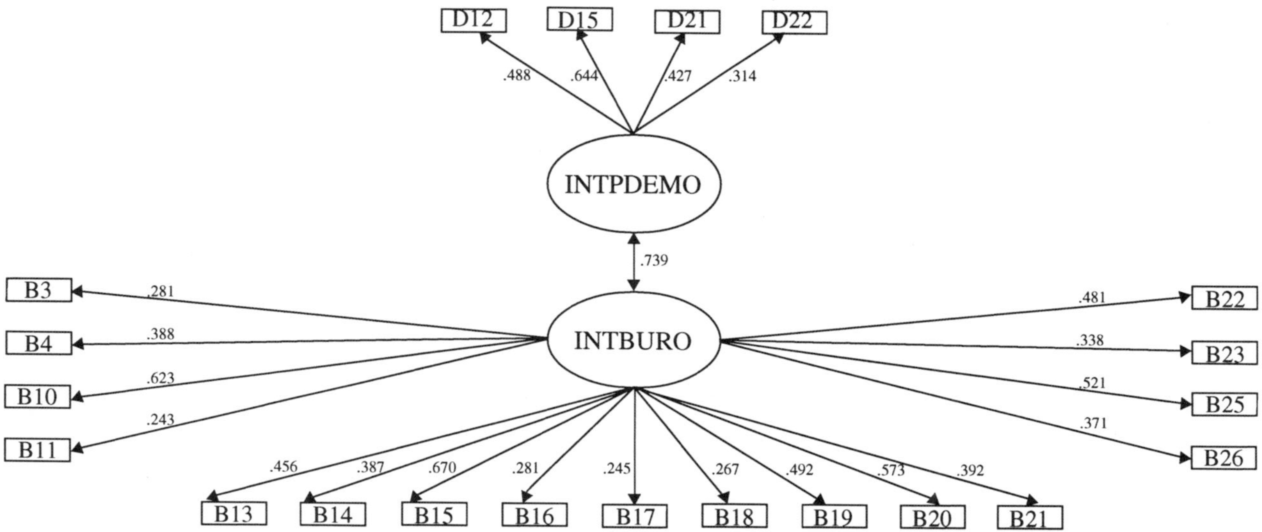

Note: Factors are circled and measures are boxed. See Fig. 4-1 for factor notation meanings. See Appen. I for specific content of measures. Coefficients estimated by maximum likelihood estimation method. All coefficient estimates at 0.1% significance level. Chi-square with 184 degrees of freedom = 431.96 (chi-square/degrees of freedom = 2.35); goodness of fit index = .875; adjusted goodness of fit index = .843; root mean square residual = .068. Errors of measures modeled as correlated with each other if measures are associated with same factor and adjacent in questionnaire. For brevity, error terms and relationships among them are not depicted in figure. Correlated with each other are errors of B3 and B18, of B4 and B17, of B10 and B25, and of B15 and B23. Estimates of covariances between these errors are all statistically significant at 0.5% significance level.

Figure 6 - 6 **LISREL Analysis of Relationships Among Conceptual Components of Bureaucratic and Democratic Ideologies**

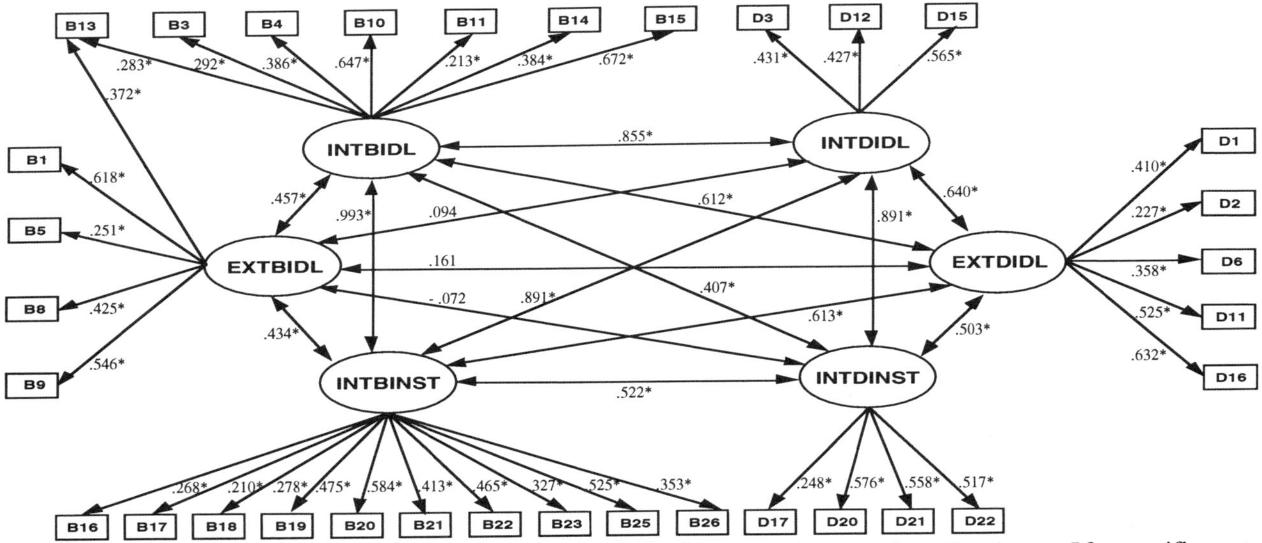

Note: Factors are circled and measures are boxed. See Fig. 4-1 for factor notation meanings. See Appen. I for specific content of measures. Coefficients estimated by maximum likelihood estimation method. Estimates at 0.1% significance level. Chi-square with 471 degrees of freedom = 905.43 (chi-square/degrees of freedom = 1.92); goodness of fit index = .845; adjusted goodness of fit index = .815; root mean square residual = .068. Errors of measures modeled as correlated with each other if measures are associated with same factor and adjacent in the questionnaire. For brevity, error terms and relationships among them are not depicted in figure. Correlated are errors of B3 and B18, of B4 and B17, of B10 and B25, of B15 and B23, of D1 and D2, of D6 and D11, of D15 and D20, and of D17 and D22. Estimates of covariances between errors are all statistically significant at 0.5% significance level.

ponents of democratic ideology. Seoul city government officials do not regard external bureaucratic ideals (EXTBIDL) as being compatible with all of the specific conceptual components of democratic ideology. That is, the factor correlations between EXTBIDL and each of the three conceptual components of democratic ideology are insignificant.

These findings reveal that the implicit reasoning behind the pro-compatibility of Preston (1987) and the critique of Simon (1973) against Argyris (1973a), which were reviewed in Chapter Two, does not stand on firm empirical grounds. The reasoning implicit in the arguments of Preston and Simon is that the Human Relations School's organizational democracy would lead to the demise of bureaucratic ideals defined in a positive sense (i.e., efficient and effective production of resources). My findings, however, suggest that this may not be the case. In my study, the concept of organizational democracy is reflected in the measures of INTDIDL and INTDINST, and the bureaucratic ideals that are reflected in the measures of INTBIDL. Thus, the positive correlations between INTBIDL and INTDIDL, and between INTBIDL and INTDINST, suggest that when bureaucrats internalize organizational democracy, they internalize bureaucratic ideals to a higher degree. In addition, the positive correlations between INTBINST and INTDIDL, and between INTBINST and INTDINST suggest that a reform aimed at driving bureaucrats to internalize organizational democracy would lead them to accept bureaucratic instrumental principles designated to attain bureaucratic ideals.

Second, the factor correlations among INTBIDL, INTBINST, INTDIDL, and INTDINST provide an interesting insight into the debates between classical organization theorists and the proponents of the Human Relations School. The debates, as I reviewed in Chapter Two, revolve around the extent to which bureaucratic and democratic instrumental principles for managing organizations can contribute to the attainment of organizational bureaucratic and democratic ideals. In the debates, they show exclusive beliefs in their own instrumental principles for managing organizations (i.e., bureaucratic instrumental principles for classical organization theorists and democratic ones for the proponents of the Human Relations School). Classical organization theorists maintain that it is bureaucratic instrumental principles rather than democratic instrumental principles that ensure the attainment of both ideals. In contrast, the proponents of the Human Relations School argue that it is not bureaucratic instrumental principles, but democratic instrumental principles that can lead to the accomplishment of both ideals.

The result of my analysis reveals that the beliefs of Seoul city government officials are consistent more with those of classical organization theorists than those of the proponents of the Human Relations School. That is, the correlation of INTBIDL with INTBINST is very high and positive (i.e., $r = .993$, $p < .001$), and greater than its correlation with INTDINST ($r = .407$, $p < .001$).[2] In contrast, INTBINST is positively correlated with INTDIDL to the same degree as INTDINST is correlated with INTDIDL ($r = .891$, $p < .001$).

Interpreted from a practical viewpoint, the result suggests that encouraging bureaucrats to accept internal bureaucratic instrumental principles will be more likely than encouraging them to internalize internal democratic instrumental principles to lead to their internalization of internal bureaucratic ideals. Thus, it suggests that in order to enhance bureaucrats' internalization of internal democratic ideals, the reformer does not necessarily have to force bureaucrats to accept internal democratic instrumental principles. Rather, according to the result, the reformer may accomplish this objective by having bureaucrats accept internal bureaucratic instrumental principles.

Third, the empirical validity of the reasoning behind some arguments about the compatibility thesis posed in the field of Public Administration is checked by the factor correlation between the external bureaucratic and democratic ideals (i.e., EXTBIDL and EXTDIDL). As I mentioned in Chapter Three, the proponents of New Public Administration and the critical theorists of Public Administration commonly observe that the goals of public adminstration have been traditionally composed of such external bureaucratic ideals as the dichotomy between public administration and politics, maintaining order in society, and maintaining the predictability of society. They maintain that the goals of modern public administration must be fundamentally reformulated by replacing these bureaucratic ideals with democratic ones.[3] The common reasoning behind these scholars' argument is, as reviewed in Chapter Four, that an emphasis upon such bureaucratic ideals leads to the demise of democratic ideals. A hypothesis implied by this reasoning is that the correlation between these bureaucratic and democratic ideals would be discernably high and negative. My empirical finding, however, rejects this hypothesis. The factor correlation between EXTBIDL and EXTDIDL is positive and statistically insignificant (i.e., $r = .161$, t-value = 1.662).[4] This indicates that Korean bureaucrats internalize the traditional external bureaucratic ideals without reducing their internalization of the democratic ideals stressed by the proponents of the New Public Administration and the critical theorists of Public Administration.[5]

Finally, the factor correlation between INTDINST and EXTDIDL provides an interesting insight that is related to Mosher's (1968) argument. As reviewed in Chapter Four, Mosher stresses the contradictory relationship between organizational democracy within government agencies and external democratic ideals. It is, however, found that the factor correlation between these conceptual components is positive and statistically significant ($r = .503$, $p < .001$). This indicates that even if the practice of organizational democracy within public agencies may be, as Mosher maintains, *logically* contradictory to the ideals of political democracy, they are not contradictory to one another in the minds of Seoul city government officials. This result suggests that implementing the instrumental principles for organizational democracy in government agencies can be accompanied by an increase in their internalization of external democratic ideals. Thus, according to the result, such implementation would set a favorable condition for the realization of external democratic ideals.

Q-Methodological Analysis of the Compatibility Between Bureaucratic and Democratic Ideologies in the Minds of Bureaucrats

As mentioned in Chapter One, the analysis presented thus far has a drawback that is typical of most R-methodological analyses. That is, the subjects' own perspectives on democratic ideology are not taken fully into account. This results from the way in which the subjects' internalization of democratic ideology is measured. It is measured by the extent to which the subjects agree with "democratic" statements which are constructed to express the conceptual components of democratic ideology. The conceptual components expressed by these statements are, as discussed in Chapter Four, ones that are abstracted from the theoretical literature on organizations and public administration. It is not, however, empirically verified whether or not the subjects responding to the "democratic" statements actually think of them as democratic. Thus, precisely speaking, what is clarified in this analysis is the relationship of bureaucratic ideology with the theoretical, not empirical, version of democratic ideology.

Omitting the subjects' own perspectives on democratic ideology is problematic in that the extent to which bureaucrats regard bureaucratic ideology as compatible with democratic ideology would largely differ by the kinds of democratic ideologies they themselves envision. This likelihood is suggested by the very source of the divergence among the theorists in their arguments about the compatibility thesis. That is, as reviewed in Chapters Two and Three, their arguments differ largely by the components of democratic ideology that they juxtapose with the components of bureaucratic ideology. In fact, as will be shown later, my Q-methodological analysis reveals that a number of perspectives on democratic ideology exist among bureaucrats, and that the differences in perspectives on democratic ideology accompany differences in understanding the relationship between bureaucratic and democratic ideologies.

I attempted to overcome this drawback by examining the same theme within the framework of Q-methodology. The raw data used for the Q-methodological analysis are the 30 Q-sorting charts obtained as a result of the Q-sorting sessions.[6] Each Q-sorting chart demonstrates how each subject sorts out the 48 "democratic" and "bureaucratic" statements used in the R-methodological analysis on an 11-point response scale in accordance with their evaluations of the statements as democratic or undemocratic. Thus, the location of a statement on a Q-sorting chart demonstrates the extent to which each subject regards the theoretical conceptual components of bureaucratic and democratic ideologies expressed by each statement. More specifically, the individual Q-sorting charts tell us about two characteristics of individual subjects. First, it tells us which of the theoretical conceptual components of democratic ideology they see as salient to their own conceptions of democratic ideology. Second, it reveals the extent to which they regard the theoretical conceptual components of bureaucratic ideology as compatible with their own conceptions of democratic ideology.

In order to describe these characteristics of individuals in a parsimonious way, I processed the raw data into factor analysis. As presented in Table 6-1, three unrotated centroid Q-factors (i.e., A, B, and C) have eigen values that are greater than one. This suggests that the individual subjects' perspectives on democratic ideology and the relationship between bureaucratic and democratic ideologies can be summarized by three major perspectives.[7] The result varimax rotation demonstrates this point more clearly. As presented in Table 6-2, nine subjects have significant factor loadings exclusively on the first Q-factor named Factor A; eight subjects have significant factor loadings exclusively on the second Q-factor named Factor B; three subjects have significant factor loadings exclusively on the third Q-factor named Factor C; and the remaining ten subjects are loaded on any two of these three Q-factors. Note here that a Q-factor, as I mentioned in Chapter Five, represents essentially a group of subjects who share a common perspective on the ideas or concepts that are presented to them. Thus, I decided to use these three Q-factors as empirical categories for grouping the perspectives of the individual subjects.[8] The appropriateness of this usage of the three Q-factors are all insignificant at the .05 level (see Table 6-3). That is, this finding indicates that the three Q-factors are mutually exclusive categories for grouping individual perspectives.

Figure 6-7 summarizes the results of Q-factor analysis. Each Q-sort presented in the figure illustrates to what extent each of the three groups of subjects collectively sort out the 48 "democratic" and "bureaucratic" statements as democratic, undemocratic, or irrelevant to the concept of democracy on the 11-point response scale.[9] The result of the Q-factor analysis presented in this figure can be interpreted as follows:

Bureaucrats' Own Perspectives on Democratic Ideology

Examination of the data presented in Figure 6-7 focusing especially on the "democratic" statements enables us to understand the perspectives on democratic ideology held by the three groups of subjects. Because the conceptual components of democratic ideology are expressed by the "democratic" statements, each group's perspective on democratic ideology can be described partic-

Table 6 - 1 **Unrotated Centroid Q-Factors**

Subjects \ Factors	A	B	C	D	E	F	G	H	I	h^2
1	.67*	-.32	-.17	-.08	-.14	.06	-.10	-.21	-.06	.67
2	.72*	-.13	-.08	-.04	-.17	.24	-.09	.10	.08	.65
3	.52*	.15	-.27	.15	.33	.19	.19	.11	.09	.59
4	.63*	-.46*	.14	-.02	.08	.15	.24	-.10	.02	.73
5	.78*	-.18	-.26	-.04	-.10	-.21	-.09	-.04	.16	.80
6	.64*	-.35	-.18	-.13	-.25	-.07	.15	-.14	.09	.70
7	.71*	-.18	.05	-.21	.40*	.06	-.01	-.15	.00	.77
8	.60*	.02	.01	-.15	-.07	-.07	-.08	.22	-.01	.45
9	.44*	-.54*	.02	.16	.25	.05	.12	.19	.10	.64
10	.25	.46*	-.26	-.19	-.11	.13	-.12	-.10	.11	.44
11	.48*	-.05	.30	.11	-.35	.09	.17	-.12	.05	.51
12	.64*	.12	.12	-.40*	-.09	.10	.02	.08	.09	.63
13	.74*	.10	.07	.23	.00	.02	-.21	-.02	.06	.66
14	.07	.51*	.11	.14	-.12	.07	-.21	-.05	.16	.39
15	.78*	.10	.04	-.02	.04	.06	.02	-.16	-.09	.66
16	.79*	-.33	-.16	-.02	.20	.19	.13	.16	.07	.88
17	.71*	.01	.11	.18	-.09	.22	.25	.04	-.01	.67
18	.54*	.23	-.02	-.07	.21	-.29	.10	.11	.02	.50
19	.52*	-.19	.38*	-.17	.07	-.29	.04	-.25	.19	.67
20	.77*	.03	-.10	.19	-.08	-.04	-.04	.09	.02	.66
21	.55*	.24	.20	.14	-.09	-.15	.32	-.16	.08	.58
22	.57*	-.10	.29	-.03	-.03	.14	-.23	.25	.08	.56
23	.43*	.25	-.58*	-.30	.23	-.04	.08	-.03	.13	.75
24	.76*	.00	.06	.19	.13	-.19	.03	.09	.07	.68
25	.64*	-.30	-.14	.18	.18	.07	-.35	.00	.21	.76
26	.39*	.41	.19	-.29	-.31	-.23	-.10	.01	.08	.61
27	.33*	.28	.18	-.15	.08	.17	.15	.15	.22	.37
28	.47*	.18	.20	.15	.10	.00	-.36	-.20	.24	.55
29	.66*	.29	-.09	.07	-.11	.11	.18	-.22	.02	.64
30	.77*	-.24	-.13	.18	-.13	-.25	.12	.14	.16	.84
Eigen Values	11.66	2.18	1.23	.87	.97	.71	.88	.60	.38	19.01
% Variance	37	7	4	3	3	2	3	2	1	62
										Totals

Note: a. N = 30; "*" indicates a loading significant at 5% significance level.
b."h^2" indicates communality that is sum of squared factor loadings for rows.
c. "%Variance" indicates percentage of total variance explained by a factor.

Table 6 - 2 **Q-Factor Loadings Rotated by Varimax Method**

Subjects \ Factors	A	B	C	h^2
1	.73*	.14	-.18	.58
2	.62*	.33	-.23	.55
4	.74*	.23	.15	.62
5	.72*	.23	-.36	.70
6	.73*	.10	-.17	.57
9	.68*	.00	.15	.48
16	.82*	.22	-.21	.76
25	.69*	.15	-.16	.52
30	.74*	.27	-.23	.67
11	.34	.45*	.11	.33
12	.36	.53*	-.17	.44
14	-.31	.38*	-.20	.28
18	.24	.44*	-.31	.35
21	.20	.58*	-.14	.40
26	-.02	.57*	-.18	.36
27	.02	.46*	-.11	.22
28	.19	.50*	-.08	.29
3	.31	.24	-.46*	.37
10	-.09	.24	-.52*	.34
23	.23	.05	-.73*	.59
7	.63*	.37*	-.09	.54
8	.42*	.39*	-.18	.36
13	.46*	.55*	-.23	.57
15	.49*	.56*	-.27	.63
17	.49*	.51*	-.14	.52
19	.45*	.44*	.23	.45
20	.55*	.43*	-.34	.60
22	.44*	.47*	.10	.42
24	.54*	.50*	-.19	.58
29	.29	.51*	-.43*	.53
Eigen Values	7.64	4.72	2.26	14.64
% Variance	25	16	8	49
				Totals

Note: a. N = 30; "*" indicates loading significant at 5% significance level.
b. "h^2" indicates communality that is sum of squared factor loadings for rows.
c. "% Variance" indicates percentage of total variance explained by a factor.

Table 6 - 3 **Q-Factor Correlations**

Factor	A	B	C
A	—		
B	.42	—	
C	.36	.40	—

Note: a. N = 30
b. All coefficients are insignificant at 5% significance level (two-tailed test).

Figure 6 - 7 **Result of Q-Methodological Analysis of Perspectives on Compatibility Between Bureaucratic and Democratic Ideologies**

1. Perspective A

most undemocratic ◄— indeterminate —► most democratic

-5	-4	-3	-2	-1	0	+1	+2	+3	+4	+5
B16	B4	B24	B6	B10	B2*	B3	B1	D2	D1	D17
B17	B18	D13	B12	B15	B7	B5	D5	D11	D16	D21
	D10*	D4*	B13	B23	B8	B19	D6	D22	D20	
			B22	B25	B9	B21	D12			
			D9*	B26	B11	D3	D15			
			D19*	D14*	B14	D7*	D18*			
					B20					
					D8*					

2. Perspective B

most undemocratic ◄— indeterminate —► most democratic

-5	-4	-3	-2	-1	0	+1	+2	+3	+4	+5
B17	D4	B12	B3	B2*	B7	B14	B11	B8	B25	B1
B24	D10*	D5	B4	B5	B13	B17	B15	B9	D11	B10
	D19*	D6	B6	B16	B18	B19	B23	D1	D16	
			D3	D9*	B26	B20	D7*			
			D12	D14*	D2	B21	D8*			
			D21	D20	D15	D22	D17			
					D18*					
					D13					

(continued on next page)

Figure 6 - 7 (continued) **Result of Q-Methodological Analysis of Perspectives on Compatibility Between Bureaucratic and Democratic Ideologies**

3. Perspective C

most undemocratic ◄—— indeterminate ——► most democratic

-5	-4	-3	-2	-1	0	+1	+2	+3	+4	+5
B17	B9	B16	B18	B7	B1	B3	B6	B13	B23	B19
D3	B26	D10*	B22	B8	B2*	B4	B10	D21	D8*	B20
	D13	D12	B24	B12	B5	B11	B14	D22	D17	
			D7*	D4*	D1	B15	B21			
			D9*	D14*	D5	D2	B25			
			D19*	D18*	D6	D16	D15			
					D11					
					D20					

Note: a. Entries in boxes are identification symbols of statements presented in Part II of Appendix I.
b. Statements pertaining to conceptual components of bureaucratic ideology start with "B": and those pertaining to conceptual components of democratic ideology start with "D".

ularly by examining the extent to which each group of subjects sorts out these "democratic" statements as democratic. For convenience of presentation, the factor scores of these statements are selected and rearranged in Table 6-4.

Democratic Ideology Viewed from Perspective A. The overall pattern of factor scores of the "democratic" statements associated with Factor A indicates that the subjects who hold Perspective A sort most of the statements into the democratic response categories. That is, as presented in Table 6-4, of the 14 positively-phrased statements, 13 statements have positive factor scores; and of the eight negatively-phrased statements, five statements have negative factor scores. More specifically, this group of subjects views the conceptual components expressed by statements D1, D2, D4, D10, D11, D16, D17, D20, D21, and D22, as highly democratic; and one conceptual component expressed by statement D13, as highly undemocratic. The conceptual components expressed by statements D3, D5, D6, D9, D12, D14, D15 and D19, are conceived as slightly democratic. The conceptual components expressed by statements D7 and D18 are conceived as slightly undemocratic. The conceptual component expressed by statement D8 is perceived as irrelevant to the concept of democratic ideology.

Note that the conceptual components of democratic ideology expressed by "democratic" statements are ones that I abstracted from the theoretical literature of organizations and Public Administration. Thus, the result that the subjects who hold Perspective A regard most of the "democratic" statements as democratic indicates that they hold a perspective on democratic ideology that is fairly consistent with the theoretical version of democratic ideology that I derived from the theoretical literature of organizations and public administration.

Table 6-5 summarizes the uniqueness of Perspective A compared with the other two perspectives. Of the 22 "democratic" statements, five statements (D3, D8, D12, D18 and D20) particularly distinguish Perspective A from the other two perspectives in that the difference between the factor scores of these statements for Factor A and those of these statements for Factors B and C are all statistically significant at the .01 level.[10] More specifically, those who are grouped by Factor A regard as highly democratic a conceptual component of democratic ideology expressed by statement D20 (participation by low-ranking officials). In contrast, within the minds of those officials holding other perspectives, this conceptual component is not conceived of as a salient ingredient of democratic ideology.

Perspective A is also distinct from other perspectives in that those who hold Perspective A view "individual freedom in the workplace" and "popular sovereignty in the workplace," which are expressed respectively by statements D3 and D12, in an opposite way from those who hold other perspectives. That is, those who hold Perspective A view these conceptual components of democratic ideologies as slightly democratic, while those who hold Perspectives B or

Table 6 - 4 **Three Perspectives on Democratic Ideology Expressed in Terms of Individual Statements**

State-ments	Conceptual Components Expressed by Individual Statements	Perspectives (Q-Factors)		
		A	B	C
D1	individual freedom in a general sense	+ 4	+ 3	0
D2	individual freedom in a general sense	+ 3	0	+ 1
D3	individual freedom in workplace	+ 1	- 2	- 5
D5	individual freedom in workplace	+ 2	- 3	0
D6	citizen's freedom of choice of public goods	+ 2	- 3	0
D11	special care for alienated citizens	+ 3	+ 4	0
D12	popular sovereignty in workplace	+ 2	- 2	- 3
D13	popular sovereignty in workplace	- 3	0	- 4
D15	openness to others in workplace	+ 2	0	+ 2
D16	openness to the public	+ 4	+ 4	+ 1
D17	self-directed task-performance	+ 5	+ 2	+ 4
D20	participation by low-ranking officials	+ 4	- 1	0
D21	consensus-based decision-making	+ 5	- 2	+ 3
D22	consensus-based decision-making	+ 3	+ 1	+ 3
D4*	individual freedom in workplace	- 3	- 4	- 1
D7*	equality in a general sense	+ 1	+ 2	- 2
D8*	equality in a general sense	0	+ 2	+ 4
D9*	equality between male and female	- 2	- 1	- 2
D10*	equality in workplace	- 4	- 4	- 3
D14*	resposibility juxtaposed with accountability	- 1	- 1	- 1
D18*	respect for unique individual personality in workplace	+ 2	0	- 1
D19*	participation by low-ranking officials	- 2	- 4	- 2

Note: a. For specific content of statements, see Part II of Appendix I.
b. Negatively phrased statements are asterisked. Conceptual components listed for these statements are those that are opposite to concepts directly expressed by these statements.
c. Entries in columns of perspectives are factor scores of each statement on three Q-factors. "+" indicates statement is evaluated as "democratic"; "-" indicates statement is evaluated as "undemocratic"; "0" indicates statement is evaluated as "irrelevant" to democratic ideology.

Table 6 - 5 **Unique Content of Perspective A on Democratic Ideology**

Statements	Q-Factors and Rounded Factor Scores		
	A	B	C
(D3) Within my department, the number of those who prevent other staff from having freedom of action should be minimized as much as possible.	+1	-2	-5
(D8) One must behave in accordance with his/her social status. (R)	0	+2	+4
(D12) The ability of the chief executive officer of an organization must be evaluated first of all by the extent to which the results induced by him/her are meaningful to all other staff within the organization.	+2	-2	-3
(D18) It is much more desirable to let the project of my department to be carried out by those staff who share similar personalities or characters than by those whose personalities and characters are quite different. (R)	+2	0	-1
(D20) All rank-and-file staff should be allowed to have a formal right to participate in meetings where people make decisions that are critical to the fate of my department as a whole.	+4	-1	0

Note: Statements noted with (R) are those that express a conceptual component in a negative way.

C commonly regard them as undemocratic.

In addition, those who hold Perspective A do not regard "equality in a general sense," which is negatively expressed by statement D8, as a salient ingredient of democratic ideology. In contrast, those who hold Perspectives B and C commonly regard this conceptual component of democratic ideology as undemocratic. In contrast, those who hold Perspective B view it as slightly undemocratic, and those who hold Perspective C view it as highly undemocratic.

Finally, those who hold Perspective A are distinguished from those who hold other perspectives in their understandings of a conceptual component of democratic ideology (i.e., respect of unique individual personality in the workplace) which is expressed negatively by statement D18. Those who hold Perspective A view this conceptual component as democratic. In contrast, those who hold Perspectives B and C view this conceptual component as undemocratic.

In sum, the perspective on democratic ideology held by the subjects grouped by Factor A may be summarized by the following conceptual components that they regard as highly democratic:

- Individual Freedom in a General Sense (D1 and D2); Individual Freedom in Workplace (D4)
- Equality in Workplace (D10)
- Special Care for Alienated Citizens (D11)
- Openness to the Public (D16)
- Self-Directed Task-Performance (D17)
- Participation by Low-Ranking Officials in Decision-Making (D20)
- Consensus-Based Decision-Making (D21, D22)

Democratic Ideology Viewed from Perspective B. Unlike those who are grouped by Factor A, those who are grouped by Factor B have a perspective on democratic ideology which is inconsistent with the theoretical version of democratic ideology. That is, as presented in Table 6-4, this group of subjects regards as democratic less than half of the theoretical conceptual components of democratic ideology (i.e., those conceptual components expressed by statements D1, D4, D9, D10, D11, D14, D16, D17, D19, and D22). They regard the remaining 12 theoretical conceptual components as irrelevant to their own conception of democratic ideology or even as undemocratic.

The unique characteristics of the perspective on democratic ideology held by this group of subjects are seen, as summarized in Table 6-6, particularly among five statements (D3, D5, D6, D13, and D21). More specifically, those who hold Perspective B regard as slightly undemocratic a democratic conceptual component, "individual freedom in the workplace (i.e., self-directed task performance)," which is expressed by statement D3. In contrast, those who hold

Table 6 - 6 Unique Content of Perspective B on Democratic Ideology

Statements	Q-Factors and Rounded Factor Scores		
	A	B	C
(D3) Within my department, the number of those who prevent other staff from having freedom of action should be minimized as much as possible.	+1	-2	-5
(D5) One's personal life goals should be more important than the goals of organization to which he/she belongs.	+2	-3	0
(D6) Just as the best economic system is one in which the consumer's freedom of choice can be maximized, so is the best public administrative system one in which the enhancement of individual citizens' freedom to choose the kinds and quantity of the public goods and services they want to purchase is treated as the number one axiom in the value scale of public administration.	+2	-3	0
(D13) A big, powerful group of persons who can run the whole show in my department without considering others should be prevented as much as possible from emerging.	-3	0	- 4
(D21) All decisions pertaining to the internal affairs of my department must be based upon wide consensus among all members of my department whose interests may be affected by the decision.	+5	-2	+3

Perspective A regard this ideal as slightly democratic, and those who hold Perspective C regard it as highly undemocratic.

Perspective B is distinct from other perspectives also in that those who hold this perspective regard as highly undemocratic the two conceptual components which are, as reviewed in Chapter Four, often regarded as important ingredients of liberal democratic ideology by many organizational and public administration theorists. These conceptual components are "individual freedom in the workplace (i.e., attaching importance to individual goals over organizational goals)" expressed by statement D5, and "application of the principle of market freedom to public administration (i.e., citizens' freedom of choice of public goods)" expressed by statement D6. In contrast, in the minds of those who hold other perspectives, these conceptual components are perceived as irrelevant to the concept of democratic ideology (Perspective C) or as slightly democratic (Perspective A).

Those who hold Perspective B are also different from those who hold other perspectives in their views on a conceptual component of popular democratic ideology. That is, those who hold Perspective B regard as irrelevant to the concept of democratic ideology the conceptual component, "popular sovereignty of the workplace (i.e., removal of priveleged powerful group within organizations)" which is expressed by statement D13. In contrast, those who hold Perspective A and those who hold Perspective C commonly believe that this component is highly undemocratic.

Finally, those who hold Perspective B regard as slightly undemocratic a conceptual component which is, as reviewed in Chapter Four, often considered by many organizational theorists as an important instrumental principle for attaining the ideals of popular democracy in organizations. This conceptual component is "decision-making based upon a wide consensus among organizational members," which is expressed by statement D21. In contrast, those who hold Perspectives A and C commonly believe that this conceptual component is highly democratic.

In sum, the perspective on democratic ideology held by the subjects grouped by Factor B can be summarized by the following conceptual components that they regard as discernably democratic:

- Individual Freedom in a General Sense (D1); Individual Freedom in Workplace (D4)
- Equality in Workplace (D10)
- Special Care for Alienated Citizens (D11)
- Openness to the Public (D16)
- Participation by Low-Ranking Officials in Decision-Making (D19)[11]

Democratic Ideology Viewed from Perspective C. The overall pattern of factor scores for Factor C indicate that, similar to those who are grouped by Factor B, those who are grouped by Factor C have a perspective on democratic ideology that is not consistent with the theoretical version of democratic ideology. That is, as presented in Table 6-4, this group of subjects understands about half of the theoretical conceptual components of democratic ideology as democratic (i.e., those expressed by statements D2, D4, D7, D9, D10, D14, D15, D16, D17, D18, D19, D21, and D22). They, however, regard the theoretical conceptual components of democratic ideology expressed by the remaining nine statements as irrelevant to the concept of democratic ideology or even as undemocratic.

The uniqueness of the perspective on democratic ideology held by this group of subjects is seen particularly among the five statements as summarized in Table 6-7. That is, they conceive the conceptual component expressed by statement D3 (i.e., self-directed performance of individual work) as highly undemocratic. In contrast, those who hold Perspective A believe that this conceptual component is slightly democratic; those who hold Perspective B think of it as slightly undemocratic.

A similar pattern of difference is found on an egalitarian democratic ideal defined in a general sense (i.e., "equality among people," which is expressed by statement D7). That is, those who hold Perspective C think of this egalitarian ideal as slightly undemocratic, while those who hold Perspectives A and B commonly view this ideal as slightly democratic.

Another distinctive characteristic of Perspective C is seen among statements D1 and D11. As indicated by the zero factor scores of these statements for Factor C, those who hold Perspective C regard as irrelevant to the concept of democratic ideology a liberal democratic ideal, "individual freedom in a general sense," which is expressed by statement D1, and an egalitarian democratic ideal highlighted in the relationships between government and the citizens (i.e., "participation in crucial governmental decision-making by a group of underpriveleged citizens," which is expressed by statement D11). In contrast, those who hold Perspectives A and B view these conceptual components as highly democratic.

Finally, Perspective C differs from the other two perspectives in that those who are grouped by Factor C regard a popular democratic ideal expressed by statement D16 (i.e., "openness to the public") as democratic to a significantly lesser degree than those who are grouped by Factor A or Factor B.

In sum, the perspective on democratic ideology held by the subjects grouped by Factor C can be summarized by the following conceptual components that they regard as discernably democratic:

- Equality in Workplace (D10)
- Self-Directed Task-Performance (D17)

Table 6 - 7 **Unique Content of Perspective C on Democratic Ideology**

Statements	Q-Factors and Rounded Factor Scores		
	A	B	C
(D1) All individual human beings must be treated as having complete free-will in determining their own fates.	+4	+3	0
(D3) Within my department, the number of those who prevent other staff from having freedom of action should be minimized as much as possible.	+1	-2	-5
(D7) We have to teach children that all people are created equal, but almost everyone knows that some are better than others. (R)	+1	+2	-2
(D11) Public administrators must make the utmost effort to protect especially the disadvantaged minority citizens from being exploited by the dominant groups within society. And diverse channels through which these citizens can directly or indirectly participate in the critical decision-making made within the government.	+3	+4	0
(D16) What is happening within this city government should be known to the public as much as possible.	+4	+4	+1

Note: Statement noted with (R) is one that expresses a conceptual component in a negative way.

- Consensus-Based Decision-Making (D21, D22)

A Common Perspective on Democratic Ideology. Thus far, I have described the content of the perspectives on democratic ideology held by the three groups of subjects especially in terms of their uniqueness. However, note that these three groups of subjects share a common view on a number of conceptual components of democratic ideology. The commonality among these groups in their perspectives on democratic ideology is seen particularly among the three statements (D9, D10, and D14) presented in Table 6-8. The factor scores of these statements among the three Q-factors are not statistically different from each other. This suggests that among the three groups of subjects, there is a consensus on the conceptual components of democratic ideology expressed by these statements. The specific content of this consensus can be summarized as follows:

First, the factor scores of statement D10 indicate that the three groups of subjects commonly believe that the conceptual component expressed by the statement is highly undemocratic. Note that this statement negatively phrases the conceptual component that I originally wished to examine. That is, what is directly expressed by this statement is an anti-egalitarian organizational democratic ideal (i.e., "*unequal* treatment between the subordinates and the superordinates on non-formal affairs"). The conceptual components that I originally wished to examine with this statement, however, is a pro-egalitarian organizational democratic ideal; that is, "equal treatment between the subordinates and the superordinates on non-formal affairs." Thus, converting the negative wording into a positive sense, the result suggests that the three groups of subjects commonly regard the egalitarian organizational democratic ideal as highly significant.

Second, statement D9, which also negatively phrases another egalitarian organizational democratic ideal (i.e., equality between males and females within organizations), has the same pattern of factor scores as D10, except that the magnitude of factor scores is not as substantially high as D10 (-2 for Perspectives A and C and -1 for Perspective B). Converting the negative wording into positive terms, the result suggests that they commonly regard this ideal as slightly democratic.

Finally, the factor scores for statement D14 indicate that the conceptual component expressed by this statement is commonly regarded as slightly undemocratic. The conceptual component that is directly expressed by this statement is "accountability," which is stressed in the argument that the dichotomy between public administration and politics is compatible with democracy (especially popular democracy). Note that the concept of "responsibility," which is the mirror image of "accountability," is indirectly expressed by the same statement. Thus, if we interpret the factor scores of this statement in terms of the concept of "responsibility," we may say that the three groups of subjects com-

Table 6 - 8 **Content of Common Perspective on Democratic Ideology**

Statements	Q-Factors and Factor Scores		
	A	B	C
(D9) It is more natural to be directed by a male boss than to be directed by a female boss. (R)	-2	-1	-2
(D10) Unequal treatment between high ranking officials and low ranking officials is natural. (R)	-4	-4	-3
(D14) Public administrators' responsibility to legislators and the citizens are confined only to those affairs for which the law requires the administrators to be responsible. It is an excessive request to ask public administrators to have even a moral responsibility to them beyond the legally defined sphere of responsibility. (R)	-1	-1	-1

Note: Statements noted with (R) are ones that express a conceptual component in a negative way.

monly regard "responsibility" as a slightly salient conceptual component of democratic ideology.

In sum, the Q-methodological analyses of bureaucrats' own understandings of democratic ideology presented thus far indicate that (1) a multiple number of perspectives on democratic ideology exist among the respondents;[12] (2) the theoretical version of democratic ideology postulated in the fields of organization theory and Public Administration is consistent with only one of the three major perspectives held by the actual practitioners of bureaucracy; (3) the respondents understand as undemocratic or irrelevant to the concept of democratic ideology many of the conceptual components which have been regarded as important ingredients of democratic ideology by the scholars in these fields; (4) except for several conceptual components, the three groups of subjects have different understandings of the extent to which the conceptual components of democratic ideology are democratic, undemocratic, or irrelevant; and (5) the three groups of subjects do not all distinguish the three types of democratic ideologies (i.e., liberal, egalitarian, and popular democratic ideologies) in their conceptualizations of democratic ideology (see the conceptual components that they regard as highly democratic).

The first two findings suggest that the clarification of the bureaucrats' own conception of democratic ideology is important in investigating the relationships between bureaucratic and democratic ideologies as understood by bureaucrats. The reasoning behind the inference of this insight is that, just as the arguments of scholars in the fields of organization theory and Public Administration about the compatibility between bureaucratic and democratic ideologies differ widely by how they understand democratic ideology, so also would bureaucrats' own understandings of compatibility differ by their own conceptions of democratic ideology. Thus, the findings suggest that the content of the relationship between bureaucratic and democratic ideologies would be richer than what is described in the previous section by the R-methodological analysis, in which only the theoretical version of democratic ideology is considered. Recall that this is a major speculation that motivates the use of Q-methodology in addition to R-methodology for investigating the theme of subjective compatibility.

The next two findings provide a practical insight.[13] That is, if we accept that all of the theoretical conceptual components of democratic ideology, expressed by "democratic" statements, are the democratic ideals and instrumental principles that should be fully internalized by bureaucrats, the third finding indicates that the ideological reorientation of Seoul city government officials is of crucial necessity. Related to this insight, the fourth finding suggests that the ideological reorientation should be put into practice selectively. That is, it suggests that the reorientation must focus particularly upon those officials who do not regard many of the conceptual components of democratic ideology as democratic, and particularly upon those democratic ideals and instrumental principles that are regarded as undemocratic or irrelevant to the concept of democratic ideology by bureaucrats. In this vein, the specific results of my Q-methodological analysis of bureaucrats' perspectives on democratic ideology suggest that the officials who need the ideological re-orientation are more those who have a perspective on democratic ideology like Perspectives B and C, rather than those who have a perspective like that of A.[14] As my examination of the uniqueness of Perspective B reveals, such democratic ideals and instrumental principles as the "importance of individuals over organizations," "citizens' freedom of choice of public goods," and "consensus-based decision-making" are regarded as undemocratic, particularly by those who hold Perspective B. Thus, this finding suggests that these ideals and instrumental principles must be emphasized in re-orienting those officials who hold a perspective on democratic ideology like Perspective B. Finally, my examination of the uniqueness of Perspective C suggests that such democratic ideals as "individual freedom in the workplace," "special care for alienated citizens," and "equality in a general sense" should be stressed in re-orienting the officials who have this kind of perspective. My examination of the common perspective on democratic ideology provides an insight that if we have to find democratic ideals that will be stressed to all Seoul city government officials, they may be "gender equality in the workplace" and "responsibility to the public citizens and legislators."

The last finding indicates that the distinction among the liberal egalitarian, and popular democratic ideologies that have been frequently made in the literature of democratic theory is analytical rather than empirical. It indicates that in reality, these three types of democratic ideologies are intermingled into a *whole* concept of democratic ideology.

Compatibility Between Bureaucratic and Democratic Ideologies in the Minds of Bureaucrats

Throughout the previous section, it has been emphasized that the subjects are divided into three groups in their perspectives on democratic ideology. I have also specified which of the theoretical conceptual components of democratic ideology are salient to bureaucrats' own conceptions of this ideology. I did this by examining the locations of the "democratic" statements on the three Q-sorts in Figure 6-7. To what extent, then, do the three groups of subjects think of the theoretical conceptual components of bureaucratic ideology as compatible with those that they regard as salient to their own conceptions of democratic ideology? This can be answered by examining the locations of the "bureaucratic" statements on the three Q-sorts in Figure 6-7 in relation to the "democratic" statements. The core logic of this examination is as follows:

The statements located on the far-right three piles of the Q-sorting charts in Figure 6-7 are ones that are evaluated as highly democratic (i.e., the factor scores are equal to or greater than +3) by each of the three groups of subjects, and that those located on the far-left three piles are ones that are evaluated as highly undemocratic (i.e., the factor scores are equal to or smaller than -3). Therefore, if a group of subjects places a "bureaucratic" statement in one of the three far-left piles, it can be said that the group regards the bureaucratic conceptual component expressed by the statement as being incompatible with democratic ideology, particularly the one that is expressed collectively by the "democratic" statements placed in the three far-right piles. Similarly, if a group of subjects places a "bureaucratic" statement in one of the three far-right piles, it can be said that the group regards the bureaucratic conceptual component expressed by the statement as compatible with democratic ideology, particularly the one that is expressed collectively by the "democratic" statements placed in the three far-right piles. In these ways, we can clarify the specific conceptual components of bureaucratic and democratic ideologies that are regarded as compatible or incompatible with each other by each of the three groups of subjects.

The overall pattern of locations of the statements indicates that, insofar as the theme of compatibility is concerned, the subjects are split into two groups: those who understand most components of bureaucratic ideology as incompatible with most components of democratic ideology and those whose understandings of them vary depending on which components of bureaucratic and democratic ideologies are considered. The former are those who hold Perspective A on democratic ideology (i.e., those who are grouped by Factor A), and the latter are those who hold Perspective B or Perspective C. That is, those who hold Perspective A place most of the "bureaucratic" and negatively phrased "democratic" statements in the piles representing undemocratic characteristics. In contrast, such a distinctive pattern of a split between "bureaucratic" and "democratic" statements is not found in the Q-sorting charts produced by those who hold Perspectives B or C. These subjects spread the bureaucratic statements across all piles along with the "democratic" statements.

More specific examinations of Figure 6-7 reveal that each of the three groups of subjects has a different understanding of specifically which conceptual components of bureaucratic and democratic ideologies are compatible or incompatible with one another.

Those who hold Perspective A place five "bureaucratic" statements (B4, B16, B17, B18, and B24) on the three far-left piles of the Q-sorting chart. This indicates that these subjects understand the theoretical conceptual components of bureaucratic ideology expressed by these statements as highly incompatible with their own conception of democratic ideology. Which conceptual components these subjects think of as highly democratic has already been clarified in the previous section. That is, they think of as highly democratic the conceptual components that are positively expressed by eight statements (D1, D2, D11, D16, D17, D20, D21, and D22) and those that are negatively expressed by two statements (D4 and D10). In Figure 6-7, the former are located on the three far-right piles, and the latter are located on the two of the three far-left piles. This finding indicates that the subjects holding Perspective A understand particularly the following conceptual components of bureaucratic and democratic ideologies as highly incompatible with one another:

Bureaucratic Ideology

- Effectiveness (B4)
- Hierarchy of Authority and Control (B16 , B17)
- Unity of Command (B18)
- Impersonal Relationships Among People (B24)

Democratic Ideology

- Individual Freedom in a General Sense (D1 and D2); Individual Freedom in Workplace (D4)
- Equality in Workplace (D10)
- Special Care for Alienated Citizens (D11); Openness to the Public (D16); Self-Directed Task-Performance (D17)
- Participation by Low-Ranking Officials in Decision-Making (D20)
- Consensus-Based Decision-Making (D21, D22)

Those who hold Perspective B on democratic ideology (i.e., those who, as clarified in the previous section, conceive democratic ideology mainly in terms of the conceptual components expressed by statements D1, D4, D10, D11, D16, and D19) placed the five bureaucratic statements (B1, B8, B9, B10, and B25) on the three far-right piles. This indicates that this group of subjects understands the following conceptual components of bureaucratic and democratic ideologies as highly compatible with one another:

Bureaucratic Ideology

- Maintenance of Order in a General Sense (B8, B9); Maintenance of Order in Workplace (B10)
- Task-Performance Based Upon Formal Rules and Regulations (B25)
- Instrumental Rationalism (B1)

Democratic Ideology

- Individual Freedom in a General Sense (D1); Individual Freedom in Workplace (D4)
- Equality in Workplace (D10)
- Special Care for Alienated Citizens (D11)
- Openness to the Public (D16)
- Participation by Low-Ranking Officials in Decision-Making (D19)

In addition, this group of subjects placed three bureaucratic statements (B12, B17, and B24) on the three far-left piles. This indicates that they understand the following conceptual components of bureaucratic ideology as incompatible with those of democratic ideology listed above:

- Emphasis on Stability (B12)
- Hierarchy of Authority and Control (B17)
- Impersonal Relationships Among People (B24)

Those who hold Perspective C (i.e., those who, as clarified in the previous section, conceive democratic ideology mainly in terms of the conceptual components expressed by statements D10, D17, D21, and D22) placed four "bureaucratic" statements (B3, B9, B20, and B23) in the three far-right piles of the Q-sorting chart. This indicates that this group of subjects understands the following components of bureaucratic and democratic ideologies as compatible with one another:

Bureaucratic Ideology	**Democratic Ideology**
- Efficiency (B3)	- Equality in Workplace (D10)
- Division of Labor (B9)	- Self-Directed Task-Performance (D17)
- The 3 S's (B20)	- Consensus-Based Decision Making (D21, D22)
- Professionalism (B23)	

In addition, that this group of subjects placed four "bureaucratic" statements (B9, B16, B17, and B26) in the far-left three piles indicates that they understand the following conceptual components of bureaucratic ideology as incompatible with those of democratic ideology listed above:

- Maintenance of Order (B9)
- Hierarchy of Authority and Control (B16, B17)
- Reliance on and Use of Written Documents (B26)

Finally, an analysis of the commonality among the three groups of subjects in their placements of the "bureaucratic" and "democratic" statements on the Q-sorting charts reveals that in all of the three charts, there is no common "bureaucratic" statement that is placed in any of the three far-right piles. This indicates that there is no consensus among the three groups of subjects about the compatibility between bureaucratic and democratic ideologies. For incompatibility, however, the analysis reveals that there is a consensus, particularly on one set of the democratic and bureaucratic conceptual components. That is, the three groups of subjects commonly placed a "bureaucratic" statement (i.e., B17) in the pile which represents the most undemocratic characteristic (i.e., -5) and a "democratic" statement that negatively expresses a conceptual component of democratic ideology (i.e., D10) in the pile which represents a highly undemocratic perception. This indicates that the three groups of subjects commonly understand "hierarchy of authority and control" as highly incompatible with "equality in the workplace."

The Q-methodological analysis clarifies specifically which conceptual components of bureaucratic and democratic ideologies are understood as compatible or incompatible with one another in the minds of bureaucrats. It does not serve very well, however, for checking the empirical validity of the theoretical arguments posed in the fields of organization theory and Public Administration. This is because the conceptual components of bureaucratic and democratic ideologies examined in this Q-methodological analysis are *substantive* ones which are expressed by *individual* statements. In contrast, however, the conceptual components that I wish to examine for checking the empirical validity of the theoretical arguments are not substantive but analytical ones which are expressed *collectively* by *sets* of the individual statements. In order to assess the empirical validity of the theoretical arguments, I thus performed another Q-methodological analysis on the results of Q-factor analysis reported in Figure 6-7.

In this second Q-methodological analysis, major attention was given to the relationships among the 25 analytical conceptual components of bureaucratic and democratic ideologies that were abstracted from the theoretical literature (see Figure 4-2). The 48 "bureaucratic" and "democratic" statements were grouped into 25 sets so that the statements in each set collectively expressed each of the 25 analytical conceptual components. The factor scores of these 25 groups of statements were then averaged for all three Q-factors[15] and processed by the mean-difference tests. The average factor scores and the results of mean-difference tests are presented in Table 6-9.

In reading the table, note that the average factor scores (i.e., whether they are positive, negative or zero) and the results of mean-difference tests (i.e., the statistical significance of t-values) are used for determining different, but interrelated things. Whether the average factor scores are positive, negative, or zero, determines two things. First, it determines whether or not a certain group of subjects are relevant to the examinations of the relationships between certain democratic and bureaucratic conceptual components. As mentioned earlier, in order to reduce the gap between measured facts and the substantive inference on them, it should be made clear that the researcher and the subjects have the same understandings about what the statements in the questionnaire are supposed to measure. If the scores of certain sets of "democratic" statements are negative or zero for a certain group of subjects, it indicates that the group regards the conceptual components of democratic ideology expressed by the sets of "democratic" statements as undemocratic or irrelevant to the concept of democratic ideo-

Table 6 - 9 **Results of Significance Tests for Difference Between Average Rounded Factor Scores of Sets of "Bureaucratic" and "Democratic" Statements**

Conceptual Components (X and Y) of Bureaucratic and Democratic Ideologies Juxtaposed with One Another		Groups of Subjects (Q Factors)								
		Factor A			Factor B			Factor C		
		Average Rounded Factor Scores of Sets of Statements Expressing Composite Conceptual Components		t-value of Difference Between Average Rounded Factor Scores	Average Rounded Factor Scores of Sets of Statements Expressing Composite Conceptual Components		t-value of Difference Between Average Rounded Factor Scores	Average Rounded Factor Scores of Sets of Statements Expressing Composite Conceptual Components		t-value of Difference Between Average Rounded Factor Scores
(X)	(Y)	($\overline{X}$)	($\overline{Y}$)		($\overline{X}$)	($\overline{Y}$)		($\overline{X}$)	($\overline{Y}$)	
Set I										
BURO -	DEMO	-1.08	2.09	- 5.47**	.42	.50	- .10	.23	.45	- .30
BURO -	LIBDEMO	-1.08	2.25	- 4.23**	.42	.13	.28	.23	.25	- .25
BURO -	EQDEMO	-1.08	2.00	- 3.80**	.42	1.14	- .64	.23	.71	- .43
BURO -	POPDEMO	-1.08	2.00	- 3.53**	.42	.29	.13	.23	.43	- .17
Set II										
INTBURO -	INTDEMO	-1.17	2.00	- 4.81**	.61	.28	.41	.22	.44	- .26
INTBURO -	INTLDEMO	-1.17	2.29	- 3.96**	.61	.57	.03	.22	.29	- .06
INTBURO -	INTEDEMO	-1.17	1.83	- 3.34**	.61	.67	- .05	.22	.83	- .49
INTBURO -	INTPDEMO	-1.17	1.80	- 2.83**	.61	- .60	.96	.22	.20	.01

(continued on next page)

Table 6 - 9 (continued) **Results of Significance Tests for Difference Between Average Rounded Factor Scores of Sets of "Bureaucratic" and "Democratic" Statements**

Conceptual Components (X and Y) of Bureaucratic and Democratic Ideologies Juxtaposed with One Another		Groups of Subjects (Q Factors)								
		Factor A			Factor B			Factor C		
		Average Rounded Factor Scores of Sets of Statements Expressing Composite Conceptual Components		t-value of Difference Between Average Rounded Factor Scores	Average Rounded Factor Scores of Sets of Statements Expressing Composite Conceptual Components		t-value of Difference Between Average Rounded Factor Scores	Average Rounded Factor Scores of Sets of Statements Expressing Composite Conceptual Components		t-value of Difference Between Average Rounded Factor Scores
(X)	(Y)	$(\bar{X})$	$(\bar{Y})$		$(\bar{X})$	$(\bar{Y})$		$(\bar{X})$	$(\bar{Y})$	
Set III										
INTBIDL -	INTDIDL	- .92	1.58	- 3.22**	1.08	.08	.98	.15	- .42	.59
INTBIDL -	EXTDIDL	- .92	2.00	- 3.42**	1.08	.63	.37	.15	.13	.03
INTBIDL -	INTDINST	- .92	2.83	- 3.51**	1.08	.67	.34	.15	2.17	- 2.20*
INTBIDL -	EXTBIDL	- .92	- .11	- 1.10	1.08	1.22	- .14	.15	.22	- .08
INTBIDL -	INTBINST	- .92	-1.50	.70	1.08	.00	.94	.15	.30	- .12
EXTBIDL -	INTDIDL	- .11	1.58	- 2.17*	1.22	.08	.13	.22	- .42	.57
EXTBIDL -	EXTDIDL	- .11	2.00	- 2.77*	1.22	.63	.49	.22	.13	.10
EXTBIDL -	INTDINST	- .11	2.83	- 2.92*	1.22	.67	.48	.22	2.17	- 1.95
EXTBIDL -	INTBINST	- .11	-1.50	1.77	1.22	.00	.65	.22	.30	- .05
INTBINST -	INTDIDL	-1.50	1.58	- 3.53**	.00	.08	- .07	.30	- .42	.51
INTBINST -	EXTDIDL	-1.50	2.00	- 3.79**	.00	.63	- .46	.30	.13	.12
INTBINST -	INTDINST	-1.50	2.83	- 3.72**	.00	.67	- .49	.30	2.17	- .62

(continued on next page)

Table 6 - 9 (continued) **Results of Significance Tests for Difference Between Average Rounded Factor Scores of Sets of "Bureaucratic" and "Democratic" Statements**

Conceptual Components (X and Y) of Bureaucratic and Democratic Ideologies Juxtaposed with One Another		Groups of Subjects (Q Factors)								
		Factor A			Factor B			Factor C		
		Average Rounded Factor Scores of Sets of Statements Expressing Composite Conceptual Components		t-value of Difference Between Average Rounded Factor Scores	Average Rounded Factor Scores of Sets of Statements Expressing Composite Conceptual Components		t-value of Difference Between Average Rounded Factor Scores	Average Rounded Factor Scores of Sets of Statements Expressing Composite Conceptual Components		t-value of Difference Between Average Rounded Factor Scores
(X)	(Y)	$(\bar{X})$	$(\bar{Y})$		$(\bar{X})$	$(\bar{Y})$		$(\bar{X})$	$(\bar{Y})$	
Set III (continued)										
INTDIDL -	EXTDIDL	1.58	2.00	- .46	.08	.63	- .45	-.42	.13	- .48
INTDIDL -	INTDINST	1.58	2.83	- 1.11	.08	.67	- .49	-.42	2.17	- 2.05
EXTDIDL -	INTDINST	2.00	2.83	- .70	.63	.67	- .03	.13	2.17	- 2.26*
Set IV										
INTBIDL -	INTLDIDL	- .92	2.60	- 3.78**	1.08	.40	.47	.15	- .60	.67
INTBIDL -	EXTLDIDL	- .92	3.00	- 3.35**	1.08	.00	.63	.15	.33	- .15
INTBIDL -	INTLDNST	- .92	1.50	- 1.38	1.08	1.00	.04	.15	2.50	- 1.54
EXTBIDL -	INTLDIDL	- .11	2.60	- 3.96**	1.22	.40	.06	.22	- .60	.66
EXTBIDL -	EXTLDIDL	- .11	3.00	- 3.82**	1.22	.00	.76	.22	.33	- .09
EXTBIDL -	INTLDNST	- .11	1.50	- 1.01	1.22	1.00	.13	.22	2.50	- 1.38
INTBINST -	INTLDIDL	-1.50	2.60	- 4.18**	.00	.40	- .25	.30	- .60	.48
INTBINST -	EXTLDIDL	-1.50	3.00	- 3.65**	.00	.00	.00	.30	.33	- .01

(continued on next page)

Table 6 - 9 (continued) **Results of Significance Tests for Difference Between Average Rounded Factor Scores of Sets of "Bureaucratic" and "Democratic" Statements**

Conceptual Components (X and Y) of Bureaucratic and Democratic Ideologies Juxtaposed with One Another		Groups of Subjects (Q Factors)								
		Factor A			Factor B			Factor C		
		Average Rounded Factor Scores of Sets of Statements Expressing Composite Conceptual Components		t-value of Difference Between Average Rounded Factor Scores	Average Rounded Factor Scores of Sets of Statements Expressing Composite Conceptual Components		t-value of Difference Between Average Rounded Factor Scores	Average Rounded Factor Scores of Sets of Statements Expressing Composite Conceptual Components		t-value of Difference Between Average Rounded Factor Scores
(X)	(Y)	($\bar{X}$)	($\bar{Y}$)		($\bar{X}$)	($\bar{Y}$)		($\bar{X}$)	($\bar{Y}$)	
Set IV - continued										
INTBINST	INTLDNST	-1.50	1.50	- 1.57	.00	1.00	- .47	.30	2.50	- .79
INTDIDL	EXTLDIDL	2.60	3.00	- .50	.40	.00	.18	- .60	.33	- .85
INTDIDL	INTLDNST	2.60	1.50	.54	.40	1.00	- .24	- .60	2.50	- .36
EXTLDIDL	INTLDNST	3.00	1.50	.55	.00	1.00	- .44	.33	2.50	- 1.81
INTBIDL	INTEDIDL	- .92	1.25	- 1.91	1.08	.25	.54	.15	.75	- .46
INTBIDL	EXTEDIDL	- .92	.67	- 1.27	1.08	.00	.61	.15	- .67	.59
INTBIDL	INTEDNST	- .92	3.00	- 2.72**	1.08	1.50	- .21	.15	1.00	- .57
EXTBIDL	INTEDIDL	- .11	1.25	- 1.43	1.22	.25	.67	.22	.75	- .36
EXTBIDL	EXTEDIDL	- .11	.67	- .79	1.22	.00	.73	.22	- .67	.57
EXTBIDL	INTEDNST	- .11	3.00	- 3.09**	1.22	1.50	- .15	.22	1.00	- .49
INTBINST	INTEDIDL	-1.50	1.25	- 2.25*	.00	.25	- .29	.30	.75	- .21
INTBINST	EXTEDIDL	-1.50	.67	- 1.62	.00	.00	.00	.30	- .67	.40

(continued on next page)

Table 6 - 9 (continued) **Results of Significance Tests for Difference Between Average Rounded Factor Scores of Sets of "Bureaucratic" and "Democratic" Statements**

Conceptual Components (X and Y) of Bureaucratic and Democratic Ideologies Juxtaposed with One Another	Groups of Subjects (Q Factors)								
	Factor A			Factor B			Factor C		
	Average Rounded Factor Scores of Sets of Statements Expressing Composite Conceptual Components		t-value of Difference Between Average Rounded Factor Scores	Average Rounded Factor Scores of Sets of Statements Expressing Composite Conceptual Components		t-value of Difference Between Average Rounded Factor Scores	Average Rounded Factor Scores of Sets of Statements Expressing Composite Conceptual Components		t-value of Difference Between Average Rounded Factor Scores
(X) (Y)	$(\bar{X})$	$(\bar{Y})$		$(\bar{X})$	$(\bar{Y})$		$(\bar{X})$	$(\bar{Y})$	
Set IV - continued									
INTBINST - INTEDNST	- 1.50	3.00	- 2.96**	.00	1.50	- .66	.30	1.00	- .25
INTEDIDL - EXTEDIDL	1.25	.67	.29	.25	.00	.09	.75	- .67	.49
INTEDIDL - INTEDNST	1.25	3.00	- .67	.25	1.50	- .54	.75	1.00	- .10
EXTEDIDL - INTEDNST	.67	3.00	- 1.18	.00	1.50	- .50	- .67	1.00	- .69
INTBIDL - INTPDIDL	- .92	.33	- .94	1.08	- .67	1.11	.15	-1.67	1.29
INTBIDL - EXTPDIDL	- .92	2.50	- 2.31*	1.08	2.50	- .73	.15	1.00	- .58
INTBIDL - INTPDNST	- .92	4.00	- 3.41**	1.08	- .50	.81	.15	3.00	- 1.96
EXTBIDL - INTPDIDL	- .11	.33	- .39	1.22	- .67	1.37	.22	-1.67	1.19
EXTBIDL - EXTPDIDL	- .11	2.50	- 2.40*	1.22	2.50	- .74	.22	1.00	- .50
EXTBIDL - INTPDNST	- .11	4.00	- 4.09**	1.22	- .50	1.00	.22	3.00	- 1.79
INTBINST - INTPDIDL	-1.50	.33	- 1.27	.00	- .67	.38	.30	-1.67	.82
INTBINST - EXTPDIDL	-1.50	2.50	- 2.55*	.00	2.50	- 1.15	.30	1.00	- .16

(continued on next page)

Table 6 - 9 (continued) **Results of Significance Tests for Difference Between Average Rounded Factor Scores of Sets of "Bureaucratic" and "Democratic" Statements**

Conceptual Components (X and Y) of Bureaucratic and Democratic Ideologies Juxtaposed with One Another	Groups of Subjects (Q Factors)								
	Factor A			Factor B			Factor C		
	Average Rounded Factor Scores of Sets of Statements Expressing Composite Conceptual Components		t-value of Difference Between Average Rounded Factor Scores	Average Rounded Factor Scores of Sets of Statements Expressing Composite Conceptual Components		t-value of Difference Between Average Rounded Factor Scores	Average Rounded Factor Scores of Sets of Statements Expressing Composite Conceptual Components		t-value of Difference Between Average Rounded Factor Scores
(X) (Y)	$(\overline{X})$	$(\overline{Y})$		$(\overline{X})$	$(\overline{Y})$		$(\overline{X})$	$(\overline{Y})$	
Set IV - continued									
INTBINST - INTPDNST	-1.50	4.00	- 3.62**	.00	- .50	.23	.30	3.00	- .98
INTPDIDL - EXTPDIDL	.33	2.50	- 1.76	- .67	2.50	- 3.41**	-1.67	1.00	- .30
INTPDIDL - INTPDNST	.33	4.00	- 2.12	- .67	- .50	- .58	-1.67	3.00	- 1.94
EXTPDIDL- INTPDNST	2.50	4.00	- .83	2.50	- .50	1.65	1.00	3.00	- 1.42

Note: a. "*" indicates $p < .05$; "**" indicates $p < .01$.

b. For substantive notation meanings of composite conceptual components, see Fig. 4-1; for content of statements expressing composite conceptual components, see questionnaire in Appendix I (especially Part II).

c. Number of statements expressing composite conceptual components are:

BURO = 26	POPDEMO = 7	EXTEDIDL= 3	INTLDIDL = 5	LIBDEMO = 8
INTBURO = 23	INTDEMO = 18	INTEDNST= 2	EXTLDIDL = 3	EQDEMO = 7
INTBIDL = 13	INTLDEMO= 7	INTPDIDL = 3	INTLDNST = 2	INTDIDL =12
EXTBIDL = 9	INTEDEMO= 6	EXTPDIDL= 2	INTEDIDL = 4	EXTDIDL = 8
INTBINST = 10	INTPDEMO= 5	INTPDNST= 2	DEMO =22	INTDINST= 6

logy. Thus, I do not make any susbstantive inferences on the understandings of this group of subjects about the relationships between these democratic conceptual components and other conceptual components.

Second, the average factor scores of the 25 sets of "bureaucratic" and "democratic" statements determine *whether* (not the extent to which) a group of subjects regards an analytical conceptual component as compatible or incompatible with another conceptual component. A group of subjects is interpreted as regarding a bureaucratic conceptual component as compatible with a democratic one, particularly if the average factor scores of the corresponding sets of "bureaucratic" and "democratic" statements are all positive.[16] The substantive reasoning behind this inference is that this condition indicates that the group of subjects regards both conceptual components as qualitatively similar and democratic. Similarly, a group of subjects is interpreted as regarding the bureaucratic conceptual component as incompatible with the democratic one if the average rounded factor score of the corresponding "bureaucratic" statement is negative or zero and that of the "democratic" statement is positive. The substantive reasoning behind this inference is that this condition indicates that the group of subjects regards the bureaucratic and democratic conceptual components as qualitatively different. That is, it indicates that they regard the bureaucratic conceptual component as undemocratic or irrelevant to the concept of democratic ideology, while regarding the democratic conceptual component as democratic.

The results of mean-difference tests determine the *extent* to which a group of subjects understands any two of the 25 composite conceptual components as compatible or incompatible with one another. This substantive interpretation of the results of these tests is different depending on whether the group of subjects is found, from the examinations of the average factor scores, to regard the two conceptual components as compatible or incompatible. Suppose that a group of subjects is found to regard the two conceptual components as compatible with one another. Given this, the statistically-significant difference between the two corresponding average rounded scores indicates that the subjects regard the two conceptual components as qualitatively the same characteristic to a different degree. If the difference is not statistically significant, it indicates that the subjects regard the two conceptual components as the same not only in a qualitative sense but also in a quantitative sense. I judge that the latter approximates more closely to the operational meaning of "compatibility" than the former. Thus, the latter is interpreted as indicating that the group of subjects regards the two conceptual components as *highly* compatible with one another; while the former is interpreted as indicating that they regard the conceptual components as *slightly* compatible.

The same reasoning is applied to the case that a group of subjects is found to regard the two conceptual components as incompatible with one another. For this case, the statistically-significant difference between the two average rounded scores indicates that the group of subjects regards the two conceptual components as different ones not only in a qualitative sense, but also in a quantitative sense. The statistically-insignificant difference indicates that they regard the two conceptual components as qualitatively different characteristics, while thinking that the qualitative difference between these conceptual components is not discernable. Thus, the former is interpreted as indicating that the group of subjects regards the two conceptual components as *highly* incompatible with one another; while the latter is interpreted as indicating that they regard the conceptual components as *slightly* incompatible.

The overall pattern of the average factor scores and the t-values reported in Table 6-9 reveals that those who are grouped by Factor A have quite a different view from that of other subjects on the relationships among the composite conceptual components of bureaucratic and democratic ideologies, and that those who are grouped by Factor B are more similar to than different from those who are grouped by Factor C in their understandings of the relationships. More specific results are as follows:

According to the results of mean-difference tests pertaining to the relationships in Set I, those who are grouped by Factor A understand the general concept of bureaucratic ideology (BURO) as incompatible with the general concept of democratic ideology (DEMO) and all of the three types of democratic ideologies [the liberal democratic ideology (LIBDEMO), the egalitarian democratic ideology (EQDEMO), and the popular democratic ideology (POPDEMO)]. In contrast, those who are grouped by Factor B or Factor C commonly view these ideologies as compatible with one another.

The same pattern is found when we are concerned with the relationships in Set II, in which the composite conceptual components of bureaucratic and democratic ideologies are specified in terms of the intra-organizational context of government agencies. That is, those who are grouped into Factor A understand internal bureaucratic ideology (INTBURO) to be incompatible with internal democratic ideology (INTDEMO) and all of its three sub-types [internal liberal democratic ideology (INTLDEMO), internal egalitarian democratic ideology (INTEDEMO), and internal popular democratic ideology (INTPDEMO)]. In contrast, those who are grouped into Factor B or Factor C commonly view them as compatible with one another.

The results of mean-difference tests for the relationships in Set III enable us to assess the extent to which the subjects regard as compatible or incompatible with each other the composite conceptual components of bureaucratic and democratic ideologies that are specified in terms of the contextual factor and the means-and-ends scheme. It is found, first, that for the relationships among the conceptual components across the two ideologies, the results are similar to those discussed above. That is, those who are grouped by Factor A pose a perspective of incompatibility on each set of relationships between the three composite conceptual components of bureaucratic ideology [internal bureaucratic ideals (INTBIDL), external bureaucratic ideals (EXTBIDL), and internal bureaucratic instrumental principles (INTBINST)], and the three composite conceptual components of democratic ideology [internal democratic ideals (INTDIDL), external democratic ideals (EXTDIDL), and internal democratic instrumental principles (INTDINST)]. In contrast, those who are grouped by Factor B and those who are grouped by Factor C commonly pose a view of compatibility on the relationships among these conceptual components.

Second, it is found that in the relationships among the conceptual components within each ideology, however, the three groups of subjects commonly pose a view of compatibility. That is, they all understand internal bureaucratic ideals (INTBIDL), internal bureaucratic instrumental principles (INTBINST), and external bureaucratic ideals (EXTBIDL) as compatible with each other. They also understand internal democratic ideals (INTDIDL), internal democratic instrumental principles (INTDINST), and external democratic ideals as compatible with each other.[17]

Of these findings, the second finding, particularly the one pertaining to the relationships among the internal and external democratic ideals and the internal democratic instrumental principles, provides an opportunity to check the empirical validity of Mosher's (1968) argument. Mosher believed that there is a logical contradiction between organizational democracy within public administrative agencies and political democracy. According to the finding, however, his belief is not consistent with any of the perspectives held by my subjects. Those subjects who are grouped by Factors A and B are found to commonly regard the internal democratic ideals and instrumental principles as democratic to the same degree as they regard the external democratic ideals as democratic. For those who are grouped by Factor C, the internal democratic ideals are regarded as undemocratic while the external democratic ideals are regarded as democratic. The mean-difference test, however, reveals that these subjects do not discriminate the democratic*ness* of the two democratic conceptual components in a significant way. Thus, Mosher's notion is also inconsistent with the perspectives of these subjects.

The first finding might be used, as in the case of the R-methodological analysis in the first section, for an overall assessment of the empirical validity of several theoretical arguments posed in the fields of organization theory and Public Administration. In this Q-methodological analysis, however, this assessment is not pursued for two reasons. First, as previously mentioned, although the fact that most of the theoretical arguments differentiate the three sub-types of democratic ideology (i.e., liberal, egalitarian, and popular), this differentiation is not reflected in the democratic conceptual components pertaining to the first finding. In other words, the first finding is not specific enough for dealing with the theoretical arguments. Second, but more importantly, the Q-methodological mean-difference tests provide findings in which the democratic conceptual components are further specified by the three sub-types of democratic ideology. These findings are provided by the test results particularly pertaining to the relationships in Set IV.

Recall that the debates between Simon (1973) and Argyris (1973a, 1973b) revolve around the relationship between bureaucratic ideology and liberal democratic ideology within organizations. Implicit in Argyris' argument is the belief that the internal liberal democratic instrumental principles are compatible with both the internal bureaucratic ideals and the internal democratic ideals, whereas the internal bureaucratic instrumental principles are compatible with neither of these ideals. In contrast, Simon's critique of Argyris is based upon the opposite belief that the internal bureaucratic ideals and the internal liberal democratic ideals, whereas the internal democratic principles are compatible with neither of these ideals. The test result pertaining to the relationships among these conceptual components in Set IV (i.e., INTBIDL-INTBINST, INTBINST-INTLDIDL, INTLDIDL-INTLDNST, and INTBIDL-INTLDNST), however, indicates that neither of these beliefs is consistent with any of the perspectives posed by those subjects who are grouped by Factors A and B.[18] That is, those who are grouped by Factor A think that internal bureaucratic instrumental principles are compatible with internal bureaucratic ideals but incompatible with internal liberal democratic ideals, and the internal liberal democratic instrumental principles are compatible with the internal liberal democratic ideals but incompatible with internal bureaucratic ideals. It is inconsistent with the perspective of those who are grouped by Factor B because they think that the internal bureaucratic instrumental principles are irrelevant to the concept of democratic ideology itself (i.e., the average rounded factor score is zero) and compatible with the internal bureaucratic ideology only. On the other hand, they think that the internal democratic instrumental principles are compatible with both the internal bureaucratic ideals and the internal liberal democratic ideals.

As mentioned in Chapter Four, the belief that the internal bureaucratic instrumental principles are compatible with not only the internal bureaucratic ideals but also with the internal popular democratic ideal, is implicit in Taylor's (1947:9) argument that "the scientific management is the best way to ensure maximum prosperity for all members of organization." As in the cases of Simon and Argyris, the test results pertaining to the relationships among these conceptual components (INTBIDL-INTBINST and INTPDIDL-INTBINST) indicate that especially the perspective of the subjects who are grouped into Factor A is relevant to the assessment of this belief,[19] and that the belief is invalid. That is, those who are grouped by Factor A regard the internal bureaucratic instrumental principles as undemocratic (the average rounded factor score is -1.50).

Implicit in the arguments of the critical organization theorists is the belief that it is the egalitarian democratic instrumental principles, not the internal bureaucratic instrumental principles, that are compatible with the egalitarian democratic ideals within organizations. The test results pertaining to the relationships among these conceptual components (i.e., INTEDIDL-INTBINST and INTEDIDL-INTEDNST) indicate that this belief is shared particularly by those subjects who are grouped by Factor A. That is, they regard, on the one hand, the internal bureaucratic instrumental principles as undemocratic and as incompatible with the internal egalitarian democratic ideals. On the other hand, they regard the internal egalitarian democratic ideals as democratic and compatible with the internal egalitarian democratic ideals. However, it is found that the critical theorists' belief is not fully consistent with the perspectives held by those who are grouped by Factors B or C. According to the test result, a part of the critical theorists' belief is shared by these two groups of subjects. That is, they commonly believe that internal egalitarian democratic ideals are compatible with the egalitarian democratic ideals within organizations. On the relationship between the internal bureaucratic instrumental principles and the internal egalitarian democratic ideals, however, they have beliefs that are different from those of the critical theorists. Those who are grouped by Factor C regard the internal bureaucratic instrumental principles as compatible with the internal egalitarian democratic ideals. Those who are grouped by Factor B regard the internal bureaucratic instrumental principles as irrelevant to the concept of democratic ideology itself.

Finally, the results of mean-difference tests for the relationship between the external bureaucratic ideal (EXTBIDL) and the external democratic ideal (EXTPDIDL) provide an opportunity to make a specific assessment of the empirical validity of several theoretical arguments posed in the field of Public Administration. One of the controversial issues addressed by the scholars of Public Administration is, as reviewed in Chapter Three, whether or not the strict separation between politics and public administration is compatible with such ideals of popular democracy as "popular sovereignty" and "openness to the public." Implicit in Jacksonianism and Frederickson's (1980) argument, a leading proponent of New Public Administration, is the belief that the dichotomy between politics and public administration is incompatible with these ideals of popular democracy. In contrast, the classical theorists of Public Administration believe that these ideals are compatible with one another. The test result indicates that the belief underlying Jacksonianism is consistent with the perspective held by those subjects who are grouped by Factor A, while the classical theorists' belief is shared by those who are grouped by Factors B or C.

Comparisons Between the Results of R-Methodological Analysis and Those of Q-Methodological Analysis

As presented thus far, both and R- and Q-methodologies provide an opportunity to obtain access to the subjective worlds of bureaucrats to examine the theme of subjective compatibility; that is, the extent to which bureaucrats regard bureaucratic and democratic ideologies as being compatible. The main focus of the R-methodological descriptive analysis was centered on the concept of Pearson's correlation. That is, in the R-methodological analysis, subjective compatibility was examined especially in terms of the extent to which the respondents' internalization of the conceptual components of bureaucratic ideology covary in association with their internalization of the conceptual components of democratic ideology. The degree of the respondents' internalization of these conceptual components was measured especially by the extent to which they agreed or disagreed with a set of statements that phrased the conceptual components. The subjective compatibility was examined differently in the Q-methodological descriptive analysis. The most different characteristic of the Q-methodological analysis is that the respondents' own perceptions of democratic ideology were taken into account in the analysis. That is, they were asked to sort out the same statements used for the R-methodological analysis in accordance with the extent to which they evaluated the statements as democratic. The extent to which the conceptual components of bureaucratic and democratic ideologies are compatible or incompatible with each other was analyzed in terms of the extent to which the respondents sorted them out into the same category of democratic*ness*.

These two methodologies were employed under the consideration that the strength of one methodology can complement the weakness of the other. As mentioned in Chapter Five, the major benefit of R-methodological descriptive analysis, compared with the Q-methodological descriptive analysis, is that the result of the analysis can be generalized to the population from which the sample subjects were randomly selected. Although, because of the small number of the subjects studied (30 subjects), the results of the Q-methodological descriptive analysis cannot be generalized as much as those of the R-methodological analysis, the Q-methodological analysis has valuable advantages over the R-methodological analysis. Q-methodology enables researchers to get deeper into the subjective worlds of respondents. To put it in Geertz's terms, this appeared in my Q-methodological analysis as a "thick description" of bureaucrats' understandings of the relationships among the conceptual components of bureaucratic and democratic ideologies. That is, as seen thus far, Q-methodology enabled us to describe these understandings in more detail than R-methodology. In the

R-methodological analysis, the differences among the respondents in their understandings of the relationship between bureaucratic and democratic ideologies were not considered. Instead, the major focus of this analysis was brought on how the respondents as a whole answered the questionnaire. In addition, what are examined in the R-methodological descriptive analysis are not the specific conceptual components of bureaucratic and democratic ideologies that are expressed individually by the statements in the questionnaire, but the more abstract and composite ones that are construed by combining the specific conceptual components in accordance with a particular theoretical scheme. In contrast, Q-methodology enabled me to bring into the analysis not only the abstract, but also the specific conceptual components of bureaucratic and democratic ideologies. It also allowed me to discern the major differences and similarities among the respondents in their understandings of the relationships between these conceptual components.

As such, the two methodologies have their own strengths and weaknesses, and they have led me to approach the theme of subjective compatibility in different ways. To what extent, then, do these two methodologically different descriptive analyses produce substantively different or similar conclusions about the relationships between bureaucratic and democratic ideologies? Another Q-methodological analysis is needed to answer this question. This is because the problem of comparison involves contrasting the results of the two Q-methodological descriptive analyses presented with those of the R-methodological analysis. For the first Q-methodological analysis, the problem of comparison is led by the fact that the conceptual components examined in these analyses are not the same. As shown in the previous section, the conceptual components examined in the first Q-methodological analysis are substantive and specific ones, which are expressed by individual statements. In contrast, those examined in the R-methodological analysis are abstract and composite ones, which are expressed collective *sets* of the individual statements. For the second Q-methodological analysis, this problem does not exist for the conceptual components examined in this analysis, and the R-methodological analysis are all the abstract and composite ones. The conceptual components examined in the R-methodological analysis are included in those reviewed in the second Q-methodological analysis. However, the results of the second Q-methodological analysis cannot be compared directly with those of the R-methodological analysis for a different reason. That is, the statements combined for observing the responses of subjects to these conceptual components in each analysis are not the same. In the second Q-methodological analysis, the statements are selected from the pool of all 48 statements used in the survey and combined for expressing each of the analytical and composite conceptual components of bureaucratic or democratic ideology. In the R-methodological analysis, however, the pool is composed of a part of the 48 statements because a number of them had to be discarded due to low reliability and validity. Thus, it becomes likely that the conceptual components examined in each analysis are the same only in a nominal sense, but different in a substantive sense. For example, in the second Q-methodological analysis, a conceptual component of democratic ideology, the liberal democratic ideology (LIBDEMO), is expressed collectively by eight statements (D1, D2, D3, D4, D5, D6, D17 and D18). In the R-methodological analysis, however, only some of these statements (D1, D2, D3, D6 and D17) are considered in measuring the respondents' internalization of the conceptual component.

In order to resolve this comparison problem, I performed another Q-methodological analysis (i.e., mean-difference tests) on the result of Q-factor analysis reported in Figure 6-7. This analysis is basically the same as the second Q-methodological analysis except that it deals with only the conceptual components and statements that are dealt with in the R-methodological analysis. The results of the third Q-methodological analysis are reported in Table 6-10, and the susbstantive interpretations of the results are compared with those of the results of the R-methodological analysis in Table 6-11.

As shown in Table 6-11, the substantive conclusions inferred from the R-methodological analysis are consistent mostly with those inferred from the Q-methodological analysis by subjects grouped into Factors B or C. Most of the substantive conclusions inferred from the Q-methodological analysis pertaining to those who are grouped by Factor A, however, are opposite to those inferred from the R-methodological analysis. This finding indicates that the reliance upon conventional R-methodological analysis alone leads to a loss of the opportunity to investigate diverse patterns of the relationships between bureaucratic and democratic ideologies that exist in the minds of bureaucrats.

Determinants of the Ideological Traits of Bureaucrats

I have examined thus far the extent to which bureaucrats internalize bureaucratic and democratic ideologies, how they understand democratic ideology, and the extent to which these ideologies are understood as compatible with each other in the minds of bureaucrats. Based upon these examinations, I have assessed the empirical validity of the basic beliefs underlying the theoretical debates about the compatibility thesis posed in the fields of organization theory and Public Administration. I have also discussed the results of this examination in terms of their practical implications for building several strategies that are useful for making bureaucracy compatible with democracy. What kinds of factors, then, affect the ideological traits of bureaucrats (i.e., the extent to which the bureaucrats internalize bureaucratic and democratic ideologies and the extent to which

Table 6 - 10 **Results of Significance Tests for Difference Between Average Rounded Factor Scores of Sets of "Bureaucratic" & "Democratic" Statements that Coincide with Those in R-Methodological Analysis**

Conceptual Components (X and Y) of Bureaucratic and Democratic Ideologies Juxtaposed with One Another		Groups of Subjects (Q-Factors)								
		Factor A			Factor B			Factor C		
				t-value of Difference Between Average Rounded Factor Scores	Average Rounded Factor Scores of Sets of Statements Expressing Composite Conceptual Components		t-value of Difference Between Average Rounded Factor Scores	Average Rounded Factor Scores of Sets of Statements Expressing Composite Conceptual Components		t-value of Difference Between Average Rounded Factor Scores
(X)	(Y)	$(\bar{X})$	$(\bar{Y})$		$(\bar{X})$	$(\bar{Y})$		$(\bar{X})$	$(\bar{Y})$	
BURO	DEMO	- 1.00	3.17	- 6.42**	.95	.33	.70	.38	.50	- .12
BURO	LIBDEMO	- 1.00	3.00	- 4.11**	.95	.00	.78	.38	.00	- .26
BURO	POPDEMO	- 1.00	3.20	- 4.39**	.95	.20	1.22	.38	1.20	- .58
INTBURO	INTDEMO	- 1.41	3.14	- 5.35**	.59	- .57	1.20	.76	.57	.14
INTBURO	INTPDEMO	- 1.41	3.00	- 4.13**	.59	- .75	1.05	.76	- 1.75	1.49
INTBIDL	INTDIDL	- 1.00	1.67	- 2.68*	.40	- 1.33	1.22	1.57	- 2.00	.88
INTBIDL	EXTDIDL	- 1.00	3.20	- 5.23**	.86	1.60	- .47	1.57	.40	2.85*
INTBIDL	INTDINST	- 1.00	4.25	- 5.80**	.86	.00	.60	1.57	2.50	- 1.25
INTBIDL	EXTBIDL	- 1.00	.20	- 1.30	.86	2.00	- .30	1.57	- .40	1.98
INTBIDL	INTBINST	- 1.00	- 1.70	.70	.86	.40	.72	1.57	.20	.93
EXTBIDL	INTDIDL	.20	1.67	- 1.60	2.00	- 1.33	2.17	- .40	- 2.00	.25
EXTBIDL	EXTDIDL	.20	3.20	- 3.94**	2.00	1.60	.23	- .40	.40	- .70
EXTBIDL	INTDINST	.20	4.25	- 4.70**	2.00	.00	1.35	- .40	2.50	- 1.96
EXTBIDL	INTBINST	.20	- 1.70	1.69	2.00	.40	1.24	- .40	.20	.32

(continued on next page)

Table 6 - 10 (continued) **Results of Significance Tests for Difference Between Average Rounded Factor Scores of Sets of "Bureaucratic" & "Democratic" Statements that Coincide with Those in R-Methodological Analysis**

Conceptual Components (X and Y) of Bureaucratic and Democratic Ideologies Juxtaposed with One Another	Groups of Subjects (Q-Factors)								
	Factor A			Factor B			Factor C		
	Average Rounded Factor Scores of Sets of Statements Expressing Composite Conceptual Components		t-value of Difference Between Average Rounded Factor Scores	Average Rounded Factor Scores of Sets of Statements Expressing Composite Conceptual Components		t-value of Difference Between Average Rounded Factor Scores	Average Rounded Factor Scores of Sets of Statements Expressing Composite Conceptual Components		t-value of Difference Between Average Rounded Factor Scores
(X) (Y)	$(\bar{X})$	$(\bar{Y})$		$(\bar{X})$	$(\bar{Y})$		$(\bar{X})$	$(\bar{Y})$	
INTBINST- INTDIDL	- 1.70	1.67	2.48*	.40	- 1.33	1.22	.20	- 2.00	.88
INTBINST- EXTDIDL	- 1.70	3.20	4.61**	.40	1.60	- .85	.20	.40	- .11
INTBINST- INTDINST	- 1.70	4.25	4.68**	.40	.00	.31	.20	2.50	- 1.14
INTDIDL - EXTDIDL	1.67	3.20	- 2.76*	- 1.33	1.60	- 1.58	- 2.00	.40	- 1.54
INTDIDL - INTDINST	1.67	4.25	- 4.09**	- 1.33	.00	- 1.10	- 2.00	2.50	- 2.23
EXTDIDL - INTDINST	3.20	4.25	- 1.76	1.60	.00	.92	.40	2.50	- 2.59*

Note: a. "*" indicates $p < .05$; "**" indicates $p < .01$.

b. For substantive meaning of composite conceptual component notations, see Figure 4-1; for composition of statements for each conceptual component, see Figure 6-1 through Figure 6-6; for substantive content of statements expressing conceptual components, see questionnaire in Appendix I (especially Part II).

c. Number of statements expressing composite conceptual components are:

BURO = 21	EXTBIDL = 5	INTDIDL = 3	LIBDEMO = 5
INTBURO = 17	INTBINST = 10	EXTDIDL = 5	POPDEMO = 5
INTBIDL = 7	DEMO = 12	INTDINST = 4	INTDEMO = 7
			INTPDEMO = 4

Table 6 - 11 **Comparison Between Q-Methodological and R-Methodolgical Analyses Results**

Conceptual Components of Bureaucratic and Democratic Ideologies Juxtaposed with One Another	Results of Q-Methodological Analysis: Groups of Subjects (Q Factors)			Results of R-Methodological Analysis
	Factor A	Factor B	Factor C	
BURO - DEMO	Incompatible	Compatible	Compatible	Compatible
BURO - LIBDEMO	Incompatible	-	Compatible	Compatible
BURO - POPDEMO	Incompatible	Compatible	Compatible	Compatible
INTBURO - INTDEMO	Incompatible	-	Compatible	Compatible
INTBURO - INTPDEMO	Incompatible	-	-	Compatible
INTBIDL - INTDIDL	Incompatible	-	-	Compatible
INTBIDL - EXTDIDL	Incompatible	Compatible	Slightly Compatible	Compatible
INTBIDL - INTDINST	Incompatible	-	Compatible	Compatible
INTBIDL - EXTBIDL	Slightly Incompatible	Compatible	Slightly Incompatible	Compatible
INTBIDL - INTBINST	Compatible	Compatible	Compatible	Compatible
EXTBIDL - INTDIDL	Compatible	-	-	Slightly Compatible
EXTBIDL - EXTDIDL	Slightly Compatible	Compatible	Slightly Incompatible	Slightly Compatible
EXTBIDL - INTDINST	Slightly Compatible	-	Slightly Incompatible	Slightly Incompatible
EXTBIDL - INTBINST	Slightly Incompatible	Compatible	Slightly Incompatible	Compatible
INTBINST - INTDIDL	Incompatible	-	-	Compatible
INTBINST - EXTDIDL	Incompatible	Compatible	Compatible	Compatible
INTBINST - INTDINST	Incompatible	-	Compatible	Compatible
INTDIDL - EXTDIDL	Slightly Compatible	-	-	Compatible
INTDIDL - INTDINST	Slightly Compatible	-	-	Compatible
EXTDIDL - INTDINST	Compatible	-	Slightly Compatible	Compatible

Note: "-" indicates case is inappropriate to assessment of relationship between two conceptual components in each set because subjects regard "democratic" conceptual components themselves as undemocratic or irrelevant to concept of democratic ideology.

they regard these ideologies as compatible with one another)? As mentioned in Chapter Five, I attempted to answer this question by focusing upon four types of traits possessed by bureaucrats: organizational, socio-economic, socialization background, and cultural traits.[20] The major focus of my explanatory analysis was brought on clarifying which of these traits is most powerful in explaining the variations among individual bureaucrats in their ideological traits that have been described in the previous chapter.

Overall Determinants of the Ideological Traits of Bureaucrats: Organization, Socio-economic Conditions, Socialization, or Culture?

In order to examine the relative explanatory power of each of the four traits, I performed the F-test for joint impact. As described in Chapter Five, the core of this test is a comparison between the R^2 of a full regression model, in which all measured independent variables are included, and that of a restricted model, which is the same as the full model except that a set of measured independent variables pertaining to a certain type of trait under investigation is excluded. If the difference between the two R^2s is statistically significant, it is inferred that the trait represented collectively by the excluded independent variables has significant power.[21]

The results of joint impact tests (see Table 6-12) indicate that the answer to the question presented above depends on what kinds of dependent variables with which we are concerned. Many of the R^2-differences are statistically insignificant. For example, R^2-differences for DEMO, LIBDEMO, POPDEMO, INTDEMO, INTPDEMO, INTDIDL, EXTDIDL, and INTDINST are all statistically significant. The fact that these are all the dependent variables representing bureaucrats' internalization of democratic ideology indicates that none of the four types of traits has significant explanatory power on the variations among individual bureaucrats in their internalization of these components of democratic ideology. Insofar as we are concerned with the dependent variables for which the R^2-difference is statistically significant, particularly two of the four types of traits have significant explanatory power: organizational and cultural traits. More specifically, organizational traits as a whole have a significant impact on the internalization of bureaucratic ideology, defined particularly in terms of the intra-organizational context of bureaucracy (INTBURO). It is also found that the two components of internal bureaucratic ideology [i.e., the internal bureaucratic ideals (INTBIDL) and the internal bureaucratic instrumental principles (INTBINST)], organizational traits as a whole have a significant impact particularly on bureaucrats' internalization of the internal bureaucratic instrumental principles. Organizational traits as a whole have a significant explanatory power, particularly for the congruity between bureacrats' internalization of the

Table 6 - 12 **Joint Impact Test Results for Organizational, Socio-Economic, Socializational and Cultural Traits of Bureaucrats**

Sets of Independent Variables / Dependent Variables	Organizational Traits: (OFFICE, INDECON, ENV, WELF, INTORD, PUBREL, YRSERVE, HIRANK MIDRANK, JOBCLAS, ROUTINE, MIDROUTN, SUPERIOR, SUBORDNT)	Socio-Economic Traits: (AGE, INCOME, PREUNIV, UNIV, SEX)	Socialization Backgrounds: (RURAL, MIDURBAN, POOR, AVECON, PARNTDIE, DIVORCE, PUBURO, PVBURO, FARMER, SELFEMP, AUTHFMLY, AVEFMLY)	Cultural Traits: (PROTEST, CATHOLIC, BUDDHIST, NONE, MATERIAL, MIXCULT, THEOX, XYMIXED)
Conceptual Components of Bureaucratic Ideology				
BURO	.077 (1.678)	.013 (.777)	.046 (1.190)	.060 (2.320)*
INTBURO	.093 (2.092)*	.012 (.776)	.040 (1.051)	.060 (2.334)*
INTBIDL	.077 (1.726)	.012 (.745)	.058 (1.504)	.052 (2.016)*
EXTBIDL	.021 (.370)	.004 (.241)	.034 (.708)	.026 (.799)
INTBINST	.089 (1.904)*	.012 (.746)	.042 (1.040)	.054 (2.031)*
Conceptual Components of Democratic Ideology				
DEMO	.047 (.897)	.035 (.765)	.035 (.765)	.055 (1.822)
LIBDEMO	.037 (.672)	.007 (.352)	.045 (.954)	.050 (1.595)
POPDEMO	.054 (1.062)	.040 (2.216)	.053 (1.218)	.036 (1.230)
INTDEMO	.047 (.870)	.024 (1.218)	.028 (.609)	.012 (.643)
INTPDEMO	.054 (1.027)	.041 (2.176)	.040 (.890)	.021 (.719)
INTDIDL	.075 (1.466)	.027 (1.461)	.024 (.541)	.032 (1.799)
EXTDIDL	.036 (.668)	.020 (1.067)	.053 (1.156)	.009 (.449)
INTDINST	.035 (.635)	.022 (1.091)	.035 (.734)	.022 (.693)

(continued on next page)

Table 6 - 12 (continued) **Joint Impact Test Results for Organizational, Socio-Economic, Socializational and Cultural Traits of Bureaucrats**

Sets of Independent Variables / Dependent Variables	Organizational Traits: (OFFICE, INDECON, ENV, WELF, INTORD, PUBREL, YRSERVE, HIRANK MIDRANK, JOBCLAS, ROUTINE, MIDROUTN, SUPERIOR, SUBORDNT)	Socio-Economic Traits: (AGE, INCOME, PREUNIV, UNIV, SEX)	Socialization Backgrounds: (RURAL, MIDURBAN, POOR, AVECON, PARNTDIE, DIVORCE, PUBURO, PVBURO, FARMER, SELFEMP, AUTHFMLY, AVEFMLY)	Cultural Traits: (PROTEST, CATHOLIC, BUDDHIST, NONE, MATERIAL, MIXCULT, THEOX, XYMIXED)
Attitudinal Congruity				
BURO-DEMO	.040 (.694)	.006 (.271)	.044 (.900)	.016 (.485)
BURO-LIBDEMO	.052 (.993)	.014 (.781)	.071 (1.597)	.016 (.849)
BURO-POPDEMO	.063 (1.133)	.015 (.768)	.029 (.600)	.008 (.262)
INTBURO-INTDEMO	.075 (1.353)	.013 (.660)	.023 (.491)	.023 (.712)
INTBURO-INTPDEMO	.066 (1.205)	.025 (1.254)	.032 (.677)	.009 (.282)
INTBIDL-INTDIDL	.049 (.942)	.008 (.434)	.071 (1.576)	.075 (2.521)*
INTBIDL-EXTDIDL	.063 (1.159)	.013 (.670)	.043 (.929)	.023 (.743)
INTBIDL-INTDINST	.061 (1.104)	.015 (.773)	.043 (.902)	.006 (.195)
EXTBIDL-INTDIDL	.057 (1.064)	.010 (.504)	.051 (1.100)	.023 (.753)
EXTBIDL-EXTDIDL	.056 (1.019)	.004 (.188)	.051 (1.080)	.024 (.752)
EXTBIDL-INTDINST	.036 (.650)	.023 (1.135)	.043 (.892)	.012 (.368)

(continued on next page)

Table 6 - 12 (continued) **Joint Impact Test Results for Organizational, Socio-Economic, Socializational and Cultural Traits of Bureaucrats**

Sets of Independent Variables / Dependent Variables	Organizational Traits: (OFFICE, INDECON, ENV, WELF, INTORD, PUBREL, YRSERVE, HIRANK MIDRANK, JOBCLAS, ROUTINE, MIDROUTN, SUPERIOR, SUBORDNT)	Socio-Economic Traits: (AGE, INCOME, PREUNIV, UNIV, SEX)	Socialization Backgrounds: (RURAL, MIDURBAN, POOR, AVECON, PARNTDIE, DIVORCE, PUBURO, PVBURO, FARMER, SELFEMP, AUTHFMLY, AVEFMLY)	Cultural Traits: (PROTEST, CATHOLIC, BUDDHIST, NONE, MATERIAL, MIXCULT, THEOX, XYMIXED)
Attitudinal Congruity (continued)				
INTBINST-INTDIDL	.056 (1.010)	.008 (.408)	.040 (.851)	.031 (.991)
INTBINST-EXTDIDL	.054 (1.006)	.034 (1.784)	.059 (1.283)	.041 (1.363)
INTBINST-INTDINST	.102 (1.905)*	.010 (.505)	.057 (1.252)	.020 (.647)
INTDIDL-EXTDIDL	.023 (.407)	.021 (1.054)	.055 (1.125)	.012 (.368)
INTDINST-EXTDIDL	.070 (1.269)	.010 (.484)	.028 (.588)	.030 (.919)

Note: Numbers without parentheses are differences between R^2 of full model where all independent variables are included and that of a restricted model where set of independent variables specified at the top of the column are excluded. Numbers within parentheses are F-value of R^2 difference. "*" indicates that F-value is at 5% significance level. For substantive notation meanings and measurement schemes for dependent and independent variables, see Table 5-2, Table 5-3, and Figure 5-2.

internal bureaucratic instrumental principles (INTBINST) and those of the internal democratic instrumental principles (INTDINST).

Cultural traits have a significant explanatory power, particularly for bureaucrats' internalization of the general concept of bureaucratic ideology (BURO). The fact that, of the conceptual components of bureaucratic ideology, the statistically-significant R^2-differences are found only for INTBURO, INTBIDL, and INTBINST, indicates that the impact of cultural traits on bureaucrats' internalization of bureaucratic ideology is confined to the components of bureaucratic ideology that are defined in terms of the internal context of bureaucracy. Cultural traits do not, however, have significant explanatory power on the internalization of external democratic ideals (EXTDIDL). Instead, they do have significant explanatory power on the congruity between bureaucrats' internalization of the internal bureaucratic ideals (INTBIDL) and the internal democratic ideals (INTDIDL).

All these findings indicate that, insofar as the bureaucrats' internalization of bureaucratic ideology is concerned, both institutional and cultural explanations are valid. That is, the findings indicate that what and how individual bureaucrats think are conditioned not only by institutional factors, but also by cultural factors surrounding them. The findings also indicate that, insofar as we are concerned with the ideological traits of bureaucrats between the bureaucratic and democratic instrumental principles defined in terms of the intra-organizational context of governmental agencies, only the institutional explanation is valid. They also indicate that, insofar as we are concerned with the ideological traits of bureaucrats between bureaucratic and democratic ideals defined in terms of the intra-organizational context of governmental agencies, only the cultural explanation is valid.

Specific Determinants of the Ideological Traits of Bureaucrats

The four types of individual bureaucrats' traits examined as the determinants of the ideological traits of bureaucrats in the previous section are composed of sub-independent variables. As mentioned in Chapter Five (see Table 5-3), the variable, "organizational traits," is composed of eight sub-independent variables which are further specified into 14 measured independent variables. The variable, "socio-economic traits," is composed of four sub-independent variables which are further specified into five measured independent variables. The variable, "socialization backgrounds," is composed of six sub-independent variables which are further specified into 12 measured independent variables. Finally, the variable, "cultural traits," is composed of three sub-independent variables which are further specified into eight measured independent variables. From the results of the joint impact tests presented in the previous section, we cannot assess the impact of these specific independent variables on the dependent variables.

The considerations of these specific independent variables in explaining the dependent variables are important not only in that they provide us detailed information about the content of determinations. They are important also in that, as will be shown below, a number of component variables of the independent variables, "socio-economic traits" and "socialization backgrounds," which were found as not having significant explanatory power in the previous section, do have significant explanatory power. In addition, as will also be shown below, a number of variables that compose the independent variables, "organizational traits" and "cultural traits," have significant explanatory power on the dependent variables which were found not to be explained by these independent variables.

I examined the explanatory power of the specific component independent variables, relying upon two types of statistical tests: the joint impact test (F-test) and the t-test. The joint impact test was performed to examine the relative explanatory power of the sub-independent variables of each type of trait because most of these variables are measured by a multiple number of component variables. The procedures and the inferential logic of this test are the same as those of the joint impact test presented in the previous section. The t-test was performed to examine the statistical significance of the impact of the individually measured independent variables. In what follows, the results of these tests are discussed by each type of trait.

The Organizational Determinants of the Ideological Traits of Bureaucrats. Of the results of the joint impact tests for the 21 sub-independent variables, those that are relevant to the organizational traits of bureaucrats are summarized in Table 6-13. The overall pattern of the R^2-differences and their statistical significance reported in this table shows which types of organizational traits of individual bureaucrats have strong and weak explanatory power on which dependent variables. Of the eight sub-independent variables of "organizational traits," three (years of service, number of superiors, and number of subordinates) do not have any significant explanatory power.[22] That is, the R^2-differences pertaining to these independent variables are all statistically insignifcant for all dependent variables. Of the remaining five sub-independent variables of "organizational traits," the significant R^2-differences are found mostly for three variables ("types of office - whether main or regional office," "official ranking," and "routinization of work procedures"). This indicates that, of the eight types of organizational traits of individual bureaucrats, these three types of organizational traits are the major determinants.

In addition, the overall pattern of the R^2-differences reported in Table 6-13 indicates that these three determinants are different from each other in the kinds of dependent variables they determine. In my study, three types of de-

Table 6 - 13 **Joint Impact Test Results for Sub-Independent Variables of Organizational Traits of Bureaucrats**

Sub-Independent Variables / Dependent Variables	Types of Office - whether main or regional office: (OFFICE)	Characteristics of Major Policy Dealt with by the Agencies: (INDECON, ENV, WELF, INTORD, PUBREL)	Years of Service: (YRSERVE)	Official Ranking: (HIRANK, MIDRANK)
Conceptual Components of Bureaucratic Ideology				
BURO	.026 (8.038)**	.036 (2.223)	.002 (.510)	.017 (2.686)
INTBURO	.027 (8.554)**	.047 (2.744)*	.001 (.345)	.019 (3.010)
INTBIDL	.027 (8.537)**	.039 (2.453)*	.006 (1.783)	.009 (1.460)
EXTBIDL	.006 (1.362)	.012 (.608)	.002 (.494)	.003 (.332)
INTBINST	.021 (6.143)*	.038 (2.244)	.000 (.000)	.022 (3.337)*
Conceptual Components of Democratic Ideology				
DEMO	.004 (1.080)	.007 (.363)	.004 (1.080)	.004 (.591)
LIBDEMO	.007 (1.798)	.008 (.424)	.001 (.273)	.006 (.785)
POPDEMO	.001 (.348)	.010 (.575)	.011 (2.988)	.004 (.595)
INTDEMO	.001 (.320)	.012 (.643)	.010 (2.626)	.006 (.735)
INTPDEMO	.002 (.485)	.016 (.882)	.009 (2.468)	.004 (.530)
INTDIDL	.001 (.389)	.033 (1.799)	.012 (3.186)	.017 (2.282)
EXTDIDL	.006 (1.571)	.009 (.449)	.000 (.101)	.001 (.116)
INTDINST	.001 (.158)	.002 (.125)	.005 (1.298)	.002 (.304)

(continued on next page)

Table 6 - 13 (continued) **Joint Impact Test Results for Sub-Independent Variables of Organizational Traits of Bureaucrats**

Sub-Independent Variables / Dependent Variables	Types of Office - whether main or regional office: (OFFICE)	Characteristics of Major Policy Dealt with by the Agencies: (INDECON, ENV, WELF, INTORD, PUBREL)	Years of Service: (YRSERVE)	Official Ranking: (HIRANK, MIDRANK)
Attitudinal Congruity				
BURO-DEMO	.007 (1.783)	.002 (.108)	.001 (.203)	.020 (2.490)
BURO-LIBDEMO	.001 (.164)	.016 (.849)	.007 (1.807)	.003 (.336)
BURO-POPDEMO	.005 (1.187)	.004 (.203)	.001 (.336)	.041 (5.086)**
INTBURO-INTDEMO	.016 (4.041)*	.016 (.808)	.003 (.663)	.021 (2.672)
INTBURO-INTPDEMO	.009 2.230)	.018 (.908)	.002 (.413)	.030 (3.800)*
INTBIDL-INTDIDL	.010 (2.571)	.012 (.616)	.001 (.352)	.000 (.006)
INTBIDL-EXTDIDL	.001 (.193)	.016 (.811)	.006 (1.523)	.005 (.619)
INTBIDL-INTDINST	.011 (2.701)	.034 (1.694)	.003 (.669)	.017 (2.105)
EXTBIDL-INTDIDL	.015 (3.961)*	.005 (.281)	.000 (.015)	.019 (2.530)
EXTBIDL-EXTDIDL	.001 (.187)	.003 (.132)	.000 (.006)	.003 (.405)
EXTBIDL-INTDINST	.009 (2.211)	.003 (.133)	.001 (.333)	.012 (1.551)
INTBINST-INTDIDL	.016 (4.043)*	.014 (.700)	.005 (1.176)	.005 (.684)
INTBINST-EXTDIDL	.000 (.243)	.002 (.105)	.014 (3.727)	.008 (1.014)
INTBINST-INTDINST	.011 (2.921)	.021 (1.112)	.000 (.001)	.040 (5.234)**
INTDIDL-EXTDIDL	.002 (.549)	.013 (.647)	.003 (.740)	.002 (.270)
INTDINST-EXTDIDL	.013 (3.346)	.042 (2.149)	.000 (.062)	.002 (.227)

(continued on next page)

Table 6 - 13 (continued) **Joint Impact Test Results for Sub-Independent Variables of Organizational Traits of Bureaucrats**

Sub-Independent Variables / Dependent Variables	Job Classification: (JOBCLAS)	Routinization of Work Procedures: (ROUTINE, MIDROUTN)	Number of Superiors: (SUPERIOR)	Number of Subordinates: (SUBORDNT)
Conceptual Components of Bureaucratic Ideology				
BURO	.000 (.007)	.010 (1.562)	.000 (.018)	.002 (.644)
INTBURO	.000 (.004)	.016 (2.445)	.000 (.000)	.002 (.521)
INTBIDL	.001 (.275)	.006 (.864)	.000 (.012)	.000 (.085)
EXTBIDL	.000 (.008)	.002 (.193)	.002 (.439)	.000 (.077)
INTBINST	.000 (.063)	.021 (3.091)*	.000 (.006)	.003 (.807)
Conceptual Components of Democratic Ideology				
DEMO	.000 (.126)	.024 (3.143)*	.000 (.003)	.007 (1.948)
LIBDEMO	.001 (.213)	.014 (1.740)	.001 (.166)	.011 (2.902)
POPDEMO	.000 (.105)	.023 (3.234)*	.001 (.265)	.002 (.477)
INTDEMO	.000 (.007)	.015 (1.981)	.000 (.000)	.009 (2.234)
INTPDEMO	.000 (.015)	.019 (2.561)	.001 (.188)	.001 (.276)
INTDIDL	.007 (1.960)	.012 (1.650)	.000 (.041)	.009 (2.400)
EXTDIDL	.001 (.333)	.020 (2.660)	.000 (.011)	.002 (.470)
INTDINST	.005 (1.346)	.012 (1.464)	.000 (.022)	.005 (1.261)

(continued on next page)

Table 6 - 13 (continued) **Joint Impact Test Results for Sub-Independent Variables of Organizational Traits of Bureaucrats**

Sub-Independent Variables / Dependent Variables	Job Classification: (JOBCLAS)	Routinization of Work Procedures: (ROUTINE, MIDROUTN)	Number of Superiors: (SUPERIOR)	Number of Subordinates: (SUBORDNT)
Attitudinal Congruity				
BURO-DEMO	.005 (1.107)	.001 (.170)	.001 (.152)	.002 (.514)
BURO-LIBDEMO	.001 (.246)	.015 (2.094)	.000 (.085)	.013 (3.470)
BURO-POPDEMO	.010 (2.586)	.008 (.988)	.000 (.079)	.000 (.084)
INTBURO-INTDEMO	.004 (1.096)	.023 (2.926)	.000 (.001)	.001 (.375)
INTBURO-INTPDEMO	.009 (2.278)	.011 (1.361)	.000 (.004)	.000 (.053)
INTBIDL-INTDIDL	.009 (2.411)	.004 (.548)	.005 (1.273)	.002 (.600)
INTBIDL-EXTDIDL	.000 (.098)	.031 (4.042)*	.001 (.167)	.012 (3.038)
INTBIDL-INTDINST	.002 (.387)	.005 (.639)	.000 (.029)	.001 (.171)
EXTBIDL-INTDIDL	.000 (.077)	.005 (.605)	.000 (.068)	.001 (.214)
EXTBIDL-EXTDIDL	.007 (1.679)	.025 (3.173)*	.003 (.680)	.009 (2.352)
EXTBIDL-INTDINST	.002 (.484)	.003 (.377)	.000 (.002)	.002 (.537)

(continued on next page)

Table 6 - 13 (continued) **Joint Impact Test Results for Sub-Independent Variables of Organizational Traits of Bureaucrats**

Sub-Independent Variables / Dependent Variables	Job Classification: (JOBCLAS)	Routinization of Work Procedures: (ROUTINE, MIDROUTN)	Number of Superiors: (SUPERIOR)	Number of Subordinates: (SUBORDNT)
Attitudinal Congruity (continued)				
INTBINST-INTDIDL	.001 (.178)	.013 (1.669)	.001 (.142)	.004 (.894)
INTBINST-EXTDIDL	.001 (.132)	.012 (1.629)	.007 (1.722)	.002 (.540)
INTBINST-INTDINST	.032 (8.319)**	.011 (1.381)	.001 (.198)	.000 (.105)
INTDIDL-EXTDIDL	.002 (.453)	.002 (.208)	.000 (.000)	.000 (.067)
INTDINST-EXTDIDL	.000 (.072)	.023 (2.936)	.001 (.367)	.004 (1.018)

Note: Numbers without parentheses are differences between R^2 of a full model where all independent variables are included and that of a restricted model where set of independent variables specified at top of the column are excluded. Numbers within parentheses are F-value of R^2 difference. "*" indicates F-value is at 5% significance level. "**" indicates F-value is at 1% significance level. For substantive notation meanings and measurement schemes for dependent and independent variables, see Tab. 5-2, Tab. 5-3, and Fig. 5-2.

pendent variables are supposed to be determined by the independent variables: (1) the extent to which individual bureaucrats internalize the conceptual components of bureaucratic ideology; (2) the extent to which they internalize the conceptual components of democratic ideology; and (3) the extent to which they regard the conceptual components of bureaucratic and democratic ideologies as compatible with one another. "Types of office" determines especially the first and third types of dependent variables. "Routinization of work procedures" determines all of the three types of dependent variables.

The t-tests for the individual components of the sub-independent variables (i.e., measured independent variables) representing the organizational traits provide us with a more detailed picture of the determinants. That is, "organizational traits" is further specified into a number of measured independent variables. Thus, the t-tests for these measured independent variables enable us to assess the extent to which the differences in these specific organizational traits lead the individual bureaucrats to have the traits represented by the dependent variables to different degrees. Of the results of the t-tests for the 39 individually measured independent variables, those that are relevant to the measured independent variables pertaining to the organizational traits are summarized in Table 6-14. The interpretations of the results reported in this table can be found below.

As mentioned in Chapter Five, most of the tasks for Seoul city government officials are performed by two *types of office*: the main office and the regional offices. These offices are interconnected within a bureaucratic institutional structure. That is, one of the major functions for the main office is planning, and the regional offices are expected to faithfully carry out the plans made by the main offfice. In addition, the main office controls the distribution of human, financial, and other resources to the regional offices, and coordinates the transactions among the regional offices.

The t-tests for the dummy variable, OFFICE, clarify the extent to which the ideological traits represented by the dependent variables differ by these two types of offices. As presented in Table 6-14, the regression coefficients of OFFICE for most dependent variables representing bureaucrats' internalization of bureaucratic ideology (BURO, INTBURO, INTBIDL, and INTBINST) are estimated as negative and statistically significant. The dummy variable is operationalized as having the value of 1; if the respondent works in the main office (0 if the respondent works in the regional offices). Thus, the result indicates that those who work in the main office internalize the four conceptual components of bureaucratic ideology to a lesser degree than those who work in the regional offices. Given the bureaucratic nature of the institutional relationships between the main and regional offices, this finding can be interpreted as indicating that bureaucratic ideology is internalized more by those who work in the office that is controlled by the higher office than by those who work at the office that exerts

Table 6 - 14 **Individual Test Results for Measured Independent Variables (Organizational Traits of Bureaucrats)**

Dependent Variables \ Measured Independent Variables	Constant	Types of Office	Characteristics of Major Policies Dealt With by Agencies		
		OFFICE	INTORD	ENV	INDECON
Conceptual Components of Bureaucratic Ideology					
BURO	89.08 (8.53)**	-6.22 (-2.84)**	5.62 (2.36)*	7.69 (2.87)**	7.53 (2.20)*
INTBURO	66.92 (7.29)**	-5.64 (-2.93)**	5.63 (2.70)**	6.98 (2.96)**	8.14 (2.70)**
INTBIDL	29.05 (7.19)**	-2.48 (-2.92)**	2.41 (2.62)**	2.57 (2.48)*	3.65 (2.75)**
EXTBIDL	26.62 (7.46)**	- .88 (-1.17)	.56 (.69)	1.14 (1.25)	- .22 (- .18)
INTBINST	37.87 (6.24)**	-3.16 (-2.48)*	3.22 (2.33)*	4.41 (2.83)**	4.49 (2.26)*
Conceptual Components of Democratic Ideology					
DEMO	58.22 (8.20)**	-1.55 (-1.04)	.40 (.25)	1.99 (1.09)	1.22 (.52)
LIBDEMO	26.15 (7.01)**	-1.05 (-1.34)	.31 (.37)	.97 (1.01)	1.00 (.81)
POPDEMO	22.50 (6.38)**	- .43 (- .59)	- .30 (- .37)	.95 (1.04)	.51 (.44)
INTDEMO	32.75 (6.61)**	- .59 (- .57)	- .60 (- .54)	1.15 (.91)	.96 (.56)
INTPDEMO	17.54 (5.49)**	- .47 (- .70)	- .31 (- .42)	.72 (.87)	.76 (.72)
INTDIDL	11.67 (4.84)**	- .32 (- .62)	- .77 (-1.41)	.87 (1.41)	.55 (.70)
EXTDIDL	25.47 (6.98)**	- .96 (-1.25)	1.00 (1.20)	.83 (.89)	.26 (.22)
INTDINST	21.08 (6.46)**	- .27 (- .40)	.17 (.22)	.28 (.33)	.41 (.38)

(continued on next page)

Table 6 - 14 (continued) **Individual Test Results for Measured Independent Variables (Organizational Traits of Bureaucrats)**

Dependent Variables \ Measured Independent Variables	Constant	Types of Office	Characteristics of Major Policies Dealt With by Agencies		
		OFFICE	INTORD	ENV	INDECON
Attitudinal Congruity					
BURO-DEMO	.66 (1.56)	- .11 (-1.34)	.02 (.26)	.03 (.24)	.04 (.32)
BURO-LIBDEMO	.78 (1.70)	- .04 (- .41)	.01 (.05)	- .05 (- .44)	.21 (1.39)
BURO-POPDEMO	.82 (1.87)	- .10 (-1.09)	- .03 (- .27)	.02 (.15)	- .06 (- .39)
INTBURO-INTDEMO	.83 (1.99)*	- .18 (-2.01)*	.09 (.98)	.10 (.92)	.01 (.04)
INTBURO-INTPDEMO	.75 (1.75)	- .13 (-1.49)	.03 (.34)	.09 (.85)	- .05 (- .33)
INTBIDL-INTDIDL	1.29 (3.25)**	- .13 (-1.60)	- .05 (- .55)	- .12 (-1.17)	- .01 (- .05)
INTBIDL-EXTDIDL	.93 (2.06)*	.04 (.44)	- .07 (- .67)	.07 (.61)	- .06 (- .39)
INTBIDL-INTDINST	.76 (1.64)	- .16 (-1.64)	.03 (.29)	.18 (1.47)	- .13 (- .87)
EXTBIDL-INTDIDL	1.30 (2.37)*	- .23 (-1.99)*	.07 (.60)	- .06 (- .39)	.12 (.67)
EXTBIDL-EXTDIDL	1.39 (2.48)*	- .05 (- .43)	- .05 (- 40)	- .09 (- .61)	.01 (.05)
EXTBIDL-INTDINST	1.06 (1.73)	- .19 (-1.49)	.09 (.67)	- .02 (- .14)	.04 (.18)
INTBINST-INTDIDL	.92 (2.40)*	- .16 (-2.01)*	.13 (1.46)	.04 (.38)	.08 (.60)
INTBINST-EXTDIDL	.62 (1.44)	- .05 (- .49)	- .03 (- .30)	- .07 (- .59)	- .03 (- .18)
INTBINST-INTDINST	.19 (.41)	- .17 (-1.71)	- .00 (- .00)	.11 (.91)	- .11 (- .68)
INTDIDL-EXTDIDL	.71 (1.57)	- .07 (- .74)	- .12 (-1.18)	.01 (.11)	- .03 (- .20)
INTDINST-EXTDIDL	.82 (1.78)	- .82 (-1.83)	.04 (.38)	.11 (.95)	- .08 (- .52)

(continued on next page)

Table 6 - 14 (continued) **Individual Test Results for Measured Independent Variables (Organizational Traits of Bureaucrats)**

Measured Independent Variables / Dependent Variables	Characteristics of Major Policies Dealt With by Agencies		Years of Service	Official Ranking	
	PUBREL	WELF	YRSERVE	HIRANK	MIDRANK
Conceptual Components of Bureaucratic Ideology					
BURO	5.43 (1.65)	4.29 (1.57)	.16 (.71)	7.86 (2.06)*	3.94 (1.80)
INTBURO	4.64 (1.60)	3.65 (1.52)	.12 (.59)	6.87 (2.05)*	3.96 (2.06)*
INTBIDL	1.55 (1.22)	1.84 (1.74)	.12 (1.34)	2.24 (1.52)	1.12 (1.33)
EXTBIDL	1.23 (1.10)	1.00 (1.07)	.05 (.70)	.99 (.76)	.02 (.03)
INTBINST	3.08 (1.61)	1.81 (1.14)	- .00 (- .00)	4.62 (2.09)*	2.84 (2.23)*
Conceptual Components of Democratic Ideology					
DEMO	2.00 (.89)	.41 (.22)	- .20 (-1.29)	2.20 (.85)	1.43 (.96)
LIBDEMO	1.12 (.96)	- .00 (- .00)	- .04 (- .52)	1.71 (1.25)	.37 (.47)
POPDEMO	.83 (.75)	- .18 (- .20)	- .13 (-1.73)	.36 (.28)	.80 (1.08)
INTDEMO	.88 (.57)	- .63 (- .49)	- .17 (-1.62)	1.64 (.90)	1.15 (1.10)
INTPDEMO	1.25 (1.24)	- .25 (- .30)	- .11 (-1.57)	.32 (.27)	.68 (1.02)
INTDIDL	.31 (.41)	- .47 (- .74)	- .09 (-1.79)	1.80 (2.04)	.70 (1.39)
EXTDIDL	1.11 (.97)	1.03 (1.09)	- .03 (- .32)	.57 (.43)	.29 (.38)
INTDINST	.57 (.56)	- .16 (- .19)	- .08 (-1.14)	- .17 (- .14)	.44 (.65)

(continued on next page)

Table 6 - 14 (continued) **Individual Test Results for Measured Independent Variables (Organizational Traits of Bureaucrats)**

Dependent Variables \ Measured Independent Variables	Characteristics of Major Policies Dealt With by Agencies		Years of Service	Official Ranking	
	PUBREL	WELF	YRSERVE	HIRANK	MIDRANK
Attitudinal Congruity					
BURO-DEMO	.09 (.68)	.05 (.43)	- .00 (- .45)	.06 (.40)	- .16 (-1.85)
BURO-LIBDEMO	.15 (1.04)	.08 (.68)	- .01 (-1.34)	- .11 (- .68)	- .07 (- .69)
BURO-POPDEMO	.08 (.59)	- .03 (- .27)	.01 (.58)	.27 (1.72)	- .16 (-1.77)
INTBURO-INTDEMO	.24 (1.87)	.05 (.47)	.01 (.81)	.14 (.93)	- .14 (-1.57)
INTBURO-INTPDEMO	.24 (1.81)	.08 (.69)	.01 (.64)	.24 (1.55)	- .13 (-1.47)
INTBIDL-INTDIDL	.09 (.69)	- .00 (- .03)	.01 (.59)	- .01 (- .10)	- .01 (- .09)
INTBIDL-EXTDIDL	.14 (1.02)	.09 (.75)	- .01 (-1.23)	- .17 (-1.03)	- .08 (- .80)
INTBIDL-INTDINST	.29 (1.99)*	- .02 (- .13)	.01 (.82)	.17 (.99)	- .12 (-1.25)
EXTBIDL-INTDIDL	.01 (.08)	- .03 (- .20)	.00 (.12)	.11 (.56)	- .20 (-1.77)
EXTBIDL-EXTDIDL	.01 (.07)	- .05 (- .35)	- .00 (- .08)	.04 (.17)	- .09 (- .74)
EXTBIDL-INTDINST	.06 (.33)	.04 (.26)	.01 (.58)	- .00 (- .00)	- .21 (-1.62)
INTBINST-INTDIDL	.14 (1.19)	.15 (1.52)	.01 (1.08)	.06 (.46)	- .06 (- .80)
INTBINST-EXTDIDL	.02 (.14)	- .02 (- .17)	- .02 (-1.93)	.00 (.02)	- .12 (-1.30)
INTBINST-INTDINST	.25 (1.71)	- .01 (- .08)	- .00 (- .03)	.22 (1.28)	- .22 (-2.21)*
INTDIDL-EXTDIDL	.08 (.59)	- .03 (- .23)	- .01 (- .86)	- .07 (- .43)	.04 (.38)
INTDINST-EXTDIDL	.41 (2.82)**	.02 (.20)	.00 (.25)	- .10 (- .60)	- .05 (- .52)

(continued on next page)

Table 6 - 14 (continued) **Individual Test Results for Measured Independent Variables (Organizational Traits of Bureaucrats)**

Dependent Variables \ Measured Independent Variables	Job Classification	Routinization of Work Procedure		Number of Superiors	Number of Subordinates
	JOBCLAS	ROUTINE	MIDROUTN	SUPERIOR	SUBORDNT
Conceptual Components of Bureaucratic Ideology					
BURO	- .17 (- .08)	6.24 (1.73)	6.84 (1.62)	.03 (.13)	-.06 (- .80)
INTBURO	- .12 (- .07)	6.82 (2.15)*	7.60 (2.05)*	.00 (.01)	-.05 (- .72)
INTBIDL	- .41 (- .52)	1.69 (1.21)	2.09 (1.28)	-.01 (-.11)	-.01 (- .29)
EXTBIDL	- .06 (- .09)	- .76 (- .61)	- .80 (- .55)	.05 (.66)	-.01 (- .28)
INTBINST	.29 (.25)	5.13 (2.44)*	5.51 (2.25)*	.01 (.08)	-.04 (- .90)
Conceptual Components of Democratic Ideology					
DEMO	- .49 (- .36)	-5.62 (2.29)*	7.04 (2.46)*	.01 (.05)	-.07 (-1.40)
LIBDEMO	- .33 (- .46)	-2.03 (1.58)	2.80 (1.86)	.03 (.41)	-.05 (-1.70)
POPDEMO	.22 (.32)	-2.66 (2.18)*	3.61 (2.54)*	-.04 (-.52)	-.02 (- .69)
INTDEMO	- .08 (- .08)	-2.75 (1.60)	3.98 (1.99)*	-.00 (-.00)	-.05 (-1.50)
INTPDEMO	.08 (.12)	-2.21 (2.00)*	2.89 (2.24)*	-.03 (-.43)	-.01 (- .53)
INTDIDL	.65 (1.40)	-1.36 (1.62)	1.75 (1.79)	-.01 (-.20)	-.03 (-1.55)
EXTDIDL	- .41 (- .58)	-2.87 (2.27)*	3.06 (2.08)*	.01 (.10)	-.02 (- .69)
INTDINST	- .73 (-1.16)	-1.39 (1.23)	2.23 (1.69)	.01 (.15)	-.03 (-1.12)

(continued on next page)

Table 6 - 14 (continued) **Individual Test Results for Measured Independent Variables (Organizational Traits of Bureaucrats)**

Dependent Variables \ Measured Independent Variables	Job Classification	Routinization of Work Procedure		Number of Superiors	Number of Subordinates
	JOBCLAS	ROUTINE	MIDROUTN	SUPERIOR	SUBORDNT
Attitudinal Congruity					
BURO-DEMO	.09 (1.05)	-.04 (- .26)	.02 (.10)	-.00 (- .39)	.00 (.72)
BURO-LIBDEMO	-.04 (- .50)	-.20 (-1.25)	-.36 (-1.96)	.00 (.29)	.01 (1.86)
BURO-POPDEMO	.14 (1.61)	.09 (.62)	.22 (1.24)	.00 (.28)	-.00 (- .29)
INTBURO-INTDEMO	.08 (1.05)	.08 (.54)	.30 (1.82)	.00 (.04)	.00 (.61)
INTBURO-INTPDEMO	.13 (1.51)	.14 (.92)	.27 (1.55)	.00 (.06)	-.00 (- .23)
INTBIDL-INTDIDL	-.12 (-1.55)	.09 (.62)	.16 (1.00)	.00 (1.13)	.00 (.77)
INTBIDL-EXTDIDL	.03 (.31)	-.34 (-2.18)*	-.52 (-2.84)**	.00 (.41)	.01 (1.74)
INTBIDL-INTDINST	.06 (.62)	.05 (.33)	.17 (.90)	.00 (.17)	.00 (.42)
EXTBIDL-INTDIDL	-.03 (- .28)	-.15 (- .82)	-.24 (-1.09)	.00 (.26)	.00 (.46)
EXTBIDL-EXTDIDL	.14 (1.30)	-.28 (-1.42)	-.54 (-2.37)	-.01 (- .83)	.01 (1.53)
EXTBIDL-INTDINST	.08 (.70)	-.05 (- .22)	-.17 (- .67)	-.00 (- .05)	.00 (.73)
INTBINST-INTDIDL	-.03 (- .42)	.13 (.96)	.26 (1.69)	-.00 (- .38)	.00 (.95)
INTBINST-EXTDIDL	-.03 (- .36)	-.09 (- .60)	-.26 (-1.48)	-.01 (-1.31)	.00 (.74)
INTBINST-INTDINST	.26 (2.88)**	.04 (.26)	.22 (1.17)	-.00 (- .45)	.00 (.32)
INTDIDL-EXTDIDL	.06 (.67)	-.10 (- .63)	-.08 (- .45)	.00 (.00)	.00 (.26)
INTDINST-EXTDIDL	.02 (.27)	-.31 (-1.94)	-.45 (-2.42)*	-.01 (- .61)	.00 (1.01)

Note: Estimated regression coefficients presented are of full models where measured independent variables listed in Fig. 5-3 are included. For convenience of presentation, however, estimation result presented by types of traits. Numbers without parentheses are estimates of partial regression coefficient. Numbers in parentheses are t-values. "*" indicates t-value is at 5% significance leve. "**" indicates t-value is at 1% significance level. For substantive notation meanings and measurement schemes for dependent and independent variables, see Tab. 5-2, Tab. 5-3, and Fig. 5-2.

control over the lower offices.

The t-tests also reveal that the regression coefficients of OFFICE for the dependent variables representing bureaucrats' internalization of the conceptual components of democratic ideology are all insignificant.

Finally, the t-tests for the impact of OFFICE on the dependent variables representing the attitudinal congruity clarified the extent to which the officials working in the two types of offices are similar to or different from one another in their internalization of a certain ideological component in relation to another. The regression coefficient of OFFICE is statistically significant especially for the three dependent variables representing attitudinal congruity (i.e., INTBURO-INTDEMO, EXTBIDL-INTDIDL, and INTBINST-INTDIDL). This indicates that those who work in the main office are less likely than those who work in the regional offices to regard the internal bureaucratic ideology (INTBURO) as compatible with the internal democratic ideology (INTDEMO). The result also indicates that those who work in the main office are less likely than those who work in regional offices to regard external bureaucratic ideals (EXTBIDL) and internal bureaucratic instrumental principles (INTBINST) as compatible with the internal democratic ideals (INTDIDL).

One of the independent variables that has been frequently considered in explaining the attitudes of bureaucrats is the "*characteristics of the major policy dealt with by the agencies* to which the bureaucrats belong" (e.g., Rinehart and Bernick, 1975 and Wynia, 1974; cf., Berger and Cummings, 1979). Implicit to this tradition are the hypotheses that the more "control"-oriented a major policy dealt with by an agency, the more bureaucratic and less democratic the attitudes of bureaucrats working in the agency will be, and that the more "service"-oriented a major policy dealt with by an agency, the less bureaucratic and the more democratic the attitudes of the bureaucrats working in the agency will be.[23]

In order to examine the empirical validity of these hypotheses, I classified the agencies that I surveyed into three groups: those that deal with control-oriented policy, those that deal with service-oriented policy, and others that were unamenable to the "control-vs.-service" scheme of classification.[24] The third group served as a common basis for a comparison between the first two groups.

According to the results of t-tests (Table 6-14), the hypotheses are partially confirmed. None of the regression coefficients of the measured independent variables pertaining to the characteristics of policies are statistically significant for all of the dependent variables representing bureaucrats' internalization of democratic ideology. This indicates that there are no significant differences between the bureaucrats who work in the agencies that deal with service-oriented policy in their internalization of the conceptual components of democratic ideology.[25] Regression coefficients of the three measured independent dummy variables that represent bureaucrats working in the control-oriented agencies are all positive and statistically significant for most of the dependent variables that represent bureaucrats' internalization of bureaucratic ideology. This indicates that the bureaucrats working in the control-oriented agency have a higher level of internalization of bureaucratic ideology than those who work in the reference agencies which are treated as an excluded dummy category. In contrast, the regression coefficients of the two measured independent dummy variables that represent those who work in the service-oriented agencies are all statistically insignificant for the same dependent variables. This indicates that there is no significant difference between those who work in the service-oriented agencies and those who work in the third group of agencies in the degree of their internalization of bureaucratic ideology. The combination of these two findings indicates that those who work in control-oriented agencies internalize bureaucratic ideology to a greater extent than those who work in the service-oriented agencies.

Finally, the results of t-tests indicate that those who work in the agencies that provide public information to citizens and that deal with complaints from citizens (i.e., those who are represented by the measured independent dummy variable, PUBREL) are more inclined than others to regard the internal democratic instrumental principles (INTDINST) as compatible with the internal bureaucratic ideals (INTBIDL) and the external democratic ideals (EXTDIDL).

How long individual bureaucrats have stayed in the bureaucracy has frequently been chosen as an independent variable for explaining the attitudes of bureaucrats with an expectation that the more years in bureaucracy, the more acceptance of bureaucratic ideology and the less acceptance of democratic ideology (cf., Wynia, 1974:160).

This expectation, however, is inconsistent with the results of my empirical tests. As presented in Table in 6-14, the regression coefficients for *years of service* (i.e., YRSERVE) are statistically insignificant for all dependent variables. "Years in service," does not explain internalization of bureaucratic and democratic ideologies.

I expect that *higher ranking* officials would show a higher level of internalization of bureaucratic ideology than lower ranking officials. My expectation is based on my speculation that those who advance in an organization may be those who internalize the norms that guide that organization better than others.

This expectation is consistent with the results of my empirical tests. That is, shown in Table 6-14, the measured dummy independent variable, HIRANK, has significant and positive regression coefficients for three out of five dependent variables that represent bureaucrats' internalization of bureaucratic ideology. Because the dummy variable that is left out of the regression model represents low-ranking officials (i.e., the sixth-graders), this finding indicates that the high-ranking officials maintain a higher level of internalization of bureaucratic ideology than do lower-ranking officials.

The t-tests also reveal that there is no significant difference between high- and low-ranking officials in their internalization of democratic ideology. That is, the regression coefficients of HIRANK and MIDRANK[26] are all insignificant for the dependent variables that represent bureaucrats' internalization of the conceptual components of democratic ideology. In addition, the results of t-tests indicate that, of the 16 regression coefficients of the measured independent variables of "official ranking" that are estimated for attitudinal congruity, only one coefficient[27] is statistically significant. This indicates that there is no difference between high- and low-ranking officials in their understandings of the compatibilities among the conceptual components of bureaucratic and democratic ideologies.

What and how one thinks would be significantly affected by what he or she is doing. One of the objective traits of individual Korean bureaucrats that generally describes what they are doing is their official *job classification*; that is, "general administrators" (called *Ilban Hangjongjig*) vs. "technicians" (called *Kisooljig*). The t-tests for this independent variable (i.e., JOBCLAS), however, indicate that there is only one significant difference of 29 tests between general administrators and technical experts in the degree of their internalization and understanding of the compatibility among most components of bureaucratic and democratic ideologies.

Another job-related trait of individual Korean bureaucrats that I expect to produce differences in what and how bureaucrats think is the *routinization of procedures* that they follow in performing their jobs. The results of t-tests indicate that the extent to which work procedures are routinized make differences in the extent to which individual bureaucrats internalize bureaucratic and democratic ideologies. That is, it is found that the regression coefficients of ROUTINE and MIDROUTN especially for the two dependent variables, INTBURO and INTBINST, are positive and significant. ROUTINE and MIDROUTN are dummy variables that represent respectively those who report that their work procedures are routinized to a high degree and those who report that their work procedures are routinized to an average degree. The excluded category pertaining to these dummy variables represents those who report that their work procedures are unroutinized or difficult to be routinized. Thus, the finding indicates that those who perform routinized work are more likely than those who perform unroutinized work to internalize internal bureaucratic ideology (INTBURO). Specifically, the internal bureaucratic instrumental principles (INTBINST), rather than the internal bureaucratic ideals (INTBIDL).

More than half of the regression coefficients of ROUTINE and MIDROUTN for the dependent variables that represent bureaucrats' internalization of democratic ideology are statistically significant and negative. This indicates that democratic ideology is internalized less by those who perform unroutinized work than by those who perform routinized work.

For the dependent variables that represent the extent to which individual bureaucrats regard the conceptual components of bureaucratic and democratic ideologies as compatible with each other, it is found that most of the regression coefficients of ROUTINE and MIDROUTN are insignificant. This indicates that there is not a considerable difference between those who deal with routinized work and those who deal with unroutinized work in their tendencies to regard bureaucratic and democratic ideologies as compatible with one another.[28]

For heuristic purposes, I examined the extent to which the *number of superiors and subordinates* affects the extent to which they internalize bureaucratic and democratic ideologies, and the extent to which they regard the conceptual components of bureaucratic and democratic ideologies as compatible with each other. The results of t-tests for SUPERIOR and SUBORDNT indicate the number of superiors and subordinates are not sources of variations among individual bureaucrats in their internalization of bureaucratic and democratic ideologies, and their tendencies to regard the conceptual components of these ideologies.

The Socio-economic Determinants of the Ideological Traits of Bureaucrats. Of the results of joint impact tests for the 21 sub-independent variables, those that are relevant to the socio-economic traits of bureaucrats are summarized in Table 6-15. The overall pattern of the R^2-differences and their statistical significance reported in this table indicates that of the six types of socio-economic traits examined in this study, "age" is the only significant determinant.

Reading the table by rows reveals that the explanatory power of this variable is detected mostly on bureaucrats' internalization of democratic ideology. The significant R^2-differences are found especially for the three dependent variables, the internalization of popular democratic ideology (POPDEMO), internal popular democratic ideology (INTPDEMO), and internal democratic ideals (INTDIDL). Combined with the finding that R^2-differences for the two dependent variables, internalization of liberal democratic ideology (LIBDEMO) and external democratic ideology (EXTDIDL) are all insignificant, indicates two things. First, "age" has significant explanatory power more on bureaucrats' internalization of democratic ideology that is defined in the intra-organizational context of governmental agencies, rather than the one defined in terms of the external relationships of these agencies with the citizens, legislators, and the market. Second, "age" has significant explanatory power more on bureaucrats' internalization of popular democratic ideology than liberal democratic ideology.

Note that the joint impact tests do not tell us about the directions of impact of the socio-economic traits of bureaucrats on the extent to which individual bureaucrats internalize bureaucratic and democratic ideologies, and on the extent to which they regard the conceptual components of these ideologies

Table 6 - 15 **Results of Joint Impact Tests for Sub-Independent Variables of Socio-Economic Traits of Bureaucrats**

Dependent Variables / Measured Independent Variables	Age: (AGE)	Annual Family Income: (INCOME)	Level of Education: (PREUNIV, UNIV)	Gender: (SEX)
Conceptual Components of Bureaucratic Ideology				
BURO	.007 (2.051)	.000 (.086)	.006 (.899)	.000 (.184)
INTBURO	.007 (2.128)	.000 (.101)	.005 (.850)	.001 (.229)
INTBIDL	.003 (.966)	.001 (.293)	.008 (1.231)	.000 (.021)
EXTBIDL	.002 (.429)	.000 (.038)	.003 (.372)	.000 (.043)
INTBINST	.008 (2.410)	.000 (.014)	.003 (.493)	.002 (.673)
Conceptual Components of Democratic Ideology				
DEMO	.010 (2.576)	.003 (.898)	.010 (1.330)	.002 (.472)
LIBDEMO	.002 (.489)	.000 (.000)	.005 (.641)	.000 (.034)
POPDEMO	.016 (4.550)*	.003 (.790)	.018 (2.555)	.002 (.620)
INTDEMO	.013 (3.299)	.000 (.022)	.010 (1.323)	.001 (.237)
INTPDEMO	.015 (3.908)*	.002 (.452)	.024 (3.155)*	.001 (.349)
INTDIDL	.019 (5.139)*	.003 (.737)	.006 (.808)	.000 (.001)
EXTDIDL	.002 (.431)	.010 (2.688)	.006 (.761)	.002 (.456)
INTDINST	.005 (1.167)	.003 (.742)	.011 (1.439)	.002 (.516)
Attitudinal Congruity				
BURO-DEMO	.000 (.053)	.000 (.058)	.001 (.067)	.004 (1.097)
BURO-LIBDEMO	.012 (3.216)	.002 (.494)	.011 (.114)	.000 (.012)
BURO-POPDEMO	.008 (2.015)	.004 (.954)	.004 (.557)	.000 (.055)

(continued on next page)

Table 6 - 15 (continued) **Results of Joint Impact Tests for Sub-Independent Variables of Socio-Economic Traits of Bureaucrats**

Dependent Variables \ Measured Independent Variables	Age: (AGE)	Annual Family Income: (INCOME)	Level of Education: (PREUNIV, UNIV)	Gender: (SEX)
Attitudinal Congruity (continued)				
INTBURO-INTDEMO	.007 (1.869)	.002 (.516)	.004 (.458)	.001 (.304)
INTBURO-INTPDEMO	.011 (2.915)	.010 (2.481)	.005 (.585)	.001 (.179)
INTBIDL-INTDIDL	.004 (.953)	.000 (.079)	.004 (.514)	.000 (.018)
INTBIDL-EXTDIDL	.005 (1.355)	.000 (.079)	.007 (.925)	.001 (.229)
INTBIDL-INTDINST	.007 (1.758)	.001 (.272)	.002 (.262)	.006 (1.585)
EXTBIDL-INTDIDL	.000 (.067)	.005 (1.370)	.002 (.250)	.002 (.432)
EXTBIDL-EXTDIDL	.002 (.484)	.000 (.045)	.002 (.224)	.000 (.000)
EXTBIDL-INTDINST	.001 (.354)	.009 (2.157)	.007 (.911)	.004 (.980)
INTBINST-INTDIDL	.006 (1.489)	.001 (.129)	.000 (.043)	.001 (.336)
INTBINST-EXTDIDL	.015 (3.978)*	.014 (3.694)	.005 (.717)	.000 (.036)
INTBINST-INTDINST	.000 (.025)	.003 (.864)	.006 (.082)	.000 (.000)
INTDIDL-EXTDIDL	.002 (.577)	.014 (3.469)	.005 (.562)	.000 (.001)
INTDINST-EXTDIDL	.000 (.027)	.005 (1.368)	.003 (.436)	.000 (.074)

Note: Numbers without parentheses are differences between R^2 of a full model where all independent variables are included and that of a restricted model where set of independent variables specified at top of the column are excluded. Numbers within parentheses are F-value of R^2 difference. "*" indicates F-value is at 5% significance level. For substantive notation meanings and measurement schemes for dependent and independent variables, see Tab. 5-2, Tab. 5-3, and Fig. 5-2.

as compatible with each other. The results of t-tests for the 39 individually measured independent variables contain information by which we can investigate the directions of impact of the socio-economic traits. Table 6-16 summarizes the results of t-tests that are related particularly to socio-economic traits. According to the results, the older the bureaucrats, the less likely that they internalize democratic ideology, especially popular democratic ideology (POPDEMO), internal popular democratic ideology (INTPDEMO), and internal democratic ideals (INTDIDL). This is indicated especially by the result that the regression coefficients of AGE for the three dependent variables that represent bureaucrats' internalization of democratic ideology (i.e., POPDEMO, INTPDEMO, and INTDIDL) are all negative and significant.

In addition, the t-tests for the dummy variables representing "levels of education" [i.e., those who have a high school diploma only (PREUNIV), those who have a bachelor's degree (UNIV), and those who have a master's degree or higher[29])] indicate that there are no differences among these three categories of educational levels in the extent to which they internalize the bureaucratic and democratic ideologies, and the extent to which they regard the conceptual components of these ideologies as compatible with each other. These findings are inconsistent with the findings reported by many other authors who have studied western bureaucrats. Wynia (1974:160), for example, studied the attitudes of U.S. federal bureaucrats toward democratic ideology, and found that "the less education, the more anti-democratic." According to the results of my t-tests, however, those who have only a high school diploma and those who have a bachelor's degrees, are not different from those who hold a master's or higher degree, in the extent to which they internalize most of the conceptual components of democratic ideology.

The Socializational Determinants of the Ideological Traits of Bureaucrats. It has been widely pointed out that values, including bureaucratic and democratic ideologies, are often learned through socialization.[30] Socialization is, as Chackerian and Abcarian (1984:29) define, "an educational or inculcative process through which one internalizes values and attitudes in the social environment." I focus especially upon childhood socialization (which is operationally defined in my study as the period during which the respondents were attending middle and high schools). Two types of socialization backgrounds are considered: the region where one grew up and the characteristics of one's family during the socialization period. Of the six sub-independent variables considered in my study (region where grown-up, family economic condition, early loss of parents, experience of parental divorce, the most influential person's job, and atmosphere of communications within family), the first represents the former, and the remaining five sub-independent variables represent the latter.[31]

Table 6 - 16 **Results of Individual Tests for Measured Independent Variables (Socio-Economic Traits of Bureaucrats)**

Measured Independent Variables / Dependent Variables	Age	Annual Family Income (in Won)	Levels of Education		Gender
	AGE	INCOME	PREUNIV	UNIV	SEX
Conceptual Components of Bureaucratic Ideology					
BURO	.33 (1.43)	-367 (- .29)	- .62 (- .21)	-2.61 (- .99)	-1.93(-.43)
INTBURO	.29 (1.46)	-349 (- .32)	- .85 (- .33)	-2.42 (-1.04)	-1.89(-.48)
INTBIDL	.09 (.99)	-263 (- .54)	- .02 (- .02)	-1.01 (- .98)	.25(.14)
EXTBIDL	.05 (.66)	- 83 (- .19)	- .00 (- .00)	- .48 (- .53)	- .32(-.21)
INTBINST	.21 (1.55)	- 87 (- .12)	- .83 (- .49)	-1.42 (- .92)	-2.14(-.82)
Conceptual Components of Democratic Ideology					
DEMO	- .25 (1.61)	-807 (- .95)	-2.28 (-1.15)	-2.92 (-1.62)	2.10(.69)
LIBDEMO	- .06 (.70)	- 8 (- .02)	- .90 (- .86)	-1.07 (-1.13)	.30(.19)
POPDEMO	- .17 (2.13)*	-376 (- .89)	-1.15 (-1.17)	-1.90(-2.12)*	1.20(.79)
INTDEMO	- .20 (1.82)	- 89 (- .15)	-1.06 (- .77)	-1.87 (-1.49)	1.04(.49)
INTPDEMO	- .14 (1.98)*	-258 (- .67)	-1.12 (-1.26)	-1.89(-2.33)*	.81(.59)
INTDIDL	- .12 (2.27)*	249 (.86)	- .00 (- .01)	- .48 (- .79)	.03(.03)
EXTDIDL	- .05 (.66)	-718 (-1.64)	-1.22 (-1.20)	-1.04 (-1.13)	1.06(.68)
INTDINST	- .08 (1.08)	-338 (- .86)	-1.06 (-1.16)	-1.39 (-1.68)	1.01(.72)
Attitudinal Congruity					
BURO-DEMO	.00 (.23)	12 (.24)	- .03 (- .22)	.00 (.00)	.19(1.05)
BURO-LIBDEMO	.02 (1.79)	- 39 (- .70)	- .05 (- .38)	- .06 (- .48)	.02(.11)
BURO-POPDEMO	- .01 (-1.42)	51 (.98)	.11 (.88)	.12 (1.05)	.04(.24)

(continued on next page)

Table 6 - 16 (continued) **Results of Individual Tests for Measured Independent Variables (Socio-Economic Traits of Bureaucrats)**

Measured Independent Variables / Dependent Variables	Age	Annual Family Income (in Won)	Levels of Education		Gender
	AGE	INCOME	PREUNIV	UNIV	SEX
Attitudinal Congruity (continued)					
INTBURO-INTDEMO	- .01 (-1.37)	36 (.72)	.05 (.44)	.09 (.87)	.10(.55)
INTBURO-INTPDEMO	- .02 (-1.71)	81 (1.58)	.11 (.88)	.12 (1.08)	.08(.42)
INTBIDL-INTDIDL	- .01 (- .98)	- 13 (- .28)	- .03 (- .30)	- .08 (- .83)	- .02(-.13)
INTBIDL-EXTDIDL	.01 (1.16)	15 (.28)	- .15 (-1.19)	- .06 (- .53)	- .09(-.48)
INTBIDL-INTDINST	- .01 (-1.33)	29 (.52)	- .00 (- .03)	.05 (.42)	.25(1.26)
EXTBIDL-INTDIDL	- .00 (- .26)	- 77 (-1.17)	- .08 (- .51)	- .01 (- .09)	.16(.66)
EXTBIDL-EXTDIDL	- .01 (- .70)	- 14 (- .21)	.01 (.08)	.07 (.47)	.00(.01)
EXTBIDL-INTDINST	- .01 (- .60)	-108 (-1.47)	- .20 (-1.16)	- .08 (- .49)	.26(.99)
INTBINST-INTDIDL	- .01 (-1.22)	17 (.36)	- .02 (- .15)	- .03 (- .27)	.10(.58)
INTBINST-EXTDIDL	- .02 (-2.00)*	100 (1.92)	- .01 (- .09)	- .09 (- .81)	.04(.19)
INTBINST-INTDINST	.00 (.16)	53 (.93)	.07 (.54)	.14 (1.13)	.00(.00)
INTDIDL-EXTDIDL	.01 (.76)	100 (1.86)	- .10 (- .83)	- .03 (- .24)	.01(.03)
INTDINST-EXTDIDL	- .00 (- .17)	65 (1.17)	- .10 (- .80)	- .11 (- .93)	.05(.27)

Note: Estimated regression coefficients presented in table are those of full models where all measured independent variables listed in Fig. 5-3 are included. For convenience of presentation, however, result of estimation is presented by types of traits. Numbers without parentheses are estimates of partial regression coefficient. Numbers in parentheses are t-values. "*" indicates t-value is at 5% significance level. For substantive notation meanings and measurement schemes for dependent and independent variables, see Tab. 5-2, Tab. 5-3, and Fig. 5-2.

Ample evidence indicating that these variables have a significant impact on the development of general human values, attitudes, and personality, has been accumulated in the field of educational psychology. It is, however, difficult to find a theoretical or empirical study that deals with the causal structures of these variables, particularly in the context of bureaucrats' internalization of bureaucratic and democratic ideologies. Given this lack of previous theoretical and empirical studies that are relevant to what I wish to study, my examination of these variables must be heuristic. That is, my examination is aimed at generating hypotheses rather than testing formal hypotheses.

The overall pattern of R^2-differences and their statistical significance reported in Table 6-17 indicates that none of the six sub-independent variables representing the socialization backgrounds of bureaucrats has significant explanatory power. That is, the table demonstrates that, of the 174 R^2-differences, only six are statistically significant, and that no sub-independent variable has more than two significant R^2-differences.

The same conclusion is reached even if we turn to the results of t-tests for the measured independent variables which are constructed as component variables of the six sub-independent variables (see Table 6-18).

Cultural Determinants of the Ideological Traits of Bureaucrats. Of the results of joint impact tests performed for all sub-independent variables that are considered in my study, those that are related to the sub-independent variables representing the cultural traits of bureaucrats are summarized in Table 6-19. The overall pattern of R^2-differences and their statistical significance reported in the table indicates a number of interesting facts pertaining to the *overall* explanatory power of the sub-categories of cultural factors.

First, it is found that, of the 29 R^2-differences for the sub-independent variable, "religious culture," only one is statistically significant. This finding indicates that religion is not a significant determinant of the extent to which the individual bureaucrats internalize bureaucratic and democratic ideologies and the extent to which they regard the conceptual components of these ideologies as compatible with each other.

Second, it is found that statistically significant R^2-differences for the sub-independent variable, "societal culture" are concentrated solely on the dependent variables that represent bureaucrats' internalization of democratic ideology. As mentioned in Chapter Five, "societal culture" is operationalized in my study into the measured independent variables following Inglehart's (1977) scheme of cultural categories; that is, materialistic culture, post-materialistic culture, and mixed culture. Thus, the finding indicates that Inglehart's scheme *as a whole* is valid especially for explaining the variations among individual bureaucrats in their internalization of democratic ideology.

Finally, it is found that statistically significant R^2-differences for the

Table 6 - 17 **Results of Impact Test for Sub-Independent Variables of Socialization Backgrounds of Bureaucrats**

Sets of Independent Variables / Dependent Variables	Region Where Grown-up: (RURAL, MIDURBAN)	Family Economic Condition: (POOR, AVECON)	Early Loss of Parents: (PARNTDIE)	Experience of Parental Divorce: (DIVORCE)	Most Influential Person's Job: (PUBURO, PV-BURO, FARMER, SELFEMP)	Atmosphere of Communication within Family: (AUTHFMLY, AVEFMLY)
Conceptual Components of Bureaucratic Ideology						
BURO	.003 (.483)	.012 (1.829)	.004 (1.364)	.006 (1.928)	.009 (.679)	.009 (1.360)
INTBURO	.002 (.345)	.012 (1.946)	.004 (1.180)	.007 (2.085)	.007 (.564)	.006 (1.000)
INTBIDL	.003 (.406)	.025 (3.908)*	.000 (.035)	.008 (2.628)	.013 (1.044)	.006 (.876)
EXTBIDL	.007 (.905)	.004 (.526)	.001 (.222)	.002 (.532)	.010 (.620)	.009 (1.064)
INTBINST	.006 (.927)	.008 (1.191)	.010 (3.130)	.004 (1.220)	.006 (.469)	.005 (.798)
Conceptual Components of Democratic Ideology						
DEMO	.014 (1.798)	.011 (1.423)	.000 (.020)	.001 (.292)	.008 (.521)	.000 (.053)
LIBDEMO	.003 (.437)	.010 (1.272)	.001 (.338)	.000 (.028)	.021 (1.342)	.009 (1.129)
POPDEMO	.016 (2.163)	.015 (2.109)	.000 (.018)	.002 (.588)	.011 (.743)	.005 (.706)
INTDEMO	.008 (.995)	.005 (.678)	.000 (.071)	.006 (1.553)	.005 (.349)	.003 (.415)
INTPDEMO	.010 (1.320)	.012 (1.633)	.000 (.043)	.002 (.605)	.008 (.541)	.005 (.671)
INTDIDL	.007 (.901)	.007 (.938)	.000 (.086)	.000 (.038)	.006 (.405)	.004 (.482)
EXTDIDL	.013 (1.708)	.011 (1.449)	.002 (.404)	.002 (.409)	.018 (1.183)	.002 (.284)
INTDINST	.007 (.907)	.002 (.285)	.002 (.385)	.012 (3.048)	.006 (.360)	.002 (.267)

(continued on next page)

Table 6 - 17 (continued) **Results of Impact Test for Sub-Independent Variables of Socialization Backgrounds of Bureaucrats**

Sets of Independent Variables / Dependent Variables	Region Where Grown-up: (RURAL, MIDURBAN)	Family Economic Condition: (POOR, AVECON)	Early Loss of Parents: (PARNTDIE)	Experience of Parental Divorce: (DIVORCE)	Most Influential Person's Job: (PUBURO, PV-BURO, FARM-ER, SELFEMP)	Atmosphere of Communication within Family: (AUTHFMLY, AVEFMLY)
Attitudinal Congruity						
BURO-DEMO	.001 (.101)	.000 (.035)	.004 (.947)	.002 (.567)	.034 (2.090)	.000 (.055)
BURO-LIBDEMO	.003 (.468)	.002 (.270)	.000 (.010)	.015 (4.080)*	.041 (2.750)*	.007 (.942)
BURO-POPDEMO	.001 (.072)	.003 (.411)	.005 (1.344)	.000 (.005)	.012 (.752)	.004 (.561)
INTBURO-INTDEMO	.002 (.203)	.005 (.658)	.002 (.430)	.000 (.029)	.008 (.528)	.002 (.226)
INTBURO-INTPDEMO	.003 (.407)	.009 (1.097)	.003 (.721)	.000 (.101)	.012 (.765)	.007 (.843)
INTBIDL-INTDIDL	.009 (1.192)	.009 (1.219)	.035 (9.343)**	.000 (.071)	.006 (.407)	.021 (2.829)
INTBIDL-EXTDIDL	.002 (.195)	.010 (1.291)	.003 (.869)	.002 (.506)	.028 (1.784)	.001 (.171)
INTBIDL-INTDINST	.013 (1.667)	.001 (.155)	.004 (.963)	.002 (.378)	.012 (.787)	.003 (.348)
EXTBIDL-INTDIDL	.005 (.636)	.004 (.547)	.002 (.480)	.003 (.808)	.029 (1.878)	.006 (.778)

(continued on next page)

Table 6 - 17 (continued) **Results of Impact Test for Sub-Independent Variables of Socialization Backgrounds of Bureaucrats**

Sets of Independent Variables / Dependent Variables	Region Where Grown-up: (RURAL, MIDURBAN)	Family Economic Condition: (POOR, AVECON)	Early Loss of Parents: (PARNTDIE)	Experience of Parental Divorce: (DIVORCE)	Most Influential Person's Job: (PUBURO, PV-BURO, FARM-ER, SELFEMP)	Atmosphere of Communication within Family: (AUTHFMLY, AVEFMLY)
Attitudinal Congruity (continued)						
EXTBIDL-EXTDIDL	.003 (.423)	.001 (.077)	.001 (.220)	.008 (1.940)	.035 (2.210)	.001 (.145)
EXTBIDL-INTDINST	.002 (.259)	.019 (2.361)	.002 (.612)	.003 (.804)	.006 (.378)	.006 (.704)
INTBINST-INTDIDL	.003 (.328)	.004 (.477)	.000 (.000)	.007 (1.715)	.019 (1.207)	.005 (.634)
INTBINST-EXTDIDL	.004 (.522)	.002 (.248)	.000 (.003)	.004 (1.135)	.047 (3.056)*	.002 (.319)
INTBINST-INTDINST	.004 (.570)	.015 (1.940)	.001 (.140)	.001 (.261)	.020 (1.339)	.004 (.543)
INTDIDL-EXTDIDL	.008 (1.046)	.012 (1.533)	.005 (1.153)	.001 (.160)	.025 (1.521)	.004 (.492)
INTDINST-EXTDIDL	.003 (.349)	.011 (1.340)	.001 (.181)	.000 (.119)	.009 (.565)	.004 (.513)

Note: Numbers without parentheses are differences between R^2 of full model where all independent variables are included and that of a restricted model where set of independent variables specified at top of column are excluded. Numbers within parentheses are F-values of R^2 difference. "*" indicates F-value is at 5% significance level. "**" indicates F-value is at 1% significance level. For substantive notation meaning and measurement schemes for dependent and independent variables, see Tab. 5-2, Tab. 5-3, and Fig. 5-2.

Table 6 - 18 **Results of Individual Tests for Measured Independent Variables (Socialization Backgrounds of Bureaucrats)**

Measured Independent Variables / Dependent Variables	Region Where Grown-up		Family Economic Condition	
	RURAL	MIDURBAN	POOR	AVECON
Conceptual Components of Bureaucratic Ideology				
BURO	- .54 (- .26)	- 1.97 (- .98)	- 5.02 (- 1.86)	- 4.36 (- 1.72)
INTBURO	.37 (.20)	- 1.20 (- .68)	- 4.66 (- 1.97)*	- 3.59 (- 1.61)
INTBIDL	.72 (.89)	.37 (.48)	- 2.70 (- 2.59)*	- 1.31 (- 1.34)
EXTBIDL	- .82 (- 1.14)	- .74 (- 1.08)	- .70 (- .75)	- .89 (- 1.02)
INTBINST	- .34 (- .28)	- 1.57 (- 1.34)	- 1.96 (- 1.25)	- 2.28 (- 1.54)
Conceptual Components of Democratic Ideology				
DEMO	- 2.70 (- 1.89)	- .75 (- .55)	- 2.97 (- 1.62)	- 2.68 (- 1.55)
LIBDEMO	- .68 (- .91)	- .39 (- .54)	- 1.42 (- 1.47)	- 1.39 (- 1.53)
POPDEMO	- 1.47 (- 2.07)*	- .36 (- .53)	- 1.86 (- 2.05)*	- 1.45 (- 1.69)
INTDEMO	- 1.39 (- 1.40)	- .63 (- .66)	- 1.42 (- 1.11)	- 1.31 (- 1.09)
INTPDEMO	- 1.03 (- 1.61)	- .22 (- .35)	- 1.49 (- 1.81)	- 1.06 (- 1.36)
INTDIDL	- .53 (- 1.10)	- .52 (- 1.11)	- .81 (- 1.31)	- .75 (- 1.27)
EXTDIDL	- 1.30 (- 1.78)	- .11 (- .16)	- 1.56 (- 1.65)	- 1.37 (- 1.54)
INTDINST	- .86 (- 1.31)	- .11 (- .18)	- .60 (- .71)	- .56 (- .71)
Attitudinal Congruity				
BURO-DEMO	- .02 (- .28)	.02 (.23)	- .01 (- .07)	- .02 (- .22)
BURO-LIBDEMO	- .07 (- .72)	.03 (.35)	- .05 (- .43)	.00 (.04)
BURO-POPDEMO	.03 (.38)	.01 (.16)	.07 (.64)	.01 (.09)

(continued on next page)

Table 6 - 18 (continued) **Results of Individual Tests for Measured Independent Variables (Socialization Backgrounds of Bureaucrats)**

Dependent Variables / Measured Independent Variables	Region Where Grown-up		Family Economic Condition	
	RURAL	MIDURBAN	POOR	AVECON
Attitudinal Congruity (continued)				
INTBURO-INTDEMO	- .04 (- .51)	- .04 (- .54)	.09 (.83)	.01 (.13)
INTBURO-INTPDEMO	- .01 (- .15)	- .07 (- .89)	.06 (.57)	- .04 (- .43)
INTBIDL-INTDIDL	.09 (1.18)	.10 (1.36)	- .12 (- 1.13)	- .15 (- 1.56)
INTBIDL-EXTDIDL	.00 (.06)	- .05 (- .56)	- .11 (- .96)	- .17 (- 1.56)
INTBIDL-INTDINST	- .10 (- 1.05)	- .16 (- 1.77)	.03 (.24)	- .02 (- .14)
EXTBIDL-INTDIDL	.07 (.62)	.12 (1.10)	.06 (.45)	.13 (.95)
EXTBIDL-EXTDIDL	.10 (.91)	.02 (.21)	.05 (.32)	.01 (.10)
EXTBIDL-INTDINST	- .04 (- .30)	- .08 (- .72)	.05 (.33)	.24 (1.62)
INTBINST-INTDIDL	.06 (.72)	- .01 (- .09)	.08 (.78)	.02 (.23)
INTBINST-EXTDIDL	.04 (.42)	.09 (1.02)	.05 (.44)	- .00 (- .01)
INTBINST-INTDINST	- .08 (- .83)	- .08 (- .92)	.24 (1.96)*	.16 (1.40)
INTDIDL-EXTDIDL	.09 (1.04)	- .05 (- .57)	.04 (.37)	- .09 (- .80)
INTDINST-EXTDIDL	.07 (.79)	.00 (.04)	.07 (.59)	- .06 (- .51)

(continued on next page)

Table 6 - 18 (continued) **Results of Individual Tests for Measured Independent Variables (Socialization Backgrounds of Bureaucrats)**

Dependent Variables \ Measured Independent Variables	Early Loss of Parents	Experience of Parental Divorce	Most Influential Person's Job	
	PARNTDIE	DIVORCE	PUBURO	PVBURO
Conceptual Components of Bureaucratic Ideology				
BURO	- 2.61 (- 1.17)	7.42 (1.39)	- .96 (- .35)	- 5.04 (- 1.28)
INTBURO	- 2.14 (- 1.09)	6.78 (1.44)	- .81 (- .34)	- 4.41 (- 1.27)
INTBIDL	.16 (.19)	3.35 (1.62)	- .40 (- .37)	- 2.66 (- 1.74)
EXTBIDL	- .36 (- .47)	1.33 (.73)	- .20 (- .21)	- 1.38 (- 1.02)
INTBINST	- 2.30 (- 1.77)	3.43 (1.11)	- .41 (- .26)	- 1.75 (- .76)
Conceptual Components of Democratic Ideology				
DEMO	.21 (.14)	- 1.96 (- .54)	1.09 (.59)	- 2.55 (- .95)
LIBDEMO	.46 (.58)	.32 (.17)	- .37 (- .38)	- 3.18 (- 2.25)
POPDEMO	.10 (.13)	- 1.38 (- .77)	1.12 (1.21)	.37 (.28)
INTDEMO	- .28 (- .27)	- 3.16 (- 1.25)	.48 (.37)	.04 (.02)
INTPDEMO	.14 (.21)	- 1.27 (- .78)	.82 (.99)	.14 (.11)
INTDIDL	.15 (.29)	- .24 (- .20)	- .02 (- .02)	- .56 (- .61)
EXTDIDL	.50 (.64)	1.20 (.64)	.62 (.65)	- 2.59 (- 1.87)
INTDINST	- .43 (- .62)	- 2.92 (- 1.75)	.49 (.58)	.59 (.48)
Attitudinal Congruity				
BURO-DEMO	.09 (.97)	- .16 (- .75)	- .27 (- 2.45)*	.07 (.47)
BURO-LIBDEMO	.01 (.10)	- .47 (- 2.02)	- .24 (- 1.99)*	.24 (1.39)
BURO-POPDEMO	.11 (1.16)	- .02 (- .07)	- .11 (- .92)	.09 (.57)

(continued on next page)

Table 6 - 18 (continued) **Results of Individual Tests for Measured Independent Variables (Socialization Backgrounds of Bureaucrats)**

Dependent Variables \ Measured Independent Variables	Early Loss of Parents	Experience of Parental Divorce	Most Influential Person's Job	
	PARNTDIE	DIVORCE	PUBURO	PVBURO
Attitudinal Congruity (continued)				
INTBURO-INTDEMO	.06 (.66)	- .04 (- .17)	- .14 (- 1.33)	.02 (.15)
INTBURO-INTPDEMO	.08 (.85)	- .07 (- .32)	- .11 (- .97)	.06 (.38)
INTBIDL-INTDIDL	.26 (3.06)**	.05 (.27)	.03 (.26)	.04 (.27)
INTBIDL-EXTDIDL	.09 (.93)	- .16 (- .71)	- .20 (- 1.68)	.01 (.08)
INTBIDL-INTDINST	.10 (.98)	.15 (.62)	- .16 (- 1.30)	- .07 (- .42)
EXTBIDL-INTDIDL	.08 (.69)	- .25 (- .90)	- .07 (- .52)	.49 (2.39)*
EXTBIDL-EXTDIDL	.06 (.47)	- .40 (- 1.39)	- .09 (- .59)	.57 (2.68)**
EXTBIDL-INTDINST	.10 (.78)	.28 (.90)	- .12 (- .74)	.11 (.48)
INTBINST-INTDIDL	- .00 (- .01)	- .26 (- 1.31)	- .12 (- 1.18)	.07 (.46)
INTBINST-EXTDIDL	- .01 (- .06)	- .24 (- 1.07)	- .38 (- 3.37)**	.01 (.05)
INTBINST-INTDINST	- .04 (- .37)	.12 (.51)	- .26 (- 2.13)*	- .13 (- .75)
INTDIDL-EXTDIDL	- .10 (- 1.07)	- .09 (- .40)	- .17 (- 1.45)	.12 (.71)
INTDINST-EXTDIDL	- .04 (- .43)	.08 (.35)	- .46 (- .38)	- .22 (- 1.24)

(continued on next page)

Table 6 - 18 (continued) **Results of Individual Tests for Measured Independent Variables (Socialization Backgrounds of Bureaucrats)**

Dependent Variables \ Measured Independent Variables	Most Influential Person's Job		Atmosphere of Communications within Family	
	FARMER	SELFEMP	AUTHFMLY	AVEFMLY
Conceptual Components of Bureaucratic Ideology				
BURO	.09 (.04)	1.62 (.73)	.41 (.21)	- 3.29 (- 1.28)
INTBURO	- .35 (- .18)	1.01 (.51)	.09 (.05)	- 2.66 (- 1.17)
INTBIDL	.45 (.53)	.11 (.13)	- .04 (- .06)	- 1.15 (- 1.15)
EXTBIDL	.54 (.72)	.43 (.57)	.51 (.77)	- .57 (- .64)
INTBINST	- .80 (- .62)	.89 (.69)	.13 (.12)	- 1.51 (- 1.00)
Conceptual Components of Democratic Ideology				
DEMO	.95 (.64)	- .44 (- .29)	.41 (.32)	.18 (.10)
LIBDEMO	- .00 (- .00)	- .19 (- .24)	.14 (.20)	1.26 (1.37)
POPDEMO	.89 (1.19)	- .28 (- .38)	.34 (.52)	- .55 (- .63)
INTDEMO	1.15 (1.10)	.02 (.02)	.61 (.67)	- .21 (- .18)
INTPDEMO	.77 (1.14)	- .14 (- .21)	.55 (.93)	- .07 (- .09)
INTDIDL	.45 (.89)	.11 (.21)	.21 (.47)	- .29 (- .48)
EXTDIDL	- .20 (- .25)	- .45 (- .58)	- .19 (- .29)	.40 (.44)
INTDINST	.70 (1.01)	- .09 (- .13)	.40 (.66)	.07 (.09)
Attitudinal Congruity				
BURO-DEMO	- .07 (- .75)	- .15 (- 1.70)	.02 (.30)	.03 (.28)
BURO-LIBDEMO	- .08 (- .80)	- .22 (- 2.27)*	- .04 (- .46)	- .15 (- 1.34)
BURO-POPDEMO	- .04 (- .44)	- .13 (- 1.39)	- .01 (- .10)	.09 (.84)

(continued on next page)

Table 6 - 18 (continued) **Results of Individual Tests for Measured Independent Variables (Socialization Backgrounds of Bureaucrats)**

Dependent Variables \ Measured Independent Variables	Most Influential Person's Job		Atmosphere of Communications within Family	
	FARMER	SELFEMP	AUTHFMLY	AVEFMLY
Attitudinal Congruity (continued)				
INTBURO-INTDEMO	- .03 (- .39)	- .06 (- .72)	.01 (.18)	.07 (.64)
INTBURO-INTPDEMO	- .00 (- .01)	- .12 (- 1.32)	.02 (.30)	.13 (1.23)
INTBIDL-INTDIDL	.07 (.87)	- .45 (- .55)	.11 (1.47)	.23 (2.37)*
INTBIDL-EXTDIDL	.04 (.43)	- .16 (- 1.64)	.01 (.09)	- .05 (- .45)
INTBIDL-INTDINST	.01 (.05)	- .11 (- 1.09)	.04 (.41)	- .05 (- .40)
EXTBIDL-INTDIDL	.12 (1.02)	.03 (.25)	- .10 (- .94)	.03 (.20)
EXTBIDL-EXTDIDL	.01 (.08)	- .07 (- .59)	- .05 (- .48)	- .06 (- .46)
EXTBIDL-INTDINST	- .03 (- .24)	- .11 (- .86)	- .13 (- 1.17)	- .07 (- .47)
INTBINST-INTDIDL	- .15 (- 1.90)	- .09 (- 1.11)	- .01 (- .15)	.08 (.87)
INTBINST-EXTDIDL	- .15 (- 1.67)	- .14 (- 1.55)	- .03 (- .41)	- .09 (- .80)
INTBINST-INTDINST	- .05 (- .47)	- .00 (- .01)	- .06 (- .72)	.03 (.26)
INTDIDL-EXTDIDL	- .09 (- .96)	- .19 (- 1.97)	.07 (.82)	.10 (.91)
INTDINST-EXTDIDL	.02 (.24)	.04 (.39)	- .07 (- .80)	- .11 (- .95)

Note: Estimated regression coefficients presented in table are those of full models where all measured independent variables listed in Fig. 5-3 are included. For convenience of presentation, however, result of estimation is presented by types of traits. Numbers without parentheses are estimates of partial regression coefficient. Numbers in parentheses are t-values. "*" indicates t-value is at 5% significance level. "**" indicates t-value is at 1% significance level. For substantive notation meanings and measurement schemes for dependent and independent variables, see Tab. 5-2, Tab. 5-3, and Fig. 5-2.

Table 6 - 19 **Results of Joint Impact Tests for Sub-Independent Variables of Cultural Traits of Bureaucrats**

Sub-Independent Variables / Dependent Variables	Religious Culture: (PROTEST, CATHOLIC, BUDDHIST, NONE)	Societal Culture: (MATERIAL, MIXCULT)	Perspectives on Work-Related Human Nature: (THEOX, XYMIXED)
Conceptual Components of Bureaucratic Ideology			
BURO	.017 (1.342)	.013 (1.946)	.031 (4.808)**
INTBURO	.016 (1.273)	.015 (2.430)	.029 (4.550)*
INTBIDL	.008 (.650)	.017 (2.701)	.027 (4.233)*
EXTBIDL	.014 (.860)	.001 (.136)	.010 (1.239)
INTBINST	.020 (1.464)	.011 (1.608)	.025 (3.681)*
Conceptual Components of Democratic Ideology			
DEMO	.005 (.363)	.033 (4.361)*	.013 (1.750)
LIBDEMO	.003 (.188)	.042 (5.263)**	.003 (.366)
POPDEMO	.006 (.426)	.013 (1.836)	.014 (1.968)
INTDEMO	.006 (.366)	.019 (2.521)	.008 (1.003)
INTPDEMO	.003 (.182)	.009 (1.159)	.009 (1.156)
INTDIDL	.014 (.929)	.013 (1.834)	.015 (1.984)
EXTDIDL	.014 (.933)	.030 (3.903)*	.014 (1.903)
INTDINST	.003 (.180)	.017 (2.110)	.002 (.249)
Attitudinal Congruity			
BURO-DEMO	.003 (.164)	.002 (.233)	.010 (1.280)
BURO-LIBDEMO	.004 (.265)	.005 (.722)	.025 (3.329)*
BURO-POPDEMO	.003 (.215)	.005 (.564)	.001 (.185)

(continued on next page)

Table 6 - 19 (continued) **Results of Joint Impact Tests for Sub-Independent Variables of Cultural Traits of Bureaucrats**

Sub-Independent Variables / Dependent Variables	Religious Culture: (PROTEST, CATHOLIC, BUDDHIST, NONE)	Societal Culture: (MATERIAL, MIXCULT)	Perspectives on Work-Related Human Nature: (THEOX, XYMIXED)
Attitudinal Congruity (continued)			
INTBURO-INTDEMO	.021 (1.350)	.001 (.076)	.002 (.258)
INTBURO-INTPDEMO	.005 (.348)	.003 (.439)	.001 (.102)
INTBIDL-INTDIDL	.050 (3.335)*	.013 (1.693)	.000 (.024)
INTBIDL-EXTDIDL	.012 (.769)	.005 (.613)	.008 (1.017)
INTBIDL-INTDINST	.005 (.336)	.000 (.062)	.000 (.034)
EXTBIDL-INTDIDL	.021 (1.343)	.000 (.056)	.000 (.007)
EXTBIDL-EXTDIDL	.006 (.373)	.013 (1.661)	.006 (.815)
EXTBIDL-INTDINST	.004 (.221)	.003 (.378)	.005 (.598)
INTBINST-INTDIDL	.027 (1.701)	.002 (.260)	.001 (.141)
INTBINST-EXTDIDL	.012 (.815)	.009 (1.241)	.018 (2.369)
INTBINST-INTDINST	.012 (.820)	.004 (.521)	.005 (.646)
INTDIDL-EXTDIDL	.003 (.163)	.003 (.404)	.004 (.467)
INTDINST-EXTDIDL	.007 (.470)	.006 (.785)	.016 (2.054)

Note: Numbers without parentheses are difference between R^2 of a full model where all independent variables are included and that of a restricted model where set of independent variables specified at the top of the column are excluded. Numbers within parentheses are F-values of R^2 difference. "*" indicates F-value is at 5% significance level. "**" indicates F-value is at 1% significance level. For substantive notation meanings and measurement schemes for dependent and independent variables, see Tab. 5-2, Tab. 5-3, and Fig. 5-2.

sub-independent variable, "perspectives on work-related human nature" are concentrated mostly on the dependent variables that represent bureaucrats' internalization of democratic ideology. As mentioned in Chapter Five, "perspectives" are operationalized in my study into the measured independent variables that reflect McGregor's (1960) categories of perspectives on work-related human nature (i.e., Theory X vs. Theory Y). Thus, the finding indicates that McGregor's categories *as a whole* are valid, especially for explaining the variations among individual bureaucrats in their internalization of bureaucratic ideology.

The results of t-tests for the measured independent variables specifying "cultural traits" enable us to examine the extent to which the ideological traits of individual bureaucrats represented by the dependent variables differ by the specific cultural categories. Of the results of joint impact tests performed for all measured independent variables that are considered in my study, those that are related to the cultural traits of bureaucrats are summarized in Table 6-20.

The results of t-tests pertaining to the measured independent variables that specify the "religious culture," indicate that there is no significant difference among Protestants, Catholics, Buddhists, Confucians, and those with no religion in the degree of their internalization of bureaucratic and democratic ideology. That is, the regression coefficients of the measured independent variables representing the sub-categories of religions, which are included in the regression models as dummy variables,[32] are statistically insignificant for all dependent variables that represent the extent to which bureaucrats internalize bureaucratic and democratic ideologies.

This finding makes a conventional tendency of Korean scholars invalid. That is, many Korean scholars who study the culture of Korean politico-administrative systems tend to ascribe a reason for the prevalence of the authoritarian, bureaucratic culture to the long tradition of Confucianism.[33] If there is a difference between Confucians and non-Confucians in the degree to which they internalize bureaucratic ideology, this ascription can be said to be correct. My empirical finding, however, indicates that there is no such difference between Confucians and non-Confucians.

The finding is also inconsistent with the Weberian notion that Protestantism contributes to the development of rational, bureaucratic ideology.[34] Like the case of Confucianism, if there is a significant difference between Protestants and non-Protestants in the degree to which they internalize bureaucratic ideology, the Weberian notion is empirically confirmed. My empirical finding, however, indicates that there is no such difference between them.[35]

As a result of the t-tests pertaining to the measured independent variables that represent Inglehart's categories of societal culture, it is found that the regression coefficients of MATERIAL, which represents "materialistic" bureaucrats, are positive and significant for INTBURO and INTBIDL, while negative and significant for DEMO, LIBDEMO, INTDEMO, and EXTDIDL.

Table 6 - 20 **Results of Individual Tests for Measured Independent Variables (Cultural Traits of Bureaucrats)**

Dependent Variables \ Measured Independent Variables	Religious Culture			
	PROTEST	CATHOLIC	BUDDHIST	NONE
Conceptual Components of Bureaucratic Ideology				
BURO	4.23 (1.07)	1.17 (.27)	4.03 (1.06)	.40 (.11)
INTBURO	3.37 (.97)	.55 (.14)	3.77 (1.13)	.56 (.17)
INTBIDL	1.05 (.69)	.62 (.37)	1.17 (.80)	.09 (.06)
EXTBIDL	1.63 (1.21)	1.45 (.97)	.72 (.55)	.45 (.35)
INTBINST	2.32 (1.01)	- .07 (- .03)	2.60 (1.18)	.47 (.21)
Conceptual Components of Democratic Ideology				
DEMO	2.26 (.84)	.50 (.17)	1.92 (.74)	1.92 (.74)
LIBDEMO	.32 (.23)	- .28 (- .18)	.46 (.34)	.02 (.01)
POPDEMO	.95 (.71)	.13 (.09)	.55 (.43)	1.05 (.82)
INTDEMO	.47 (.25)	.30 (.14)	1.33 (.74)	1.25 (.69)
INTPDEMO	.18 (.15)	- .30 (- .22)	.07 (.06)	.37 (.32)
INTDIDL	.75 (.82)	.43 (.42)	1.34 (1.53)	.97 (1.11)
EXTDIDL	1.78 (1.29)	.21 (.14)	.58 (.44)	.67 (.51)
INTDINST	- .27 (- .22)	- .13 (- .10)	- .01 (- .01)	.28 (.23)
Attitudinal Congruity				
BURO-DEMO	- .05 (- .32)	- .07 (- .43)	- .10 (- .68)	- .09 (- .58)
BURO-LIBDEMO	- .08 (- .46)	- .04 (- .20)	- .03 (- .18)	.02 (.10)
BURO-POPDEMO	- .04 (- .23)	- .08 (- .45)	- .09 (- .55)	- .11 (- .68)

(continued on next page)

Table 6 - 20 (continued) **Results of Individual Tests for Measured Independent Variables (Cultural Traits of Bureaucrats)**

Dependent Variables \ Measured Independent Variables	Religious Culture			
	PROTEST	CATHOLIC	BUDDHIST	NONE
Attitudinal Congruity (continued)				
INTBURO-INTDEMO	- .09 (- .57)	- .27 (-1.54)	- .25 (-1.66)	- .17 (-1.14)
INTBURO-INTPDEMO	.02 (.15)	- .10 (- .56)	- .05 (- .30)	- .06 (- .39)
INTBIDL-INTDIDL	- .39 (-2.62)**	- .44 (-2.65)**	- .52 (-3.58)**	- .39 (-2.70)**
INTBIDL-EXTDIDL	.07 (.43)	.23 (1.20)	.10 (.63)	.18 (1.12)
INTBIDL-INTDINST	.06 (.32)	- .02 (- .11)	- .06 (- .37)	.02 (.11)
EXTBIDL-INTDIDL	- .40 (-1.92)	- .49 (-2.13)*	- .35 (-1.79)	- .44 (-2.20)*
EXTBIDL-EXTDIDL	- .19 (- .88)	- .03 (- .12)	- .10 (- .50)	- .12 (- .57)
EXTBIDL-INTDINST	- .05 (- .20)	.05 (.18)	- .00 (- .01)	- .08 (- .37)
INTBINST-INTDIDL	- .20 (-1.41)	- .34 (-2.14)*	- .23 (-1.64)	- .14 (-1.00)
INTBINST-EXTDIDL	- .15 (- .92)	- .03 (- .14)	.02 (.13)	- .02 (- .10)
INTBINST-INTDINST	.06 (.35)	- .15 (- .76)	.02 (.13)	- .05 (- .31)
INTDIDL-EXTDIDL	- .11 (- .63)	- .12 (- .65)	- .13 (- .79)	- .12 (- .76)
INTDINST-EXTDIDL	.03 (.17)	.10 (.52)	.16 (.94)	.08 (.48)

(continued on next page)

Table 6 - 20 (continued) **Results of Individual Tests for Measured Independent Variables (Cultural Traits of Bureaucrats)**

Dependent Variables \ Measured Independent Variables	Societal Culture		Perspective on Work-Related Human Nature	
	MATERIAL	MIXCULT	THEOX	XYMIXED
Conceptual Components of Bureaucratic Ideology				
BURO	5.56 (1.89)	3.70 (1.25)	- 7.91 (-3.06)**	- 2.49 (- 1.45)
INTBURO	5.41 (2.09)*	3.50 (1.35)	- 6.72 (-2.96)**	- 2.27 (- 1.51)
INTBIDL	2.56 (2.25)*	1.75 (1.53)	- 2.91 (-2.91)**	- .56 (- .84)
EXTBIDL	.47 (.47)	.52 (.52)	- 1.39 (-1.57)	- .29 (- .50)
INTBINST	2.85 (1.67)	1.74 (1.02)	- 3.82 (-2.54)*	- 1.71 (- 1.72)
Conceptual Components of Democratic Ideology				
DEMO	- 5.35 (-2.67)**	- 3.04 (-1.52)	- 3.01 (-1.71)	- 1.48 (- 1.27)
LIBDEMO	- 2.75 (-2.62)**	- 1.16 (-1.10)	- .79 (- .85)	- .13 (- .22)
POPDEMO	- 1.83 (-1.84)	- 1.22 (-1.22)	- 1.42 (-1.63)	- .92 (- 1.60)
INTDEMO	- 3.03 (-2.17)*	- 2.06 (-1.47)	- 1.25 (-1.02)	- 1.02 (- 1.26)
INTPDEMO	- 1.37 (-1.52)	- 1.08 (-1.19)	- 1.04 (-1.31)	- .60 (- 1.15)
INTDIDL	- 1.30 (-1.91)	- 1.06 (-1.55)	- .94 (-1.58)	- .66 (- 1.66)
EXTDIDL	- 2.32 (-2.26)*	- .98 (- .95)	- 1.76 (-1.95)	- .45 (- .76)
INTDINST	- 1.72 (-1.87)	- 1.00 (-1.08)	- .31 (- .38)	- .37 (- .69)
Attitudinal Congruity				
BURO-DEMO	- .04 (- .37)	- .07 (- .62)	- .14 (-1.31)	- .09 (- 1.30)
BURO-LIBDEMO	- .13 (-1.01)	.02 (.10)	- .04 (- .34)	- .19 (- 2.53)*
BURO-POPDEMO	- .00 (- .04)	- .11 (- .68)	- .01 (- .07)	.04 (.55)

(continued on next page)

Table 6 - 20 (continued) **Results of Individual Tests for Measured Independent Variables (Cultural Traits of Bureaucrats)**

Dependent Variables \ Measured Independent Variables	Societal Culture		Perspective on Work-Related Human Nature	
	MATERIAL	MIXCULT	THEOX	XYMIXED
Attitudinal Congruity (continued)				
INTBURO-INTDEMO	.01 (.13)	- .17 (-1.14)	- .07 (- .72)	- .02 (- .23)
INTBURO-INTPDEMO	.03 (.24)	- .06 (- .39)	- .03 (- .33)	.01 (.19)
INTBIDL-INTDIDL	- .09 (- .78)	- .39 (-2.70)**	.02 (.22)	.00 (.07)
INTBIDL-EXTDIDL	- .11 (- .85)	.18 (1.12)	- .10 (- .91)	- .10 (- 1.34)
INTBIDL-INTDINST	.04 (.28)	.02 (.11)	.01 (.09)	.02 (.26)
EXTBIDL-INTDIDL	- .05 (- .31)	- .44 (-2.20)*	.02 (.12)	.00 (.03)
EXTBIDL-EXTDIDL	.19 (1.19)	- .12 (- .57)	- .07 (- .54)	- .12 (- 1.27)
EXTBIDL-INTDINST	.02 (.09)	- .08 (- .37)	- .02 (- .10)	- .11 (- 1.06)
INTBINST-INTDIDL	- .08 (- .72)	- .14 (-1.00)	- .01 (- .13)	- .03 (- .53)
INTBINST-EXTDIDL	- .18 (-1.44)	- .12 (- .10)	- .08 (- .73)	- .15 (- 2.18)*
INTBINST-INTDINST	.13 (1.00)	- .05 (- .31)	- .13 (-1.34)	- .03 (- .43)
INTDIDL-EXTDIDL	- .08 (- .60)	- .12 (- .76)	- .06 (- .56)	- .07 (- .93)
INTDINST-EXTDIDL	.16 (1.23)	.08 (.48)	.07 (.63)	- .12 (- 1.62)

Note: Estimated regression coefficients presented in table are those of full models where all measured independent variables listed in Fig. 5-3 are included. For convenience of presentation, however, estimation result is presented by types of traits. Numbers without parentheses are estimates of partial regression coefficient. Numbers in parentheses are t-values. "*" indicates t-value is at 5% significance level. "**" indicates t-value is at 1% significance level. For substantive notation meanings and measurement schemes for dependent and independent variables, see Tab. 5-2, Tab. 5-3, and Fig. 5-2.

The excluded category of the dummy variable for measured independent variables represents "post-materialistic" bureaucrats. Thus, the finding indicates that "materialistic" bureaucrats are more likely than "post-materialistic" bureaucrats to internalize the internal bureaucratic ideology (INTBURO), especially the internal bureaucratic ideals (INTBIDL) rather than the external bureaucratic ideals (EXTBIDL). The finding also indicates that "materialistic" bureaucrats are less likely than "post-materialistic" bureaucrats to internalize the general concept of democratic ideology (DEMO); more specifically, the liberal democratic ideology (LIBDEMO) is defined both in internal and external contexts of governmental agencies.

Recall here that, as reviewed in Chapter Two, Morrow and Thayer (1978) equate bureaucratic ideals (i.e., organizational efficiency and effectiveness) with "materialism." In addition, they argue that bureaucratic ideals are in conflict with "humanism," the substantive content of which is quite similar to Inglehart's "post-materialism." Morrow and Thayer's position is confirmed by a part of my empirical findings that "materialistic" bureaucrats are more likely than "post-materialistic" bureaucrats to internalize internal bureaucratic ideals (INTBIDL).

The t-tests for the measured independent variables representing the subcategories of "perspectives on work-related human nature," produce a result that is consistent with an implicit belief underlying the classical organization theories. As characterized by McGregor (1960) in a critical tone, classical organization theorists view the individuals within organizations as "Theory X"-types, and maintain that for this type of people, bureaucratic managerial principles are the best means for attaining bureaucratic ideals of organizations (i.e., efficiency and effectiveness). If McGregor's characterization is true, an implicit belief underlying this position of classical theorists is that "Theory X"-type individuals are ones who do not internalize the intra-organizational bureaucratic ideals to a significant degree. This belief is especially consistent with the test result that the regression coefficient of THEOX, which represents the "Theory X"-type bureaucrats, is negative and statistically significant for the dependent variable, INTBIDL that represents intra-organizational bureaucratic ideals. This result indicates that "Theory X"-type bureaucrats internalize the intra-organizational bureaucratic ideals less than non-"Theory X"-type bureaucrats, including those who hold the "Theory Y"-type perspective on work-related human nature and those who hold the mixed type perspective.[36]

That the test result of the regression coefficient of THEOX for the dependent variable INTBINST is negative and statistically significant suggests that implementing the recommendation of classical organization theorists (i.e., managing the "Theory X"-type bureaucrats with the bureaucratic managerial principles) may not be an easy task. This is because the result indicates that of the three types of bureaucrats, those who hold the "Theory X" perspective on work-related human nature agree with the bureaucratic managerial principles to the least degree. In other words, the result suggests that "Theory X"-type bureaucrats are the most likely to experience value conflicts as bureaucratic managerial principles are implemented, and thus, to resist it.

Finally, the t-tests for measured independent variables representing the sub-categories of "perspectives on work-related human nature" reveal that the regression coefficients of THEOX for the dependent variables that are classified in the second and third sets are all statistically insignificant. This result indicates that there is an insignificant difference between "Theory X"-type and "Theory Y"-type bureaucrats in the extent to which they internalize democratic ideology and in the extent to which they regard the conceptual components of bureaucratic and democratic ideologies as compatible with each other.

Theoretical Implications of the Explanatory Analysis

The findings from the explanatory analysis presented thus far have two theoretical implications. First, one of the major concerns in my analysis is which theory of human psychology is the most powerful in explaining the ideological traits of bureaucrats. The results of my analysis suggest that organization theory and cultural theory are better than macro-sociological theories, such as socio-economic theory and socialization theory.

Second, as discussed earlier, the objective approach to the compatibility thesis is prevalent in the fields of organization theory and Public Administration. The finding that both organizational and cultural traits are significant factors that affect the ideological traits of bureaucrats, however, highlights the necessity of a new approach in which the objective and subjective approaches are intermingled. In order to develop this new approach, serious attention should be given to clarifying the nature and dynamics of the link between bureaucrats' subjective worlds and the objective organizational structures surrounding them.

Third, the results of the explanatory analysis also highlight the importance of developing a cultural theory of organization and public administration. Although the cultural theory has been recently resurrected in many other fields, it has not received any serious attention in the fields of organization and Public Administration.[37] Given the finding that cultural traits of bureaucrats are salient determinants of their ideological traits, it may be said that culture is one of the important keys to understanding, explaining, and handling the tension between bureaucracy and democracy in modern societies. This cultural theory can be established firmly by clarifying the nature of the links between culture and the operation of institutions, including organizations and public administrative agencies, and between culture and the ideological traits of bureaucrats.

Practical Implications of the Explanatory Analysis

Reformers who wish to find ways to drive bureaucrats to highly internalize both bureaucratic and democratic ideologies would welcome the finding that the organizational traits of individual bureaucrats are significant determinants of their ideological traits. This is because the organizational traits are essentially the managable ones. Personnel management, for example, may directly determine what kinds of organizational traits individual bureaucrats come to have.

The results of joint impact tests for the sub-independent variables representing the sub-categories of organizational traits help reformers determine the key organizational traits for an effective reform. As previously mentioned, it is found that, of the eight sub-categories of organizational traits, types of office (whether at the main or regional offices), official ranking, and routinization of work procedures are the major determinants of the ideological traits of individual bureaucrats. This finding indicates that reformers would be better off by focusing upon these three types of organizational traits of individual bureaucrats rather than on other types.

In addition, the results of joint impact tests clarify what kinds of ideological traits of individual bureaucrats are contingent upon the management of these key organizational traits. It is found that "types of office" and "official ranking" are significant determinants of the extent to which individual bureaucrats internalize bureaucratic ideology and how they regard the conceptual components of bureaucratic and democratic ideologies. These organizational traits, however, are not found as significant determinants of the extent to which the individual bureaucrats internalize democratic ideology. In contrast, "routinization of work procedures" is found as a significant determinant of all these ideological traits of bureaucrats. Given these findings, it may be said that insofar as the reformers are concerned with the enhancement of bureaucrats' internalization of democratic ideology, a reform that is based upon the management of work procedures is more effective than the one that is based upon the management of promotion, or the one that is based on transferring individual bureaucrats between the main and regional offices.

The results of t-tests for the measured independent variables representing the sub-categories of organizational traits also help reformers determine the target groups for their reforms. That is, the results of t-tests clarify who has more or less of which ideological traits than others. For example, it is found that those who work in the main office internalize few conceptual components of bureaucratic ideology as compared to those who work in the regional offices. If, for example, the goal of a reform is to enhance the level of bureaucrats' internalization of bureaucratic ideology, the finding suggests that the major target of the reform would be those who work in the main office, rather than those who work in the regional offices. This kind of inference of practical implications can be applied to the results of t-tests for all other measured independent variables representing the sub-categories of organizational traits.

NOTES

1 The results of my LISREL analyses are summarized by six figures (i.e., Figures 6-1 through 6-6). These figures commonly display two types of relationships. First, they show the relationships among factors that represent the conceptual components of bureaucratic and democratic ideologies. In the figures, the factors are depicted by circles, and the relationships among these factors are depicted by double arrows. The numbers beside these double arrows are the coefficients of correlations among the factors that are estimated by the maximum likelihood method. Second, the figures display the relationships between the conceptual components and their empirical indicators. The empirical indicators, which are depicted by boxes, are the individual items in the questionnaire. If, and only if, an item is empirically verified as a reliable and valid measure of a certain conceptual component of bureaucratic or democratic ideology, a single arrow is drawn between the indicator that represents the item and the factor that represents the conceptual component. In the methodological literature these relationships are called "factor loadings." A factor loading is essentially a measure of the extent to which a factor is responsible for the variations of responses to a certain questionnaire item. Thus, the factor loading (the sign and the statistical significance of its magnitude) illustrates the extent to which we can take a questionnaire item as a reliable and valid indicator of a certain conceptual component.

2 In my study, the bureaucratic ideals and instrumental principles addressed by classical organization theorists are reflected in the conceptual components, INTBIDL and INTBINST, respectively. The democratic ideals and the instrumental principles addressed by neo-classical organization theorists are reflected in the conceptual components, INTDIDL and INTDINST, respectively.

3 For the proponents of New Public Administration, competition as a primary principle for producing public goods and services, citizens' freedom of choice, and openness to the public; for the critical theorists of Public Administration, special care for the poor, alienated, and underprivileged people.

4 The bureaucratic ideals and democratic ideals addressed by the proponents of anti-compatibility argument in the field of Public Administration are reflected in my conceptual components INTBIDL and INTDIDL, respectively.

5 The bureaucratic and democratic ideals covered in the arguments of these authors are reflected generally and particularly in my measures of EXTBIDL and EXTDIDL. A dichotomy between public administration and politics is reflected particularly in B5 and generally in B1. Maintenance of order in society is generally reflected in B5 and B8. Maintaining predictability by planning is generally reflected in B13. The liberal democratic ideals, competition as a primary principle for producing public goods and services and citizens' freedom of choice, are directly reflected in D6 and generally in D1 and D2. A popular democratic ideal, openness to the public, is particularly reflected in D16. Finally, an egalitarian democratic ideal, special care for the poor, alienated, and underprivileged people, is particularly reflected in D11.

6 For a detailed description of this Q-sorting procedure, see Chapter Five.

7 Brown (1980:222-223) warns that determining the number of Q-factors based upon the size of eigen values may not be a good method because it "can frequently result in leaving behind sizeable residuals and significant factors." Thus, he recommends that, even if a Q-factor is identified as insignificant under this method, the factor should be chosen as a significant Q-factor if it meets one of the following two criteria: (a) if the factor has at least two significant loadings, and (b) if the cross-product of the factor's two highest loadings (ignoring sign) exceeds twice the standard error. Following this recommendation, I have applied these two criteria to the factors having the eigen values that are smaller than one. As shown in Table 6-1, none of these factors met these criteria.

8 The perspective represented by Factor A will be called Perspective A; another perspective represented by Factor B will be called Perspective B; and another perspective represented by Factor C will be called Perspective C. Because most subjects are loaded on Factors A and B, it may be said that, of these three perspectives, Perspectives A and B are dominant group perspectives and Perspective C is a minor group perspective.

9 Note that the values used for representing the response scale are not the conventional factor scores, but what Brown (1980) calls "the rounded factor scores" of the statements. The rounded factor scores are obtained

through a series of converting procedures (cf., Brown, 1980:239-247). The factor scores of statements for each Q-factor are standardized and arranged by their relative size. Each of the 11 values of the response scale used for the original Q-sorting chart (-5, -4, -3, -2, -1, 0, +1, +2, +3, +4, +5) are assigned for groups of statements in accordance with the relative size of the statements' standardized factor scores and the number of cells assigned to each of the 11 response categories used in the original Q-sorting chart. In my case, for example, the original Q-sorting chart is composed of 48 cells with two cells for ±5, three cells for ±3 and ±4, six cells for ±1 and ±2, and eight cells for 0. Thus, the two statements of the standardized factor scores of which are the two highest receive the response scale value +5, and are placed in the two cells located on the far-right piles of the Q-sorting chart. Similarly, the two statements that have a rounded factor score of -5 (i.e., those placed in the two cells of the far-left piles) are ones that have the two lowest standardized factor scores for each Q-factor. The eight statements that have the rounded factor score of 0 (i.e., those placed in the eight cells of the middle pile) are ones that have the eight middle standardized factor scores.

A major benefit of using the rounded scores instead of the conventional factor scores is that the factor scores of the statements can be interpreted directly in terms of the original response scale. That is, the rounded factor score +5 means that the corresponding statement is evaluated as "the most democratic" *collectively* by a group of subjects factored by a Q-factor. -5 indicates that the corresponding statement is evaluated as "the most undemocratic." 0 indicates that the statement is evaluated as "irrelevant" to the concept of democratic ideology, and so on. In addition, the conversion does not result in losing the property of normal distribution that is obtained when using the standardized factor scores. This is because the cells in the original Q-sorting response scale chart are forced to be distributed normally. That is, the rounded factor scores of statements are distributed on the Q-sorting chart have a mean score of 0 and a standard deviation of 1. Because of this property, the conventional method of checking the statistical significance of factor scores still works well for the rounded factor scores. That is, the statements of rounded factor scores of which are equal to or greater than +3 are interpreted as indicating that they are evaluated as highly democratic. Similarly, the statements of the rounded factor scores of which are equal to or less than -3 are interpreted as indicating that they are evaluated as highly undemocratic. The scores approaching zero (i.e., ±1 and ±2) are interpreted as indicating that the statements are sorted out as "slightly democratic" for positive scores or "slightly undemocratic" for negative scores.

Note here that the interpretation of the rounded factor scores of statements is focused not upon the statements themselves, but the conceptual components of bureaucratic and democratic ideologies expressed by the statements. Insofar as these conceptual components are concerned, the interpretation of the rounded factor scores takes two forms depending upon the ways in which the conceptual components are phrased in the statements. Most conceptual components are positively worded. In order to avoid socially-predetermined responses, however, several conceptual components are worded in a negative way. For the positively-phrased statements, the positive rounded factor scores indicate that the conceptual components expressed by these statements are evaluated as "democratic." The negative rounded factor scores indicate that the conceptual components expressed by the statements are evaluated as "undemocratic." For the negatively-phrased statements, however, the interpretation regarding the conceptual components that I originally wished to deal with before having them negatively expressed is opposite to that of the rounded factor scores of the statements. That is, the positive scores of these statements are interpreted as indicating that, although the statements themselves are sorted out as democratic, the original conceptual components expressed by these statements are regarded as undemocratic by the subjects. Similarly, the negative scores indicate that the original conceptual components are regarded as democratic. The interpretation of the magnitudes of rounded factor scores are the same for both types of statements. For example, while preparing my survey, the issue of democracy within government organizations had been given wide media coverage as a group of mid-level officials in the Ministry of Construction revolted against the minister (cf., *Hangyorye Shinmun*, August 22, 23, 28; see also the five major Korean newspapers issued between August 20 and August 31). A conceptual component of democratic ideology, "individual freedom in the workplace," is negatively expressed by statement D4 as "It is not desirable to treat every member of my department as an independent being who has complete free-will because if so, the management of internal affairs will become a mess." A positive score of this statement is interpreted as indicating that the subjects regard the concept, "individual freedom in the workplace," as "undemocratic"; and the negative factor score of this statement is interpreted as indicating that the subjects regard it as "democratic."

The effect of question wording upon my results is not significant. For example, the conceptual component, "individual freedom in the workplace," is phrased both positively (statement D5) and negatively (statement D4). As illustrated in Table 6-4, the factor score of D5 for Factor A is +2. On the other hand, the factor score of D4 for the same Q-factor is -3. Converting a negative factor score of D4 into a positive one, the factor score of D4 indicates that those who are grouped into Factor A regard the conceptual component as democratic by +3. Therefore, the difference between the factor score of positively-phrased statements and that of negatively-phrased statements is one that is negligible. Finally, note that the term, factor scores, used hereafter, indicates the rounded factor scores unless otherwise noted.

10 The statistical significance of rounded factor score differences is calculated by referring to Brown (1980:244-246). In order to determine whether the rounded factor scores associated with two Q-factors are significantly different, it is necessary to combine their respective errors into the standard error of difference:

$$SED_{X\text{-}Y} = \sqrt{SE_X^2 + SE_Y^2}, \text{ where}$$

$SED_{X\text{-}Y}$ = standard error of difference between the rounded factor scores associated with a Q-factor, X and those associated with another Q-factor, Y,
SE_X = standard error of the rounded factor scores associated with a Q-factor, X,
SE_Y = standard error of the rounded factor scores associated with a Q-factor, Y.

Because three Q-factors are identified, there are three possible comparisons, three standard errors of the rounded factor scores for each Q-factor, and three standard errors of rounded factor score difference:

$$SE_A = .45; \quad SE_B = .45; \quad SE_C = .73$$

$$SE_{A\text{-}B} = \sqrt{(.45)^2 + (.45)^2} = .64$$

$$SE_{A\text{-}C} = \sqrt{(.45)^2 + (.73)^2} = .86$$

$$SE_{B\text{-}C} = \sqrt{(.45)^2 + (.73)^2} = .86$$

Under these conditions, difference scores are expected to follow a normal curve. Thus, applying the 1% significance level, I accept as significantly different the scores that differ by an amount in excess of 2.58 (SED):

$$2.58\ (SED_{A\text{-}B} = .64) = 1.65 \approx 2$$

$$2.58\ (SED_{A\text{-}C} = .86) = 2.22 \approx 3$$

$$2.58\ (SED_{B\text{-}C} = .86) = 2.22 \approx 3$$

Since the rounded factor scores can only differ by whole numbers, the figures are rounded upward to remain on the conservative side. Consequently, when comparing Perspective A with Perspective B, the rounded factor scores differing by 2 or more are considered to be significantly different. When comparing Perspective A with Perspective C or when comparing Perspective B with Perspective C, the rounded factor scores differing by 3 or more are considered significantly different.

Based upon this result, the uniqueness of Perspective A is described by those "democratic" statements, the rounded factor scores of which differ by 2 or more between Factor A and Factor B and simulatneously by 3 or more between Factor A and Factor C. Similarly, the uniqueness of Perspective B is described by those "democratic" statements, the rounded factor scores of which differ by 2 or more between Factor A and Factor B and, at the same time, by 3 or more between Factor B and Factor C. The uniqueness of Perspective C is described by those statements, the rounded factor scores associated with Factor C of which differ by 3 or more from the same statements' factor scores associated with Factor A and Factor B.

11 To some readers, Perspective B may be interpreted as similar to Perspective A in that what is regarded as highly democratic by those who hold Perspective B is also regarded as highly democratic by those who hold Perspective A. But note that those who hold Perspective B regard a smaller number of democratic conceptual components as highly democratic than those who hold Perspective A. In addition, some readers may think that Perspective B is consistent with the theoretical version of democratic ideology in that the conceptual components regarded as highly democratic by those who hold this perspective coincide with those that are emphasized by the organizational and Public Administration theorists. But note that the conceptual components regarded as highly democratic by those who hold Perspective B are a fairly small portion of the entire theoretical conceptual components of democratic ideology examined in this study.

12 The theoretical conceptual components of democratic ideology rejected by each group of subjects are illustrated in Table 6-4. For the positively-expressed conceptual components, they are ones where the rounded factor scores are negative or zero. For the negatively-expressed conceptual com-

ponents, they are ones where the factor scores are positive or zero. For example, those who hold Perspective A reject "popular sovereignty in the workplace" expressed by statement D13 (i.e., factor score is -3), and "equality in a general sense" expressed by statement D8 (i.e., factor score is 0). Those who hold Perspective B reject "individual freedom in the workplace" expressed by statements D3 and D5 (i.e., factor scores are -2 and -3, respectively). Those who hold Perspective C reject "popular sovereignty in the workplace" expressed by statements D12 and D13. Many other theoretical conceptual components of democratic ideology are rejected by the subjects.

13 My inference of practical implications from the empirical findings presented hereafter is more speculative than definitive. It is based upon simple hypotheses that *ceteris paribus*, those who highly internalize bureaucratic or democratic ideology, would behave bureaucratically or democratically. It clearly needs further elaborate empirical evidence of the link between the ideological traits of bureaucrats and their actual behaviors.

14 It may be said that those who hold Perspective A also need the ideological reorientation in that, as will be shown later, of the three groups of subjects, they are ones who regard most of the conceptual components of bureaucratic and democratic ideologies as being incompatible with each other. Note, however, that the desirability of whether they regard the conceptual components of bureaucratic and democratic ideologies as being compatible or incompatible should not be determined in a general sense. If the major concern is the effectiveness of the objective measures to make bureaucracy be compatible with democracy, the existence of many bureaucrats who regard the bureaucratic and democratic conceptual components as being incompatible with one another is undesirable. This is because, other things being equal, imposition of the objective measures to these bureaucrats will curtail value conflicts in their minds. Therefore, these bureaucrats are likely to resist the implementation of the objective measures. In addition, if the subjective incompatibility is led by low internalization of bureaucratic ideology and high internalization of democratic ideology, then one might say that the incompatibility is desirable. Even for this case, however, the determination must be cautious. This is because the positive aspect of bureaucratic ideology (e.g., efficiency and effectiveness) is still desirable. In sum, whether subjective incompatibility is desirable or not depends on what kinds of ideology the evaluator is aimed at.

15 In calculating the average score, the signs for the statements that negative-

ly express the conceptual components were reversed. The substantive meaning of the average rounded factor score of each set of statements is the overall evaluation of a group of subjects on the democratic-*ness* of a composite conceptual component of bureaucratic or democratic ideology expressed *collectively* by the set of statements.

16 When the relationships among the conceptual components of bureaucratic ideology are the major concerns, a group of subjects are interpreted as regarding any two conceptual components of bureaucratic ideology as compatible with one another if the signs of the average rounded factor scores of the sets of statements pertaining to these conceptual components are the same (it does not matter whether they are positive or negative). They are interpreted so also if the scores are all zero. The substantive reasoning behind this inference is that, when such relationships are the major concern, the conceptual components can be compatible with each other, even if they are undemocratic or irrelevant to the concept of democratic ideology.

17 The comparisons between the bureaucratic and democratic conceptual components in the signs of average rounded factor scores, however, reveals that there is a difference between those who are grouped by Factor A and those who are grouped by Factor B or Factor C in the reasoning behind their common view of compatibility. Those who are grouped by Factor A pose the view of compatibility regarding all of the three conceptual components of bureaucratic ideology as undemocratic, and all the three conceptual components of democratic ideology as democratic. In other words, their view of compatibility is based upon a sharp distinction between the bureaucratic and democratic conceptual components in the property of democratic-*ness*. In contrast, those who are grouped by Factor B pose the view of compatibility without making this sharp distinction. That is, they regard all of the three democratic conceptual components and two of the three bureaucratic conceptual components (i.e., the internal and external bureaucratic ideals) as democratic, and one bureaucratic conceptual component (i.e., the internal bureaucratic instrumental principles) as irrelevant to the concept of democratic ideology. For those who are grouped by Factor C, all of the three bureaucratic conceptual components and the two conceptual components of democratic ideology (i.e., the external democratic ideals and the internal democratic instrumental principles) are regarded as democratic; and one conceptual component of democratic ideology (i.e., the internal democratic ideals) is regarded as undemocratic.

18 The perspective of those who are grouped by Factor C is irrelevant to this assessment. This is because they regard the internal liberal democratic ideals themselves as undemocratic (i.e., the average rounded factor score is -.60).

19 The perspectives of those who are grouped by Factors B or C are not relevant to this assessment. This is because they do not regard the internal popular democratic ideals as democratic (i.e., the average rounded factor score for those who are grouped by Factor B and those who are grouped by Factor C are -.67 and -1.67, respectively).

20 For the specific content of these types of traits, see Table 5-3.

21 As presented in Table 35-2, I consider 29 dependent variables. The number of measured independent variables that I consider is 39. I regressed each of the 29 dependent variables on all of the 39 measured independent variables. Thus, the total number of full regression models that I dealt with is 29. For each of these 29 full regression models, I considered the four sets of restricted models. For example, the full regression model that I considered in examining the joint impact of the four types of traits on a dependent variable, bureaucrats' internalization of bureaucratic ideology (BURO), is:

$$BURO_i = \alpha_0 + \alpha_1 OFFICE_i + \alpha_2 INDECON_i + \alpha_3 ENV_i + \alpha_4 WELF + \alpha_5 INTORD_i + \alpha_6 PUBREL_i + \alpha_7 YRSERVE_i + \alpha_8 HIRANK_i + \alpha_9 MIDRANK_i + \alpha_{10} JOBCLAS_i + \alpha_{11} ROUTINE_i + \alpha_{12} MIDROUTN_i + \alpha_{13} SUPERIOR_i + \alpha_{14} SUBORDNT_i + \alpha_{15} AGE_i + \alpha_{16} INCOME_i + \alpha_{17} PREUNIV_i + \alpha_{18} UNIV_i + \alpha_{19} SEX_i + \alpha_{20} RURAL_i + \alpha_{21} MIDURBAN_i + \alpha_{22} POOR_i + \alpha_{23} AVECON_i + \alpha_{24} PARNTDIE_i + \alpha_{25} DIVORCE_i + \alpha_{26} PUBURO_i + \alpha_{27} PVBURO_i + \alpha_{28} FARMER_i + \alpha_{29} SELFEMP_i + \alpha_{30} AUTHFMLY_i + \alpha_{31} AVEFMLY_i + \alpha_{32} PROTEST_i + \alpha_{33} CATHOLIC_i + \alpha_{34} BUDDHIST_i + \alpha_{35} NONE_i + \alpha_{26} MATERIAL_i + \alpha_{37} MIXCULT_i + \alpha_{38} THEOX_i + \alpha_{39} XYMIXED_i + \varepsilon_i$$

The restricted model that I considered in order to examine the impact of the organizational traits as a whole is:

$$BURO_i = \beta_0 + \beta_1 AGE_i + \beta_2 INCOME_i + \beta_3 PREUNIV_i + \beta_4 UNIV_i + \beta_5 SEX_i + \beta_6 RURAL_i + \beta_7 MIDURBAN_i + \beta_8 POOR_i + \beta_9 AVECON_i + \beta_{10} PARNTDIE_i + \beta_{11} DIVORCE_i +$$

β_{12}PUBURO$_i$ + β_{13}PVBURO$_i$ + β_{14}FARMER$_i$ + β_{15}SELFEMP$_i$ + β_{16}AUTHFMLY$_i$ + β_{17}AVEFMLY$_i$ + β_{18}PROTEST$_i$ + β_{19}CATHOLIC$_i$ + β_{20}BUDDHIST$_i$ + β_{21}NONE$_i$ + β_{22}MATERIAL$_i$ + β_{23}MIXCULT$_i$ + β_{24}THEOX$_i$ + β_{25}XYMIXED$_i$ + υ_i

Notice that except for the first 14 indepedent variables that are supposed to collectively measure the organizational traits, all indepedent variables in the full model are included in the restricted model. If the R^2 of the full model is significantly greater than that of the restricted model, then the null hypothesis, $H_0: \alpha_1 = \alpha_2 = \alpha_3 = \alpha_4 = \alpha_5 = \alpha_6 = \alpha_7 = \alpha_8 = \alpha_9 = \alpha_{10} = \alpha_{11} = \alpha_{12} = \alpha_{13} = \alpha_{14} = 0$, is rejected. It is then inferred that the organizational traits as a whole have a significant impact on bureaucrats' internalization of bureaucratic ideology. If the R^2-difference is not statistically significant, then the null hypothesis is accepted. For this case, it is inferred that the organizational traits as a whole do not have a significant impact on bureaucrats' internalization of bureaucratic ideology.

The same logic is applied to the examinations of the impacts of the other three types of traits. The only difference is the content of the null hypothesis and the independent variables specified in the restricted models. For the socio-economic traits, the null hypothesis is: $\alpha_{15} = \alpha_{16} = \alpha_{17} = \alpha_{18} = \alpha_{19} = 0$, and the restricted model is the same as the full model except that the independent variables associated with these coefficients (i.e., AGE, INCOME, PREUNIV, UNIV, and SEX) are excluded as follows:

BURO$_i$ = γ_0 + γ_1OFFICE$_i$ + γ_2INDECON$_i$ + γ_3ENV$_i$ + γ_4WELF$_i$ + γ_5INTORD$_i$ + γ_6PUBREL$_i$ + γ_7YRSERVE$_i$ + γ_8HIRANK$_i$ + γ_9MIDRANK$_i$ + γ_{10}JOBCLAS$_i$ + γ_{11}ROUTINE$_i$ + γ_{12}MIDROUTN$_i$ + γ_{13}SUPERIOR$_i$ + γ_{14}SUBORDNT$_i$ + γ_{15}RURAL$_i$ + γ_{16}MIDURBAN$_i$ + γ_{17}POOR$_i$ + γ_{18}AVECON$_i$ + γ_{19}PARNTDIE$_i$ + γ_{20}DIVORCE$_i$ + γ_{21}PUBURO$_i$ + γ_{22}PVBURO$_i$ + γ_{23}FARMER$_i$ + γ_{24}SELFEMP$_i$ + γ_{25}AUTHFMLY$_i$ + γ_{26}AVEFMLY$_i$ + γ_{27}PROTEST$_i$ + γ_{28}CATHOLIC$_i$ + γ_{29}BUDDHIST$_i$ + γ_{30}NONE$_i$ + γ_{31}MATERIAL$_i$ + γ_{32}MIXCULT$_i$ + γ_{33}THEOX$_i$ + γ_{34}XYMIXED$_i$ + ν_i

For the socialization backgrounds, the null hypothesis is: $\alpha_{20} = \alpha_{21} = \alpha_{22} = \alpha_{23} = \alpha_{24} = \alpha_{25} = \alpha_{26} = \alpha_{27} = \alpha_{28} = \alpha_{29} = \alpha_{30} = \alpha_{31} = 0$, and the restricted model is the same as the full model except that the independent variables associated with these coefficients (i.e., RURAL, MIDURBAN,

POOR, AVECON, PARNTDIE, DIVORCE, PUBURO, PVBURO, FARMER, SELFEMP, AUTHFMLY, and AVEFMLY) are excluded as follows:

$$\begin{aligned} BURO_i = {} & \varpi_0 + \varpi_1 OFFICE_i + \varpi_2 INDECON_i + \varpi_3 ENV_i + \varpi_4 WELF_i + \\ & \varpi_5 INTORD_i + \varpi_6 PUBREL_i + \varpi_7 YRSERVE_i + \varpi_8 HIRANK_i \\ & + \varpi_9 MIDRANK_i + \varpi_{10} JOBCLAS_i + \varpi_{11} ROUTINE_i + \\ & \varpi_{12} MIDROUTN_i + \varpi_{13} SUPERIOR_i + \varpi_{14} SUBORDNT_i + \\ & \varpi_{15} AGE_i + \varpi_{16} INCOME_i + \varpi_{17} PREUNIV_i + \varpi_{18} UNIV_i + \\ & \varpi_{19} SEX_i + \varpi_{20} PROTEST_i + \varpi_{21} CATHOLIC_i + \\ & \varpi_{22} BUDDHIST_i + \varpi_{23} NONE_i + \varpi_{24} MATERIAL_i + \\ & \varpi_{25} MIXCULT_i + \varpi_{26} THEOX_i + \varpi_{27} XYMIXED_i + \omega_i \end{aligned}$$

For the cultural traits, the null hypothesis is: $\alpha_{32} = \alpha_{33} = \alpha_{34} = \alpha_{35} = \alpha_{36} = \alpha_{37} = \alpha_{38} = \alpha_{39} = 0$, and the restricted model is the same as the full model except that the independent variables associated with these coefficients (i.e., PROTEST, CATHOLIC, BUDDHIST, NONE, MATERIAL, MIXCULT, THEOX, and XYMIXED) are excluded as follows:

$$\begin{aligned} BURO_i = {} & \delta_0 + \delta_1 OFFICE_i + \delta_2 INDECON_i + \delta_3 ENVI_i + \delta_4 WELF_i + \\ & \delta_5 INTORD_i + \delta_6 PUBREL_i + \delta_7 YRSERVE_i + \delta_8 HIRANK_i + \\ & \delta_9 MIDRANK_i + \delta_{10} JOBCLAS_i + \delta_{11} ROUTINE_i + \\ & \delta_{12} MIDROUTN_i + \delta_{13} SUPERIOR_i + \delta_{14} SUBORDNT_i + \\ & \delta_{15} AGE_i + \delta_{16} INCOME_i + \delta_{17} PREUNIV_i + \delta_{18} UNIV_i + \\ & \delta_{19} SEX_i + \delta_{20} RURAL_i + \delta_{21} MIDURBAN_i + \delta_{22} POOR_i + \\ & \delta_{23} AVECON_i + \delta_{24} PARNTDIE_i + \delta_{25} DIVORCE_i + \\ & \delta_{26} PUBURO_i + \delta_{27} PVBURO_i + \delta_{28} FARMER_i + \\ & \delta_{29} SELFEMP_i + \delta_{30} AUTHFMLY_i + \delta_{31} AVEFMLY_i + \tau_i \end{aligned}$$

This set of joint impact tests were performed for each of the remaining 28 dependent variables.

22 This is the finding when the 5% significance level is used. When the 10% significance level is used, only one variable (i.e., number of superiors) is found as not having a significant explanatory power.

23 A similar hypothesis was tested by Wynia (1979). He hypothesized that "the less 'social' oriented the agency, the more 'anti-democratic' the attitudes [of the bureaucrats working in the agency]." He found that "social agency bureaucrats consistently agree less with the [anti-democratic] items than either defense or other agency bureaucrats" (Wynia, 1979:160).

24 This classification was heavily relied upon the opinions of the experts on the organizational functions of Seoul city government agencies. Classified as dealing with the control-oriented policy are those agencies which are in charge of maintaining the internal order of Seoul city government (e.g., the Bureau of Internal Affairs in the main office, the Office of Inspection and the Bureau of General Affairs in the regional offices), regulating pollution and environmental protection (e.g., the Bureau of Parks and Environments in the main office, the Section of Public Health and Environments in the main offices), and maintaining economic order and security (e.g., the Bureau of Industrial and Economic Affairs in the main office and the Section of Industrial Affairs in regional affairs). Classified as dealing with the service-oriented policy are agencies which are in charge of providing special care for the poor (e.g., the Bureau of Social Welfare in the main office, the Section of Social and Family Welfare and the Regional City Hospital in the Main offices) and providing public information to the citizen and handling their complaints (e.g., Office of Public Relations in the main office and the Office of Public Relations and Citizen Counseling in the main offices).

25 Viewed from the methodological stance, this finding suggests that the control-vs.-service scheme used for classifying the characteristics of policies may not be appropriate for explaining the variations of the internalization of democratic ideology among bureaucrats.

26 MIDRANK represents the mid-ranking officials (i.e., the 5th graders).

27 This is the coefficient of MIDRANK for the dependent variable that represents the congruity between bureaucrats' internalization of the internal bureaucratic instrumental principles and those of the internal democratic instrumental principles.

28 The only notable difference between these two groups of bureaucrats is found in the extent to which they regard the internal bureaucratic ideals (INTBIDL) and the external democratic ideals (EXTDIDL) as compatible with one another. The negative sign of the regression coefficients of ROUTINE and MIDROUTN for this dependent variable indicates that those who deal with routinized work are less likely than those who deal with unroutinized work to regard these conceptual components of bureaucratic and democratic ideologies as compatible.

29 This third group of officials is treated as the category that is excluded from the regression model.

30 For an extensive review of socialization theory and research, see Goslin (1971).

31 For specific explanations of the measurement scheme by which I operationalize these variables, see Table 5-3.

32 "Confucian" is treated as a category of the dummy variable that is excluded from the regression model.

33 See, for example, Paik (1982), Ahn (1984), and Kim (1981). These authors commonly ascribe the reason for the link between Confucianism and bureaucratic psychology and culture to the hierarchical relations to the theological elements of Confucianism such as the world view of orderliness and the emphasis on the hierarchical relationships among people as a major means for maintaining the order of the world.

34 See, for example, Weber (1958) and Inglehart (1988).

35 Another notable finding is that the regression coefficient pertaining to the dependent variable, INTBIDL-INTDIDL, is consistently significant and negative for all measured independent variables representing the subcategories of religious culture. This indicates that non-Confucian bureaucrats are less likely than Confucian bureaucrats to regard bureaucratic and democratic ideologies defined in the intra-organizational context of governmental agencies as compatible with one another. This is an interesting finding, but one that awaits reasonable theological explanations.

36 "Theory Y"-type bureaucrats are treated as a category of the dummy variable that is excluded in the regression models. Those who hold the mixed perspective are represented by the measured independent variable, XYMIXED.

37 For the recent re-focus on the cultural theory in other fields, see Chapter One.

Part III

Conclusion

Chapter 7

Summary and Suggestions for Further Research

Summary

The major premise that has guided my study presented thus far is that the extent to which bureaucracy can be compatible with democracy depends not only upon how it is institutionally structured, but also upon how the key officials within bureaucracy understand the ideologies (i.e., ideals and instrumental principles) embedded in the institutional structures. Following this premise, I have examined the subjective dimension of the compatibility thesis, focusing on two types of research questions: descriptive and explanatory questions. The descriptive questions examined in this research are: "To what extent are bureaucratic and democratic ideologies regarded as compatible or incompatible with one another in the minds of bureaucrats?" "How do bureaucrats understand the theoretical conceptual components that have been emphasized as important ingredients of democratic ideology in the fields of organization theory and Public Administration?" "To what extent are bureaucrats' own conceptions of democratic ideology consistent with the theoretical conceptions of democratic ideology?" The explanatory questions examined in this research are: "What kinds of factors affect the ideological traits incorporated in the descriptive research questions?" "To what extent are the cultural factors like religion, societal culture, and perspectives on work-related human nature more or less powerful than the objective factors like organizational, socio-economic, and socializational traits of bureaucrats in determining the ideological traits of bureaucrats?"

I have examined these research questions using the data that I collected from a series of surveys of randomly selected Seoul city government officials. For the descriptive research questions, I have analyzed the data both within the conventional R-methodological framework and within Q-methodological analysis. For the explanatory research questions, I have analyzed the data using the techniques of multiple regression analysis. The results of these empirical analyses were used for assessing the empirical validity of a number of conflicting debates about the compatibility thesis posed in the fields of organization theory and Public Administration. In addition, a number of practical strategies for making bureaucracy compatible with democracy were inferred from the results of analyses.

As a result of the R-methodological descriptive analyses, it was found that Seoul city government officials perceive most of the conceptual components of bureaucratic and democratic ideologies addressed in the fields of organization theory and Public Administration as compatible with each other.[1] The results of Q-methodological descriptive analyses, however, revealed that this R-methodological finding may be true only for a part of Seoul city government officials. That is, it was found that a substantial portion of the subjects investigated within the framework of Q-methodology regard many of conceptual components of bureaucratic and democratic ideologies as incompatible with each other. In addition, the Q-methodological descriptive analyses revealed that a multiple number of perspectives on democratic ideology exist among Seoul city government officials, and the theoretical version of democratic ideology is consistent with only one of these perspectives. That is, it was found that a substantial portion of the subjects investigated within the framework of Q-methodology, regard as undemocratic or irrelevant to the concept of democratic ideology, many conceptual components which have been emphasized as salient ingredients of democratic ideology in the theoretical literature of organizations and public administration.

Based upon the comparison between R- and Q-methodological results, I maintained that both R- and Q-methodologies are useful for exploring the subjective dimension of the compatibility thesis. That is, Q-methodology enables us to do what we can hardly do with R-methodology; that is, "thick descriptions" of the subjective understandings of bureaucrats about the conceptual components of bureaucratic and democratic ideologies and the compatibility among the conceptual components. On the other hand, R-methodology enables us to overcome a drawback of Q-methodology; that is, generalization of the results of analysis to population.

As a result of the explanatory analyses, it was found that of the four types of individual bureaucrats' traits (organizational, socio-economic, socializational, and cultural), the organizational and cultural traits are the most significant determinants of the ideological traits of bureaucrats. I interpreted this finding as an indication that insofar as Seoul city government officials are concerned, the reformers who wish to make bureaucracy compatible with democracy may have to deal with two factors: one that is managable (i.e., organizational traits) and the other that is beyond direct management (i.e., cultural traits). The finding that the impact of cultural factors on the ideological traits of bureaucrats is discernable, even if the other three types of traits are controlled, and highlights the significance of cultural studies. That is, the finding suggests that, unlike the critique of structuralists against cultural studies, cultural factors are not the negligible residue of social phenomena that is left out after being explained by structural factors like the organizational, socio-economic, and socializational aspects of social life.

In sum, my study has implications in three areas: methodological, practical, and theoretical. First, my study suggests that in exploring the subjective dimension of the compatibility thesis, reliance upon the R-methodological approach combined with the Q-methodological approach is better than using the former alone.

Second, although further elaborate research is needed, my descriptive analyses suggest that ideological reorientation may be of crucial necessity for Seoul city government officials and Korean bureaucrats as a whole, if the results of my study can be generalized to the whole population of Korean bureaucrats. It is found that there are considerable variations in who internalizes what kinds of democratic ideology. This suggests that the attempt toward this ideological orientation should be selective, or to put it in other terms, strategic. The simplest strategies, for example, would be that the democratic ideological components that must be emphasized are ones that are not highly internalized, and that those who have to be targeted are ones who do not highly internalize many components of democratic ideology. In addition, my explanatory analyses highlight the significance of personnel management in handling the ideological traits of bureaucrats. The analysis suggests that the effective measures are particularly promotional systems and rotation of bureaucrats across the main and regional offices, and across routinized and unroutinized jobs.

Third, my study has several theoretical implications. First, it reveals that democratic theory is one thing and the empirical reality is another. That is, there is a gap between the theoretical version of democratic ideology and the conception of the ideology construed within the minds of bureaucrats. Second, the objective approach to the compatibility thesis which is prevalent in the fields of organization theory and Public Administration should be replaced by a new theoretical framework in which objective and subjective approaches are intermingled. In order to develop this new framework, serious attention should be given to clarifying the nature and dynamics of the link between bureaucrats' subjective worlds and the objective, institutional structures surrounding them. Third, my study also highlights the importance of developing the cultural theory of organization and administration. Although it has been resurrected in many fields, cultural theory has not received any serious attention in the fields of organization and Public Administration. The links between culture and the operation of institutions, including organizations and public administrative agencies, and between culture and the ideological traits of bureaucrats, and the influence of culture on the link between institutions and the ideological traits of bureaucrats are keys to understanding, explaining, and handling the tension between bureaucracy and democracy in modern societies.

Suggestions for Further Research

Mosher (1968:1) laid down the premise that the kinds of decisions and actions key administrative officials take, depend on their orientations and their values. If we accept this premise, then my study needs additional and extensive research that is aimed at clarifying the link between the ideological traits of bureaucrats identified by my research and their actual decisions and actions. To what extent do those officials, who are identified as regarding bureaucratic and democratic ideologies as (in)compatible with one another, actually make decisions that are (in)compatible with the ideals of democracy? To what extent do those officials who are identified as internalizing bureaucratic or democratic ideology to a high degree actually make decisions that are bureaucratic or democratic? What kinds of factors affect the link between the ideological traits of bureaucrats and their actual decisions? One might be able to study these questions effectively by combining the methods used in this research will enable us to assess the validity of basic beliefs underlying my inference of the practical implications for democratic reforms of bureaucracy from the empirical findings.

Another interesting research project that is worth being pursued as an extension of my study is comparative in nature. My study is confined to Korean bureaucrats. This characteristic of my study is limiting in two respects. First, because it focuses upon bureaucrats only, my study lacks a reference group by which we can assess the extent to which the ideological traits identified in my study are desirable. Second, because it focuses upon bureaucrats in only one country, the wide variety of cultural and institutional factors that are often found at the inter-country level, cannot be incorporated into the study. These kinds of limits can be overcome by a comparative research design in which the ideological traits of bureaucrats are compared to those of other groups of people such as politicians, interest group leaders, and general citizens across several countries that are culturally and institutionally different from each other.

My explanatory analyses also suggest an important thesis for future research. As presented in the previous chapter, it was found that the ideological traits of bureaucrats are not determined by the same independent variables. For example, the significant impact of the organizational traits were detected mostly on the dependent variables representing the extent to which the respondents internalize bureaucratic ideology and the extent to which they regard the conceptual components of bureaucratic and democratic ideologies as compatible with each other. The dependent variables representing the extent to which the respondents internalize democratic ideology were found as not being significantly determined by most of the organizational traits. I suspected that this might be caused by the variations in response scores associated with the dependent variables representing the bureaucrats' internalization of democratic ideology. I could not, however, find any consistent pattern of response scores that supports this suspicion. Given the rejection of such methodological reason, a substantive reason might be the next possibility. Existing research and theories, however, are not specific enough to assist in the search for this reason. I envision that further intensive and extensive research about the substantive reasons will provide valuable information which can enrich existing explanatory theories about the determinants of ideological traits of bureaucrats and even other groups of people.

Finally, but not the least importantly, the timing of my research and the events that have recently occurred in Korea suggests that further research can be built upon my findings. After my survey research was done, very important institutional changes have occurred in the Korean politico-administrative systems. Nationwide elections for constituting local legislators were held in March and June 1991, the first to be scheduled since the early 1960s. Elections for city mayors were held soon afterwards. As noted earlier in Chapter Five, these elections signal fundamental institutional changes in the Seoul city government. It will be out of the direct control of the central government. Seoul city government officials will no longer be enshrined in the institutional layers, safeguarding them against the external demands from citizens for direct and indirect voices in critical policy decisions. Internally, the regional offices of the Seoul city government will no longer be under the direct control of the main office. Further research that is worth being pursued after these institutional changes are combined with my study, this further research will enable us to examine such important issues as the extent to which institutional change affects the subjective beliefs and attitudinal systems of individuals, including bureaucrats.

NOTES

1 Compatible in the sense that their internalization of a conceptual component are significantly and positively correlated with those of another conceptual component.

Appendix I

Questionnaire

PART I: Items for Measuring Independent Variables

Socio-economic Traits

1-1. (Age) How old are you? ______________ years old

1-2. (Annual Family Income) How much is your annual family income? (in ten thousand won) ______________

1-3. (Level of Education) Which of the following educational institutions is the one from which you graduated most recently?
(1) elementary school (2) middle school (3) high school
(4) college (5) graduate school
(6) others (specify ______________)

1-4. (Gender) I am: (1) male (2) female

Socialization Backgrounds

2-1. (Region Where Grown-Up) Where did you mostly live when you were between the ages of 12 and 18?
(1) small town (i.e., eup or myon) (2) medium-size city (i.e., all cities other than the six biggest cities)
(3) large metropolitan city (i.e., the six biggest cities) (4) other (specify ______________)

Note: Original questionnaire written in Korean. Format and content of questionnaire presented here are slightly different from ones used for actual survey. For convenience of reference, variable names are added and sequence of items are rearranged by variable name. Also, items used in actual survey but deleted in final analysis are omitted. Specific coding scheme is presented in Table 5-3.

2-2. (Family Economic Conditions) How was the economic condition of your family when you were between the ages of 12 and 18?
(1) very poor (2) poor (3) slightly poor (4) ordinary
(5) slightly rich (6) rich (7) very rich

2-3. (Early Loss of Parents) Were your parents alive when you were between the ages of 12 and 18?
(1) both parents were alive (2) father was dead
(3) mother was dead (4) both parents were dead

2-4. (Experience of Parental Divorce) What was your parents' marital status when you were between the ages of 12 and 18?
(1) never divorced (2) divorced

2-5. (The Most Influential Person's Job) When you were between the ages of 12 and 18, what was the job of the person who made the most significant influence on your future? Be as specific as possible. ____________
____

2-6. (Family Atmosphere Pertaining to Freedom of Self-Expression) When you were between the ages of 12 and 18, what was the atmosphere of your family like in terms of freedom of self-expression?
(1) very strict (2) strict (3) slightly strict (4) average
(5) slightly free (6) free (7) very free

Organizational Traits

3-1. (Types of Office and Major Policy) I work at:
(1) a regional office
(2) a main office (specify name of Bureau and Section ____________)

3-2. (Length of Service) How long have you been a government official?
__________ years

3-3. (Hierarchical Rank and Job Classification) What is your job classification and official ranking?
(1) general administrative (2) technical (Grade: __________)

3-4. (Degree of Routinization of Work Procedures) How routinized are the procedures of the work you usually do?
(1) very routinized (2) routinized (3) slightly routinized
(4) average (5) slightly unroutinized
(6) unroutinized (7) very unroutinized

3-5. (Number of Superiors) How many superiors affect your task performance? Specify number of persons ___

3-6. (Number of Subordinates) How many subordinates do you have whose task performance you can directly affect? Specify number of persons ___

Cultural Traits

4-1. (Religious Cultural Traits) What kind of religion do you have?

(1) Protestantism	(2) Catholicism	(3) Confucianism
(4) Buddhism	(5) no religion	(6) others

4-2. (Inglehart's Cultural Categories: "Materialistic Culture" vs. "Post-Materialistic Culture") Which of the following 12 goals do you consider most or least important? Please write a number (1 to 12) beside each item. 1 indicates "the most important" and 12 indicates "the least important."

__ Maintain order in the nation
__ Give people more say in government decisions
__ Fight rising prices
__ Protect freedom of speech
__ Maintain strong defense forces
__ Give people more say in work and community decisions
__ Maintain high economic growth rate
__ Make our cities and countryside more beautiful
__ Maintain a stable economy
__ Fight against crime
__ Move toward a friendlier, less impersonal society
__ Move toward a society where ideas count more than money

4-3. (Perspectives on Work-Related Human Nature) How much do you agree with each of the following statements? Write a number from 1 to 7, where a smaller number indicates you agree with the statement to a lesser degree.

(Theory X Perspective)

"Intrinsically, humans do not like to work. Whether they come to like work depends on external conditions."	Answer: ___

Note: For brevity, each indicator is designated in the main text by the notation presented in front of it (e.g., B1, B2, D1, D2, etc.). Indicators noted with one asterick are those pertaining to external context of public administration; those noted with two astericks are those that are context neutral; and indicators having no asterick are those pertaining to internal context. Indicators to be coded reversely are noted with "(R)."

(Theory Y Perspective)

"Intrinsically, humans like to work. Whether they come to dislike work depends on external conditions."

Answer: ____

PART II: Indicators for Examining Bureaucrats' Attitudes and Beliefs About, and Subjective Understandings of, the Conceptual Components of Bureaucratic and Democratic Ideologies

I. The Bureaucratic Ideology Scales

(1) Bureaucratic Ideals:

a. Instrumental Rationalism

**(B1) "One's life should be centered more around the attainment of substantive goals than around the processes of achieving goals." (R) (cf., Chackerian and Abcarian, 1984:16)

(B2) "In performing a task, it is more important to think of how one's task performance contributed to the overarching goals of the department and the city government than to think of how to achieve these goals." (R)

a-1. Efficiency

(B3) "The best honor should be given to the one who has produced the largest amount of output with the least amount of input, no matter what kinds of tasks are given to him/her."

a-2. Effectiveness

(B4) "At all times, any mission given to the staff in my department must be accomplished 100%."

a-3. Dichotomy Between Politics and Public Administration

*(B5) "Politics is one thing, public administration is another. Politicians should devote themselves to finding which policy goals are the most desirable to the development of society; while public administrators should devote themselves to finding the best means for accomplishing the policy goals given by the politicians."

*(B6) "Public administrators must perform faithfully the policy-missions given by the legislators, regardless of whether he/she likes or dislikes the missions."

*(B7) "Just as management in private companies should be separated from ownership in private companies, so the administration of public affairs must be separated from the affairs of politics."

b. Maintenance of Order

**(B8) "One should not like diversity without order, because it means chaos."

**(B9) "In order for diversity to be meaningful, it must exist within the framework of order."

(B10) "Every staff member in my department must perform the tasks given to him or her in a well-ordered way."

b-1. Stability

**(B11) "In most cases, 'stability' should be preferred to 'change'."

(B12) "Any situation or persons who push me to change my own work style or procedures which I have firmly established for a fairly long time should be minimized."

b-2. Planned Predictability

**(B13) "Every action must be planned thoroughly before it is taken."

**(B14) "The consequences of all actions must be predicted as accurately as possible."

(B15) "Every task within my department must be planned so that it can be performed in a predictable way."

(2) Bureaucratic Instrumental Principles

a. Hierarchy of Authority and Control

(B16) "As a person's rank becomes higher, he/she deserves to exercise more authority to command and control those who are lower than him/her in rank."

(B17) "All official activities of any public administrator must be thoroughly checked by those who are above him/her in rank."

b. Unity of Command

(B18) "All missions within my department must be ordered not by a multiple number of bosses, but by a single boss."

c. Division of Labor

(B19) "All functions within my department should be arranged according to the principle of division of labor."

d. Simplification, Standardization, and Specialization of Task-Performance

(B20) "All procedures for task-performance should be simplified, standardized, and specialized."

e. Technical Competence

(B21) "All persons within my department should be selected, positioned, and promoted according to their technical competence."

(B22) "All persons within my department should be periodically evaluated to see how well they are doing." (cf., Hall, 1963:35)

(B23) "The public administrator should become a real 'pro' who can handle the task given to him in the most expert way."

f. Impersonality

(B24) "The relationships among all personnel must be official. All types of private and personal relationships must be minimized."

g. Task-Performance Based Upon Formal Rules and Regulations

(B25) "Every task within my government must be performed strictly according to well-defined rules and regulations."

h. Reliance on and Use of Written Documents

(B26) "All work should be done in the form of written documents."

2. *The Democratic Ideology Scales*

(1) Democratic Ideals

a. Liberal Democratic Ideal (Individual Freedom)

**(D1) "All individual human beings must be treated as having complete free will in determining their own fates."

**(D2) "All individual human beings must be protected so that they can choose freely their own courses of action without being interfered with by others."

(D3) "Within my department, the number of those who prevent other staff from having freedom of action should be minimized as much as possible."

(D4) "It is not desirable to treat every member of my department as an independent being who has complete free-will, because, if so, the management of internal affairs will become a mess." (R)

(D5) "One's personal life goals should be more important than the goals of organization to which he/she belongs."

*(D6) "Just as the best economic system is one in which the consumer's freedom of choice can be maximized, so is the best public administrative system, one in which the enhancement of individual citizens' freedom to choose the kinds and quantity of public goods and services they want to purchase is treated as the number one axiom in the value scale of public administration."

b. Egalitarian Democratic Ideal (Equality)

**(D7) "We have to teach our children that all people are created equal, but almost everyone knows that some are better than others." (R) (cf., Wynia, 1974:158)

**(D8) "One must behave in accordance with his/her social status." (R)

c. Popular Democratic Ideals

c-1. Popular Sovereignty

(D12) "The ability of the chief executive officer of an organization must be evaluated first of all by the extent to which the results induced by him/her are meaningful to all other staff members within the organization."

(D13) "A big, powerful group of persons who can run the whole show in my department without considering others should be prevented as much as possible from emerging."

*(D14) "Public administrators' responsibility to legislators and citizens are confined only to those affairs for which the law requires the administrators to be responsible. It is an excessive request to ask public administrators to have even a moral responsibility to them beyond the legally defined sphere of responsibility." (R)

c-2. Openness

(D15) "It is much better for the details of one's task not to be known too much to other staff members."

*(D16) "What is happening within this city government should be known to the public as much as possible."

(2) Democratic Instrumental Principles

a. Liberal Democratic Instrumental Principle (Self-Directed Task-Performance)

(D17) "Every individual staff member of my department must be encouraged as much as possible to use his/her own judgement in performing his/her task."

(D18) "It is much more desirable to let projects of my department be carried out by those staff members who share similar personalities or characteristics than by those whose personalities and characteristics are quite different." (R)

b. Equalitarian Democratic Instrumental Principle (Participation by the Disadvantaged Minority)

(D19) "It is not necessary to be concerned with every detail of the rank-and-files' opinions in making a crucial decision which may affect their interests." (R)

(D20) "All rank-and-file staff members should be allowed to have a formal right to participate in meetings where people make decisions that are critical to the fate of my department as a whole."

c. Popular Democratic Instrumental Principle (Consensus-Based Decision-Making

(D21) "All decisions pertaining to the internal affairs of my department must be based upon wide consensus among all members of my department whose interests may be affected by the decision."

(D22) "Even if a decision is made by high-ranking officials in my department, the decision should not be implemented if the majority of staff in my department oppose it."

Appendix II

Reliability and Validity of Questionnaire: A Multiple Indicator Approach

Composition of Multiple Indicators

Respondents' attitudes and beliefts about the conceptual components of bureaucratic and democratic ideologies which I theoretically construed in Chapter Four were measured with 48 questionnaire items (i.e., 26 items pertaining to bureaucratic ideology notated B1 through B26, and 22 items pertaining to democratic ideology notated D1 through D22.) Following the multiple indicator approach, I group the items into sets of multiple items (each set is called a multiple indicator) under a supposition that items included in a set will collectively measure the attitudes and beliefs about a conceptual component (see those checked in Tables AII-1 and AII-2).

I empirically tested the appropriateness of the composition of these original multiple inidicators in two ways. I used the reliability of each questionnaire item as a criterion for determining the appropriateness of each item to be a part of the multiple indicators. I judged that an item can be an appropriate component of a multiple indicator if, and only if, the item is reliable. As I mentioned in Chapter Five, I performed this test within the framework of the test-retest method, using the data obtained from the first and second tasks performed by the 30 respondents in Office C. As presented in Table AII-1, it was found that most of the questionnaire items are reliable. Of the 22 democratic items, only one item (D3) did not pass this test. Of the 26 bureaucratic items, four items did not pass this test.[1]

In addition, the inappropriateness was also tested within the framework of confirmatory factor analysis. In this test, each conceptual component was treated as a common factor producing the variations of, and covariations among, the response scores on the component items that construe a multiple indicator. The core logic of this test was that in order for an item to be an appropriate com-

Table AII - 1 **Reliability of Individual Questionnaire Items**

Items	Reliability Coefficients	Items	Reliability Coefficients	Items	Reliability Coefficients
B1	.5050*	B18	.5675*	D9	.5866*
B2	.4982*	B19	.5170*	D10	.5647*
B3	.5948*	B20	.6627*	D11	.5833*
B4	.5189*	B21	.6698*	D12	.4881*
B5	.5340*	B22	.8073*	D13	.5895*
B6	.3529	B23	.6927*	D14	.7525*
B7	.2881	B24	.2091	D15	.6966*
B8	.4609*	B25	.4627*	D16	.9061*
B9	.7815*	B26	.7247*	D17	.5078*
B10	.6692*	D1	.5258*	D18	.8016*

(continued on next page)

Table AII - 1 (continued) **Reliability of Individual Questionnaire Items**

Items	Reliability Coefficients	Items	Reliability Coefficients	Items	Reliability Coefficients
B11	.6119*	D2	.6870*	D19	.4974*
B12	.2990	D3	.5483*	D20	.8105*
B13	.5480*	D4	.3374	D21	.5984*
B14	.7247*	D5	.7263*	D22	.6108*
B15	.6633*	D6	.7216*	Theory-X	.5983*
B16	.6512*	D7	.4870*	Theory-Y	.7694*
B17	.6171*	D8	.5470*		

Note: a. Reliability coefficients are correlations between response scores obtained from first task and those obtained from second task.
b. Two-tailed test with N=30; "*" indicates coefficients are at 1% significance level; non-asterisked coefficients are insignificant at 5% significance level.
c. Notations for items are equivalent to those in Appendix I.

Table AII - 2 **Composition and Reliability of Multiple Indicators Pertaining to Conceptual Components of Bureaucratic Ideology**

Items \ Conceptual Components	BURO	INTBURO	INTBIDL	EXTBIDL	INTBNST
B1	x *	x	x	x *	
B2	x	x	x		
B3	x *	x *	x *		
B4	x *	x *	x *		
B5	x *			x *	
B6	x			x	
B7	x			x	
B8	x *	x	x	x *	
B9	x *	x	x	x *	
B10	x *	x *	x *		
B11	x *	x *	x *	x	
B12	x	x	x		
B13	x *	x *	x *	x *	
B14	x *	x *	x *	x	
B15	x *	x *	x *		
B16	x *	x *			x *
B17	x *	x *			x *

(continued on next page)

Table AII - 2 (continued) **Composition and Reliability of Multiple Indicators Pertaining to Conceptual Components of Bureaucratic Ideology**

Conceptual Components / Items	BURO	INTBURO	INTBIDL	EXTBIDL	INTBNST
B18	x *	x *			x *
B19	x *	x *			x *
B20	x *	x *			x *
B21	x *	x *			x *
B22	x *	x *			x *
B23	x *	x *			x *
B24	x	x			x *
B25	x *	x *			x *
B26	x *	x *			x *
Reliability of Original Indicator	.7774	.7727	.6154	.5567	.6600
Reliability of Reconstructed Indicator	.7950	.7874	.6037	.5761	.6672

Note: Items marked by "X" are those initially supposed to measure conceptual components. Items asterisked are those selected on grounds of having significant and postive factor loadings on conceptual components treated as factors. Items marked by "X" without astersiks are those dropped since they had insignificant or negative factor loadings. Reliability coefficient in last two rows is Cronbach's standardized item "a." "n/a" means reliability coefficient cannot be computed since multiple indicator has no or only one component item.

ponent of a multiple indicator, its factor loading should be positive and significantly different from zero. I estimated factor loading(s) of each item on its corresponding factor(s) using the LISREL 7 computer program. This test produced a result that was more conservative than the first one. That is, as presented in Tables AII-2 and AII-3, a number of items including those that failed to pass the reliability test were found to have insignificant or negative factor loadings.

Following the conservative result, I dropped the items that failed the second test, and reconstructed the multiple indicators only with those items that passed the test. In sum, the multiple indicators actually utilized for my study are composed only of those questionnaire items which were found to be highly reliable and which have significant and positive factor loadings on the conceptual components which the items are supposed to measure (i.e., those asterisked in Tables AII-2 and AII-3).

Note that this saturation procedure resulted in discarding several multiple indicators, either because no or only one item was left (i.e., INTEDIDL, INTEDEMO, INTLDIDL, INTLDNST, EXTEDIDL, INTEDNST, and EXTPDIDL), or because the reliability of the multiple indicator reconstructed after saturation became too low (i.e, INTLDEMO). Thus, the R-methodological analyses of bureaucrats' attitudes and beliefs, which I initially intended to measure with these multiple indicators, were not pursued.

Reliability and Validity of Multiple Indicators

I tested the reliability of both original and reconstructed multiple indicators in terms of Cronbach's standardized item α. Considering that the sample size for this test (i.e., 298) was relatively small, I judged a multiple indicator as reliable if the a was greater than or equal to 0.4. As presented in Tables AII-2 and AII-3 (refer to the last two rows of the tables), the reliablility of most original multiple indicators were enhanced after they were saturated. Of 25 multiple indicators, 16 of them were identified as reliable. I checked the validity of each multiple indicator identified as reliable using Campbell and Fiske's (1959) multitrait-multimethod matrix method. By equating my conceptual components with their conception of "traits," I judged a multiple indicator as valid especially when it met the following three criteria:[2]

a. The validity coefficients [i.e., correlations among the same traits measured by different methods (in my case, self-recording and card sorting methods were used) must be significantly different from zero)
b. Each validity coefficient should be greater than all different-trait, different-method correlations

Table AII - 3 **Composition & Reliability of Multiple Indicators Pertaining to Conceptual Components of Democratic Ideology**

Conceptual Components / Items	DEMO	LIB-DEMO	EQ-DEMO	POP-DEMO	INT-DEMO	INTL-DEMO	INTE-DEMO	INTP-DEMO	INT-DIDL	EXT-DIDL
D1	x *	x *			x	x			x	x *
D2	x *	x *			x	x			x	x *
D3	x *	x *			x *	x *			x *	
D4	x	x			x	x			x	
D5	x	x			x	x			x	
D6	x *	x			x					x *
D7	x		x		x		x		x	x
D8	x		x		x		x		x	x
D9	x		x		x		x		x	
D10	x		x		x		x		x	

(continued on next page)

Table AII - 3 (continued) **Composition & Reliability of Multiple Indicators Pertaining to Conceptual Components of Democratic Ideology**

Conceptual Components / Items	DEMO	LIB-DEMO	EQ-DEMO	POP-DEMO	INT-DEMO	INTL-DEMO	INTE-DEMO	INTP-DEMO	INT-DIDL	EXT-DIDL
D11	x *		x *							x *
D12	x *			x *	x *			x *	x *	
D13	x			x	x			x *	x	
D14	x			x						x
D15	x *			x *	x *			x	x *	
D16	x *			x *						x *

(continued on next page)

Table AII - 3 (continued) **Composition & Reliability of Multiple Indicators Pertaining to Conceptual Components of Democratic Ideology**

Conceptual Components / Items	DEMO	LIB-DEMO	EQ-DEMO	POP-DEMO	INT-DEMO	INTL-DEMO	INTE-DEMO	INTP-DEMO	INT-DIDL	EXT-DIDL
D17	x *	x *			x *	x *				
D18	x	x			x	x				
D19	x		x		x		x			
D20	x *		x *		x *		x *			
D21	x *			x *	x *			x *		
D22	x *			x *	x *			x *		
Reliability of Original Indicator	.5774	.4842	.1613	.4583	.5361	.4161	.1933	.5546	.3501	.3336
Reliability of Reconstructed Indicator	.7101	.4681	.1082	.5795	.6636	.2266	n/a	.5459	.4453	.4545

(continued on next page)

Table AII - 3 (continued) **Composition & Reliability of Multiple Indicators Pertaining to Conceptual Components of Democratic Ideology**

Conceptual Components / Items	INTD-INST	INTL-DIDL	EXTL-DIDL	INTL-DNST	INTE-DIDL	EXTE-DIDL	INTE-DNST	INTP-DIDL	EXTP-DIDL	INTP-DNST
D1		x	x *							
D2		x	x *							
D3		x *								
D4		x								
D5		x								
D6			x *							
D7					x	x				
D8					x	x				
D9					x					
D10					x					

(continued on next page)

Table AII - 3 (continued) **Composition & Reliability of Multiple Indicators Pertaining to Conceptual Components of Democratic Ideology**

Conceptual Components / Items	INTD-INST	INTL-DIDL	EXTL-DIDL	INTL-DNST	INTE-DIDL	EXTE-DIDL	INTE-DNST	INTP-DIDL	EXTP-DIDL	INTP-DNST
D11						x *				
D12								x *		
D13								x		
D14									x	
D15								x *		
D16									x	*
D17	x *			x *						
D18	x			x						
D19	x						x			
D20	x *						x *			

(continued on next page)

Table AII - 3 (continued) **Composition & Reliability of Multiple Indicators Pertaining to Conceptual Components of Democratic Ideology**

Conceptual Components / Items	INTD-INST	INTL-DIDL	EXTL-DIDL	INTL-DNST	INTE-DIDL	EXTE-DIDL	INTE-DNST	INTP-DIDL	EXTP-DIDL	INTP-DNST
D21	x *								x	*
D22	x *								x	*
Reliability of Original Indicator	.4072	.4474	.4545	-.3849	.2891	-.2022	.1524	.3829	-.1640	.3960
Reliability of Reconstructed Indicator	.5383	n/a	.4545	n/a	n/a	n/a	n/a	.4685	n/a	.3960

Note: Items marked "X" are those initially supposed to measure conceptual components. Items asterisked are those selected on grounds of having significant and positive factor loadings on conceptual components treated as factors. Items marked "X" without asterisks are those dropped since they had insignificant or negative factor loadings. Reliability coefficient in last two rows is Cronbach's standardized item "a." "n/a" means reliability coefficient cannot be computed since multiple indicator has no or only one component item.

c. Each validity coefficient should be greater than all different-trait, same-method correlations

According to the result of this test, the reconstructed multiple indicators are fairly valid. As presented in Table AII-4, the validity coefficients of all multiple indicators are significantly different from zero (thus, the first criterion is met completely). As summarized in Table AII-5, of 364 cases of comparisons between the validity coefficients and the different-trait, different-method correlations, only 16 cases indicate that the different-trait, different-method correlations are greater than the validity coefficients (thus, the second criterion is met fairly well). Of 364 cases of comparisons between the validity coefficients and the different-trait, same-method correlations, 114 cases indicate that the latter is greater than the former (see Table AII-6). Thus, of the three criteria, the third criterion is met to the least degree.[3]

Note that in the comparisons for this test, all multiple indicators are assumed to measure different traits. This assumption, however, seems to make the test too conservative. As I described in Chapter Four (see especially Figure 4-1), the conceptual components were construed deductively starting from the most abstract and inclusive ones to the most susbstantive and specific ones. Thus, the more specific conceptual components are parts of the more inclusive conceptual components. For example, INTBURO, INTBIDL, EXTBIDL, and INTBINST all constitute parts of the more inclusive conceptual component, BURO. Similarly, INTBIDL and INTBINST are included in INTBURO. This pattern is also reflected in the composition of the multiple indicators. For example, multiple indicators of BURO include all components of other indicators of sub-conceptual components of bureaucratic ideology. This suggests that the trait differences would lie more acutely between the conceptual components of bureaucratic ideology and those of democratic ideology, than among the conceptual components within each type of ideology. When this speculation was applied, my multiple indicators met both of the second and third criteria. That is, all of the validity coefficients pertaining to bureaucratic multiple indicators were greater than the different-trait, different-method correlations pertaining to democratic multiple indicators, and vice versa. Also, all of the validity coefficients pertaining to bureaucratic multiple indicators are greater than the different-trait, same-method correlations pertaining to democratic multiple indicators, and vice versa.

Table AII - 4 **Validity of Multiple Indicators**

Multiple Indicators	Valididity Coefficients	Multiple Indicators	Valididity Coefficients
BURO	.7768**	INTPDEMO	.5645**
DEMO	.6613**	INTBIDL	.7495**
LIBDEMO	.5116**	EXTBIDL	.4193*
POPDEMO	.6406**	INTBINST	.7764**
INTBURO	.8212**	INTDIDL	.4305*
INTDEMO	.6688**	EXTDIDL	.7019**
INTLDEMO	.4550*	INTDINST	.7926**

Note: a. Validity coefficient is correlation between response scores on a multiple indicator measured by self-recording method and response scores on the same multiple indicator measured by card-sorting method.
b. N = 30.
c. "*" indicates significant at 5%significance level; "**" indicates significant at 1% significance level.
d. See Table A2 - 3 for specific components of the multiple indicators.

Table AII - 5 **Comparisons of Validity Coefficients & Correlations Among Different Traits Measured by Different Methods**

Multiple Indicators	Validity Coefficient	Correlations among Different Traits Measured by Two Different Methods								
		.2333	.1415	.1868	.8072	.2111	.1466	.1901	.7205	.5006
BURO	.7768**	.7700	.2242	.1766	.1410	-.0416	-.2184	.0730	.7708	-.0359
		-.1435	.0408	.6510	.4280	.7444	-.0055	-.0337	-.0504	
		-.0416	.4915	.4427	-.0321	.6007	.3989	.3737	.1342	-.0198
DEMO	.6613**	-.1424	.2867	.4976	.6576	.2333	.3954	.6034	.1823	.5599
		.1448	.5549	.2863	.1868	.0868	.3497	.5505	.6028	
		-.2184	.3954	.0655	-.1815	.2772	.3668	.0351	-.0134	-.2125
LIBDEMO	.5116**	-.2752	.0630	.3971	.3540	.1415	.4915	.2749	.1438	.2821
		.0661	.2365	.2275	.0153	.0674	.0974	.6073	.3588	
		.0730	.6034	.2749	.0735	.6203	.2389	.5667	.1930	.0607
POPDEMO	.6406**	-.0173	.3722	.3664	.6235	.1868	.4427	.0655	.1382	.4725
		.0078	.5912	.2110	.1394	.0698	.3177	.2242	.4928	
		.7708	.1823	.1438	.1382	.1216	.0776	.1461	.7632	.4467
INTBURO	.8212**	.7626	.1974	.1906	.0314	.8072	-.0321	-.1815	.0735	-.0130
		-.1205	.0589	.7019	.3932	.7876	-.0047	-.0477	-.0164	
		-.0359	.5599	.2821	.4725	-.0130	.4369	.4578	.1059	-.0570
INTDEMO	.6688**	-.0930	.2832	.2267	.7584	.2111	.6007	.2772	.6203	.1216
		.3015	.6247	.2210	.3154	.0376	.4897	.2633	.6696	
		-.1435	.1448	.0661	.0078	-.1205	.3015	.0086	-.0900	-.1162
INTLDEMO	.4550*	-.1270	-.0338	-.0975	.4596	.1466	.3989	.3668	.2389	.0776
		.4369	.2594	.0981	.2737	.0530	.3775	.1856	.3972	

(continued on next page)

Table AII - 5 (continued) **Comparisons of Validity Coefficients & Correlations Among Different Traits Measured by Different Methods**

Multiple Indicators	Validity Coefficient	Corrélations among Different Traits Measured by Two Different Methods								
INTPDEMO	.5645**	.0408	.5549	.2365	.5912	.0589	.6247	.2594	.1717	-.0077
		-.0256	.3409	.2710	.6526	.1901	.3737	.0351	.5667	.1461
		.4578	.0086	.2243	.1378	.0731	.2874	.1020	.4919	
INTBIDL	.7495**	.6510	.2863	.2275	.2110	.7019	.2210	.0981	.2243	.3790
		.5850	.2310	.2629	.1505	.7205	.1342	-.0134	.1930	.7632
		.1059	-.0900	.1717	.2548	.6663	-.0094	.1232	.1668	
EXTBIDL	.4193*	.4280	.1868	.0153	.1394	.3932	.3154	.2737	.1378	.2548
		.4412	.1301	-.0365	.3601	.5006	.0198	-.2125	.0607	.4467
		-.0570	-.1162	-.0077	.3790	.4303	.0376	.0428	-.1125	
INTBINST	.7764**	.7444	.0868	.0674	.0698	.7876	.0376	.0530	.0731	.6663
		.4303	.1474	.1154	-.0533	.7700	-.1424	-.2752	-.0173	.7626
		-.0930 -	.1270 -	.0256	.5850	.4412	.0009	.1593	.1402	
INTDIDL	.4305*	-.0055	.3497	.0974	.3177	-.0047	.4897	.3775	.2874	-.0094
		.0376	-.0009	.0541	.5077	.2242	.2867	.0630	.3722	.1974
		.2832 -	.0338	.3409	.2310	.1301	.1474	.1788	.2379	

(continued on next page)

Table AII - 5 (continued) **Comparisons of Validity Coefficients & Correlations Among Different Traits Measured by Different Methods**

Multiple Indicators	Validity Coefficient	Correlations among Different Traits Measured by Two Different Methods								
		-.0337	.5505	.6073	.2242	-.0477	.2633	.1856	.1020	.1232
EXTDIDL	.7019**	.0428	-.1593	.1788	.2495	.1766	.4976	.3971	.3664	.1906
		.2267	-.0975	.2710	.2629	-.0365	.1154	.0541	.3053	
		-.0504	.6028	.3588	.4928	-.0164	.6696	.3972	.4919	.1668
INTDINST	.7926**	-.1125	-.1402	.2379	.3053	.1410	.6576	.3540	.6235	.0314
		.7584	.4596	.6526	.1505	.3601 -	.0533	.5077	.2495	

Note: a. Validity coefficient is correlation between same traits measured by two different methods.
b. N = 30; two-tailed test; "*" indicates significant at 5% significance level; "**" indicates significant at 1% significance level.
c. Correlations boxed are those that are greater than corresponding validity coefficient.

Table AII - 6 **Comparisons of Validity Coefficients & Correlations Among Different Traits Measured by Same Methods**

Multiple Indicators	Validity Coefficient	Correlations Among Different Traits Measured by Two Different Methods								
BURO	.7768**	.3706	.1550	.4002	.9742	.2791	.0265	.3874	.8734	.8248
		.9266	.4078	.3488	.1053	.1185	.0267	.1256	.9713	.1236
		.1371	.1140	.8469	.6433	.9202	.1451	.0642	.0856	
DEMO	.6613**	.3706	.7727	.7892	.3689	.8695	.5044	.7538	.4289	.3101
		.2835	.7205	.7998	.7290	.1185	.7988	.8116	.0388	.8973
		.6124	.7984	.2496	.2192	-.1087	.7407	.7578	.8399	
LIBDEMO	.5116**	.1550	.7727	.3147	.1520	.4917	.6305	.3018	.2262	.1165
		.0829	.4394	.8368	.3890	.0267	.7988	.3573	.0145	.5812
		.6542	.3759	.2492	.0485	-.1458	.5383	.8056	.5032	
POPDEMO	.6406**	.4002	.7892	.3147	.4145	.8218	.1300	.9693	.4174	.3036
		.3628	.7508	.4664	.6381	.1256	.8116	.3573	.0329	.8709
		.3425	.9736	.1592	.2073	-.0568	.6550	.4041	.8599	
INTBURO	.8212**	.9742	.3689	.1520	.4145	.3024	.0139	.4240	.8953	.6817
		.9521	.4031	.3174	.1424	.9713	.0388	.0145	.0329	.0065
		.0265	.0225	.8752	.4592	.9453	.0081	.0713	.0041	
INTDEMO	.6688**	.2791	.8695	.4917	.8218	.3024	.5729	.8496	.3211	.1945
		.2533	.7667	.3988	.8836	.1236	.8973	.5812	.8709	.0065
		.7022	.9111	.1659	.3187	-.1020	.8406	.3918	.9255	
INTLDEMO	.4550*	.0265	.5044	.6305	.1300	.0139	.5729	.1678	.0187	.0699
		.0089	.4556	.2403	.4942	.1371	.6124	.6542	.3425	.0265
		.7022	.3972	.0925	.4179	-.0218	.8197	.2383	.4894	

(continued on next page)

Table AII - 6 (continued) **Comparisons of Validity Coefficients & Correlations Among Different Traits Measured by Same Methods**

Multiple Indicators	Validity Coefficient	Correlations Among Different Traits Measured by Two Different Methods								
INTPDEMO	.5645**	.3874	.7538	.3018	.9693	.4240	.8496	.1678	.4047	.2346
		.3863	.7611	.3669	.6707	.1140	.7984	.3759	.9736	.0225
		.9111	.3972	.1715	.1999	-.0812	.6802	.3172	.9032	
INTBIDL	.7495**	.8734	.4289	.2262	.4174	.8953	.3211	.0187	.4047	.6204
		.7161	.3479	.4061	.2096	.8469	.2496	.2492	.1592	.8752
		.1659	.0925	.1715	.4360	.6694	.1238	.2748	.1645	
EXTBIDL	.4193*	.8248	.3101	.1165	.3036	.6817	.1945	.0699	.2346	.6204
		.6421	.3494	.3393	.0257	.6433	.2192	.0485	.2073	.4592
		.3187	.4179	.1999	.4360	.4110	.4702	-.0143	.1535	
INTBINST	.7764**	.9266	.2835	.0829	.3628	.9521	.2533	.0089	.3863	.7161
		.6421	.3927	.2184	.0792	.9202	-.1087	-.1458	-.0568	.9453
		-.1020	-.0218	-.0812	.6694	.4110	-.0710	-.0758	-.1046	
INTDIDL	.4305*	.4078	.7205	.4394	.7508	.4031	.7667	.4556	.7611	.3479
		.3494	.3927	.4058	.3769	.1451	.7407	.5383	.6550	.0081
		.8406	.8197	.6802	.1238	.4702	-.0710	.3011	.5729	

(continued on next page)

Table AII - 6 (continued) **Comparisons of Validity Coefficients & Correlations Among Different Traits Measured by Same Methods**

Multiple Indicators	Validity Coefficient	Correlations Among Different Traits Measured by Two Different Methods								
EXTDIDL	.7019**	.3488	.7998	.8368	.4664	.3174	.3988	.2403	.3669	.4061
		.3393	.2184	.4058	.2795	.0642	.7578	.8056	.4041	.0713
		.3918	.2383	.3172	.2748 -	.0143 -	.0758	.3011	.3824	
INTDINST	.7926**	.1053	.7290	.3890	.6381	.1424	.8836	.4942	.6707	.2096
		.0257	.0792	.3769	.2795	.0856	.8399	.5032	.8599	.0041
		.9255	.4894	.9032	.1645	.1535	-.1046	.5729	.3824	

Note: a. Validity coefficient is correlation between same traits measured by two different methods.
b. N = 30; two-tailed test; "*" indicates significant at 5% significance level; "**" indicates significant at 1% significance level.
c. Ccorrelations boxed are those that are greater than corresponding validity coefficient.

NOTES

1 Of the items that failed to pass the test, the p-values of two items are approximately .05 (i.e., D3 and B7).

2 In addition to these three criteria, Campbell and Fiske suggested another criterion. It is that the same pattern of correlations (i.e., the order of size) should be evidenced within each cluster of the different-trait, different-method correlations and the different-trait, same-method correlations. This criterion is useful especially when causal relationships are presumed among the traits (Sullivan and Feldman, 1979:23). I did not employ this criterion because I did not presume any causal relationships among the conceptual components.

3 The results are shown without presenting the matrix because the correlation matrix was so large (i.e., 50 x 50). The matrix can be made available from the author upon request.

Bibliography

Aberbach, J.D., Putnam R.D., and Rockman B.A. (1981), *Bureaucrats and Politicians in Western Democracies*, Cambridge, Mass., Harvard University Press.

Adamson, W. (1980), *Hegemony and Revolution: A Study of Antonio Gramsci's Political and Cultural Theory*, Berkeley, CA, University of California Press.

Ahn, Hae-Kyun (1984), *Introduction to Policy Studies*, Seoul, Dasan.

Allison, G. (1971), *Essence of Decision*, Boston, Little, Brown.

Allensworth, D. (1973), *Public Adminisitration: The Execution of Public Policy*, New York, J.B. Lippincott.

Almond, G. and Verba, S. (eds.) (1980), *The Civic Culture Revisited*, Boston, Little, Brown.

_____ and Verba, S. (eds.) (1963), *The Civic Culture: Political Attitudes and Democracy in Five Nations*, Boston, Little, Brown.

Althusser, L. (1970), *For Marx*, New York, Vintage.

Amariglio, J., Resnick, S. and Wolff, R. (1988), 'Class, Power, and Culture', in Nelson, C. and Grossberg, L. (eds.), *Marxism and Interpretation of Culture*, Urbana, IL, University of Illinois Press.

Argyris, C. (1973a), 'Some Limits of Rational Man Organizational Theory', *Public Administration Review*, 33:3, pp. 253-267.

_____ (1973b), 'Organization Man: Rational *and* Self-Actualizing', *Public Administration Review*, 33:4, pp. 354-357.

Bardach, E. (1977), *The Implementation Game: What Happens After a Bill Becomes a Law*, Cambridge, Mass., MIT Press.

Barley, S. (1983), 'Semiotics and the Study of Occupational and Organizational Culture', *Administrative Science Quarterly*, 28:3, pp. 393-413.

Beckwith, B. (1972), *Government By Experts: The Next Stage in Political Evolution*, New York, Exposition Press.

Beetham, D. (1987), *Bureaucracy*, Minneapolis, MN, University of Minnesota Press.

Bell, D. (1975), 'The Revolution of Rising Entitlements', *Fortune*, April 1975, pp. 98-103.

Bellone, C. (ed.) (1980), *Organization Theory and the New Public Administration*, Boston, Allyn and Bacon.

_____ and Nigro, L. (1980), 'Theories of Value Formation and Administrative Theory', in Bellone, C. (ed.), *Organization Theory and the New Public Administration*, Boston, Allyn and Bacon, pp. 52-67.

Bennis, W. (ed.) (1970a), *American Bureaucracy*, Hawthorne, NY, Aldine.

_____ (1970b), 'A Funny Thing Happened on the Way to the Future', *American Psychology*, 25, pp. 595-608.

_____ (1968), 'The Coming Death of Bureaucracy', in Athos, A. and Coffy, R. (eds.), *Behavior in Organizations*, Englewood Cliffs, NJ, Prentice Hall, pp. 256-266.

_____ and Slater, P. (1968), *The Temporary Society*, New York, Harper and Row.

Berger, C. and Cummings, L. (1979), 'Organizational Structure, Attitudes, and Behaviors', in Staw, B. (ed.), *Research in Organizational Behavior: An Annual Series of Annalytical Essays and Critical Reviews*, 1, Greenwich, CT, JAI Press, pp. 169-208.

Berger, P. and Luckmann, T. (1966), *The Social Construction of Reality*, New York, Doubleday.

Bhagat, R. and McQuaid, S. (1982), 'Role of Subjective Culture in Organizations: A Review and Directions for Future Research', *Journal of Applied Psychology*, Monograph, 67, pp. 653-685.

Blau, P. (1956), *Bureaucracy in Modern Society*, New York, Random House.

_____ (1955), *The Dynamics of Bureaucracy: A Study of Interpersonal Relations in Two Government Agencies*, Chicago, University of Chicago Press.

Bolan, R. (1987), 'Social Welfare, Dependency and Social Development', *Social Development Issues*, 11:1, pp. 3-20.

Brayfield, A. and Crockett, J. (1955), 'Employee Attitudes and Employee Performance', *Psychological Bulletin*, 52, pp. 284-290.

Broms, H. and Gahmberg, H. (1983), 'Communication to Self in Organizations and Cultures', *Administrative Science Quarterly*, 28:3, pp. 482-495.

Brown, S. (1980), *Political Subjectivity: Applications of Q-Methodology in Political Science*, New Haven, CT, Yale University Press.

_____ (1970), 'On the Use of Variance Designs in Q Methodology', *Psychological Record*, 20, pp. 179-189.

Burnham, J. (1960), *Managerial Revolution*, Bloomington, IN, Indiana University Press.

Buroway, M. (1985), *The Politics of Production: Factory Regimes Under Capitalism and Socialism*, London, Verso.

Burrel, G. and Morgan, G. (1979), *Sociological Paradigms and Organizational Analysis*, London, Heinemann Educational Books.

Burris, B. and Heyderbrand, W. (1979), 'Technocratic Administration and Educational Control', in Wilson, J. (ed.), *New Directions for Higher Education: Management Science Applications to Academic Administration*, San Francisco, CA, Jossey-Bass. (Also in Fischer, F. and Sirianni, C. (eds.) (1984), *Critical Studies in Organization and Bureaucracy*, Philadelphia, PA, Temple University Press, pp. 191-210.

Calder, B. and Schurr, P. (1981), 'Attitudinal Process in Organizations', in Cummings, L. and Staw, B. (eds.), *Research in Organizational Behavior*, Greenwich, CT, JAI Press, 3, pp. 283-302.

Campbell, D. and Fiske, D. (1959), 'Convergent and Discriminant Validation by the Multitrait-multimethod Matrix', *Psychological Bulletin*, 56, pp. 81-105.Carnoy, M. (1984), *The State and Political Theory*, Princeton, NJ, Princeton University Press.

Carroll, S. and Tosi, H. (1970), 'Goal Characteristics and Personality Factors in a Management-By-Objectives Program', *Administrative Science Quarterly*, 15:3, pp. 295-305.

Chackerian, R. and Abcarian, G. (1984), *Bureaucratic Power in Society*, Chicago, Nelson-Hall.

Cho, Suk-Jun, (1991), *Korean Public Administration*, Seoul, Bakyoungsa.

Clark, M. (1977), *Antonio Gramsci and the Revolution that Failed*, New Haven, CT, Yale University Press.

Clegg, S. and Dunkerly, D. (1980), *Organization, Class and Control*, London, Routledge and Kegan Paul.

Crozier, M., Huntington, S. and Watanuk, J. (1975), *The Crisis of Democracy*, New York, New York University Press.

D'Andrade, R. (1984), 'Cultural Meaning System', in Shweder, R. and LeVine, R. (eds.), *Culture Theory: Essays on Mind, Self and Emotion*, Cambridge, Cambridge University Press, pp. 88-119.

Dannhauser, W. (1980), 'Reflections on Statesmanship and Bureaucracy', in Goldwin, R. (ed.), *Bureaucrats, Policy Analysts, Statesmen: Who Leads?* Washington D.C., American Enterprise Institute for Public Policy Research, pp. 114-132.

Denhardt, R. (1981), 'Toward a Critical Theory of Public Organization', *Public Administrative Review*, 41:6, pp. 628-635.

_____ and Denhardt, K. (1979), 'Public Administration and the Critique of Domination', *Administration and Society*, 11:1, pp. 107-120.

Dennis, J., Lindberg, L., McCrone, D. and Stiefbold, R. 'Political Socialization to Democratic Orientations in Four Western Systems', *Comparative Political Studies*, 1:1, pp. 71-101.

DiTomaso, N. (1984), 'Class and Politics in the Organization of Public Administration: The U.S. Department of Labor', in Fischer, F. and Sirianni, C. (eds.) *Critical Studies in Organization and Bureaucracy*,

Philadelphia, PA, Temple University Press, pp. 334-355.

Donnellon, A., Gray, B. and Bougon, M. (1986), 'Communication, Meaning, and Organized Action', *Administrative Science Quarterly*, 31:1, pp. 43-55.

Dowling, W. (1977), 'Conversation with B. F. Skinner', in Staw, B. (ed.), *Psychological Foundations of Organizational Behavior*, Glenview, IL, Scott, Foresman, pp. 30-38.

Dunn, W. and Fozouni, B. (1976), *Toward a Critical Administrative Theory*. Beverly Hills, CA, Sage.

Durkheim, E. (1964), *The Rules of Sociological Method*, New York, Free Press.

Edwards, R. (1978), 'The Social Relations of Production at the Point of Production', *Work and Labor* (special issue of *The Insurgent Sociologist*, 8:2-3, pp. 109-125. (Also in Fischer, F. and Sirianni, C. (eds.) (1984), *Critical Studies in Organization and Bureaucracy*, Philadelphia, PA, Temple University Press, pp. 109-142.)

Elmore, R. (1978), 'Organizational Models of Social Program Implementation', *Public Policy*, 26:2, pp. 185-228.

Ettlie, J. and O'Keefe, R. (1982), 'Innovative Attitudes, Values, and Interventions in Organizations', *Journal of Management Studies*, 19:2, pp. 163-182.

Etzioni-Halevy, E. (1985), *Bureaucracy and Democracy* (rev. ed.), London, Routledge and Kegan Paul.

Fainstein, S. and Fainstein, N. (1980), 'The Political Economy of American Bureaucracy', in Weiss, C. and Barton, A. (eds.) *Making Bureaucracues Work*, Beverly Hills, CA, Sage, pp. 279-298.

Fayol, H. (1949), *General and Industrial Management* (tr. C. Storrs), London, Sir Isaac Pitman and Sons.

Fine, G. (1984), 'Negotiated Orders and Organizational Cultures', *Annual Reviews of Sociology*, 10, pp. 239-262.

Fishbein, M. (ed.) (1967), *Readings in Attitude Theory and Measurement*, New York, Wiley and Sons.

Fleishman, E. and Peters, P. (1962), 'Interpersonal Values, Leadership Attitudes and Managerial Success', *Personal Psychology*, 15, pp. 127-143.

Forester, J. (1983), 'Critical Theory and Organizational Analysis', in Morgan, G. (ed.), *Beyond Method: Strategies for Social Research*, Beverly Hills, CA, Sage, pp. 234-246.

Frederickson, H. (1980), *New Public Administration*, University, AL, University of Alabama Press.

_____ (1971), 'Toward a New Public Administration', in Marini, F. (ed.), *Toward a New Public Administration: The Minnowbrook Perspective*, Scranton, PA, Chandler, pp. 319-331.

Friedrich, C. (1976), 'Reflections on Democracy and Bureaucracy', in Griffth, J. (ed.), *From Policy to Administration: Essays in Honor of William A. Robson*, London, Allen & Unwin, pp. 39-54.

_____ and Cole, T. (1932), *Responsible Bureaucracy - A Study of Swiss Civil Service*, Cambridge, Mass., Harvard University Press.

Frost, P., *et al.* (1985), *Organizational Culture*, Beverly Hills, CA, Sage.

Geertz, C. (1964), *The Interpretation of Culture*, New York, Basic Books.

Gerth, H. and Mills, C. (eds.) (1946), *From Max Weber: Essays in Sociology*, New York, Oxford University Press.

Golembiewsky, R. (1977), *Public Administration as a Developing Discipline*, (parts 1 and 2), New York, Marcel Dekker.

Goodnow, F. (1900), *Politics and Administration*, New York, Macmillan.

Goslin, D. (ed.) (1971), *Handbook of Socialization Theory and Research*, Chicago, Rand McNally.

Gouldner, A. (1957), 'Cosmopolitans and Locals: Toward an Analysis of Latent Social Roles', *Administrative Science Quarterly*, 2:3, pp. 282-292.

Gramsci, A. (1971), *Selections from the Prison Notebooks*, (ed. and tr. Q. Hoare and F. Smith), New York, International Publishers.

Gregory, K. (1983), 'Native-View Paradigms: Multiple Cultures and Culture Conflicts in Organizations', *Administrative Science Quarterly*, 28:3, pp. 359-376.

Griffith, J. (ed.) (1976), *From Policy to Administration: Essays in Honor of William A. Robson*, London, Allen & Unwin.

Gruber, J. (1987), *Controlling Bureaucracies: Dilemmas in Democratic Governance*, Berkeley, CA, University of California Press.

Gulik, L. (1937a), 'Notes on the Theory of Organization', in Gulik, L. and Urwick, L. (eds.), *Papers on the Science of Administration*, New York, Institute of Public Administration, pp. 3-45.

_____ and Urwick, L. (eds.) (1937a), *Papers on the Science of Administration*, New York, Institute of Public Administration.

Habermas, J. (1981), *The Theory of Communicative Action Vol. 1: Reason and the Rationalization of Society*, (tr. T. McCarthy), Boston, Mass., Beacon Press.

_____ (1979), *Communication and the Evolution of Society*, (tr. T. McCarthy), Boston, Beacon Press.

Hall, R. (1963), 'The Concept of Bureaucracy: An Empirical Assessment', *American Journal of Sociology*, 69:1, pp. 32-40.

Hall, S. (1988), 'The Road in the Garden: Thatcherism Among the Theorists', in Nelson, C. and Grossberg, L. (eds.), *Marxism and Interpretation of Culture*, Urbana, IL, University of Illinois Press, pp. 35-73.

_____ (1982), 'The Discovery of 'Ideology': Return of the Repressed in Media Studies', in Gurevitch, M., Bennet, T., Curran, J. and Woollacott, J. (eds.),

Culture, Society, and the Media, London, Methuen, pp. 56-90.

Harmon, M. and Mayer, R. (1986), *Organization Theory for Public Administration*, Boston, Little, Brown.

_____ (1981), *Action Theory for Public Administration*, New York, Longman.

_____ (1980), 'Toward an Active Social Theory of Administrative Action: Some Empirical and Normative Implications', in Bellone, C. (ed.), *Organization Theory and the New Public Administration*, Boston, Allyn and Bacon, pp. 176-218.

Harring, S. (1981), 'Taylorization of Police Work: Prospects of the 1980s', *The Insurgent Sociologists*, 10:4-11, pp. 25-32. (Also in Fischer, F. and Sirianni, C. (eds.), *Critical Studies in Organization and Bureaucracy*, Philadelphia, PA, Temple University Press.)

Harvey, D. (1982), *The Limits to the Capital*, Chicago, IL, University of Chicago Press.

Hegedus, A. (1976), *Socialism and Bureaucracy*, London, Allison and Busby.

Herzberg, F. (1968), 'One More Time: How Do You Motivate Employees?', *Harvard Business Review*, 46:1, pp. 53-62.

_____ (1966), *Work and the Nature of Man*, Cleveland, OH, World.

Heyderbrand, W. (1983), 'Organization and Praxis', in Morgan, G. (ed.) *Beyond Method: Strategies for Social Research*, Beverly Hills, CA, Sage, pp. 306-320.

_____ (1977), 'Organizational Contradictions in Public Bureaucracies: Toward a Marxian Theory of Organizations', *Sociological Quarterly*, 18, pp. 83-107.

Hodges, D. (1970), 'The Relevance of 'Capital' to the Study of Bureaucracy', *Telos*, 6, pp. 234-242.

Holzner, B. (1968), *Reality Construction in Society* (rev. ed.), Cambridge, Mass., Schenkman.

Hummel, R. (1977), *The Bureaucratic Experience*, New York, St. Martin's Press.

Hwang, Sung-Don (1981), 'Korean Bureaucrats' Attitudes Toward Efficiency - Effectiveness and Democratic*ness*' (master's thesis), Graduate School of Public Administration, Seoul National University (unpublished).

Inglehart, R. (1977), *The Silent Revolution: Changing Values and Political Styles Among Western Publics*, Princeton, NJ, Princeton University Press.

Jakubouski, F. (1936), *Ideology and Superstructure in Historical Materialism*, (tr. A. Booth), New York, St. Martin's Press.

Jelinek, M., Smircich, L. and Hirsch, P. (1983), 'Introduction: A Code of Many Colors', *Administrative Science Quarterly*, 28:3, pp. 331-338.

Jessop, B. (1982), *The Capitalist State: Marxist Theories and Methods*, New York, New York University Press.

_____ (1979), 'Corporatism, Parliamentarism and Social Democracy', in

Schmitter, P. and Lehmbruch, G. (eds.), *Trends Toward Corporatist Interpretation*, Beverly Hills, CA, Sage, pp. 185-212.

_____ (1978), 'Capitalism and Democracy', in John, G., Smath, B., Wakeford, J. and Yuval-Davis, N. (eds.), *Power and the State*, New York, St. Martin's Press, pp. 10-51.

Kanter, R. (1977), *Men and Women of the Corporation*, New York, Basic Books.

Karl, Berry. (1976), 'Philanthropy, Policy Planning, and the Bureaucratization of the Democratic Ideal', *Daedulus*, 105:4, pp. 129-149.

Kim, Kwang-Woong (1981), 'Public Administrative Culture', *Korean Journal of Public Administration*, 19:2, pp. 248-265.

King, A. (1975), 'Overload: The Problem of Governing in the 1970's', *Political Studies*, 23, pp. 284-296.

Knott, J. and Miller, G. (1987), *Reforming Bureaucracy: The Politics of Institutional Choice*, Englewood Cliffs, NJ, Prentice-Hall.

Kranz, H. (1976), 'Conflict Between Bureaucracy and Democratic Theory', in Kranz, H. (ed.), *The Participatory Bureaucracy*, Lexington, Mass., D.C. Heath, pp. 31-65.

LaPier, R. (1935), 'Attitudes vs. Actions', *Social Forces*, 13, pp. 230-237.

Lee, Manwoo (1990), *The Odyssey of Korean Democracy*, New York, Praeger.

Lenin, V. (1975), *On Socialist Ideology and Culture*, Moscow, Progress Publishers.

Levi-Strauss, C. (1967), *The Scope of Anthropology*, London, Jonathan Cape.

Levine, R. (1984), 'Properties of Culture: An Ethnographic View', in Shweder, R. and Levine, R. (eds.), *Culture Theory: Essays on Mind, Self, and Emotion*, Cambridge, Cambridge University Press, pp. 67-87.

Likert, R. (1967), *The Human Organizations*, New York, McGraw-Hill.

Lindblom, C. (1979), 'Still Muddling, Not Yet Through', *Public Administration Review*, 39:6, pp. 517-526.

Lippit, R. and White, R. (1968) 'Leader Behavior and Member Reaction in Three 'Social Climates'', in Cartwright, D. and Zander, A. (eds.) *Group Dynamics* (3rd ed.), New York, Harper and Row.

Lipset, S. (1963), 'The Value Patterns of Democracy: A Case Study in Comparative Analysis', *American Sociological Review*, 28:4, pp. 515-531.

Lukacs, G. (1971), *History and Class Consciousness: Studies in Marxist Dialectics* (tr. R. Livingstone), Cambridge, Mass., MIT Press.

Lundgren, E. (1974), *Organizational Management: Systems and Process*, New York, Canfield Press.

Maclagan, P. (1983), 'The Concept of Responsibility: Some Implications of Organizational Behavior and Development', *Journal of Management Studies*, 20:4, pp. 411-423.

Mali, P. (1972), *Managing by Objectives*, New York, Wiley and Sons.
Mandel, E. (1975), *Late Capitalism* (tr. J. deBres), London, New Left Books.
Mansbridge, J. (1984), 'Feminism and the Forms of Freedom', in Fischer, F. and Sirianni, C. (eds.), *Critical Studies in Organization and Bureaucracy*, Philadelphia, PA, Temple University Press, pp. 472-481.
March, J. and Simon, H. (1958), *Organizations*, New York, Wiley and Sons.
Marini, F. (ed.) (1971), *Toward a New Public Administration: The Minnowbrook Perspective*, Scranton, PA, Chandler.
Marx, K. (1984), 'The Spirit of Bureaucracy and Beyond Bureaucracy: The Paris Commune', reprinted in Fischer, F. and Sirianni, C. (eds.), *Critical Studies in Organization and Bureaucracy*, Philadelphia, PA, Temple University Press, pp. 40-47.
_____ (1978), 'The German Ideology', in Tucker, R. (ed.), *The Marx and Engels Reader* (2nd ed.), New York, W.W. Norton, pp. 146-200.
Maslow, A. (1970), 'The Superior Person', in Bennis, W. (ed.) *American Bureaucracy*, Hawthorne, NY, Aldine, pp. 27-37.
_____ (1965), *Eupsychian Management*, Homewood, IL, Richard D. Irwin.
_____ (1962), *Toward a Psychology of Being*, Princeton, NJ, D. Van Nostrand.
_____ (1954), *Motivation and Personality*, New York, Harper and Brothers.
Mazmanian, D. and Sabatier, P. (1983), *Implementation and Public Policy*, Glenview, IL, Scott, Foresman.
_____ (ed.) (1981), *Effective Policy Implementation*, Lexington, Mass., D.C. Heath.
McClosky, H. (1964), 'Consensus and Ideology in American Politics', *American Political Science Review*, 58:2, pp. 362-382.
McConkie, M. (1979), 'A Clarification of the Goal Setting and Appraisal Process in MBO', *Academy of Management Review*, 4:1, pp. 29-40.
McCorduck, P. (1979), *Machines Who Think*, San Francisco, CA, Freeman.
McGregor, D. (1960), *The Human Side of Enterprise*, New York, McGraw-Hill.
McKeown, B. and Thomas, D. (1988), *Q-Methodology*, Beverly Hills, CA, Sage.
Medeiros, J. and Schmitt, D. (1977), *Public Bureaucracy: Values and Perspectives*, North Scituate, Mass., Duxbury Press.
Meier, K. (1987), *Politics and the Bureaucracy: Policymaking in the Fourth Branch of Government*, Monterley, CA, Books/Cole.
Merkle, J. (1968), 'The Taylor Strategy: Organizational Innovation and Class Structure', *Berkeley Journal of Sociology*, 8, pp. 59-81.
Merton, R. (1957), 'Bureaucratic Structure and Personality', in Merton, R. (ed.), *Social Theory and Social Structure* (rev. ed.), Glencoe, IL, Free Press, pp. 195-206.
Michels, R. (1915), *Political Parties* (tr. E. Paul and C. Paul), London, Jarrold and Sons.

Miliband, R. (1973), *Class Power and State Power: Political Essays*, London, Verso.

Morgan, G. (ed.) (1986), *Images of Organization*, Beverly Hills, CA, Sage.

_____ (1984), 'Opportunities Arising from Paradigm Diversity', *Administration and Society*, 16, pp. 306-327.

_____ (ed.) (1983), *Beyond Method: Strategies for Social Research*, Beverly Hills, CA, Sage.

_____ (1980), 'Paradigms, Metaphors and Puzzle Solving in Organization Theory', *Administrative Science Quarterly*, 25, pp. 605-622.

Morris, M. (1985), *Immigration: The Beleagured Bureaucracy*, Washington, D.C., Brookings Institution.

Morrow, A. and Thayer, F. (1978), 'Materialism and Humanism: Organization Theory's Odd Couple', *Administration and Society*, 10:1, pp. 86-106.

Mosher, F. (ed.) (1975), *American Public Administration: Past, Present, Future*, University, AL, University of Alabama Press.

_____ (1968), *Democracy and the Public Service*, New York, Oxford University Press.

Moskos, C. Jr. and Bell, W. (1964), 'Attitudes Towards Democracy Among Leaders in Four Emergent Nations', *British Journal of Sociology*, 15:4, pp. 317-337.

Mouzelis, N. (1967), *Organisation and Bureaucracy: An Analysis of Modern Theories*, New York, Aldine De Gruyter.

Mullet, S. (1970), 'Bureaucracy and Technocracy in the Socialist Countries', *Socialist Revolution*, 1, pp. 44-75.

Nemeth, T. (1980), *Gramsci's Philosophy: A Critical Study*, Atlantic Highlands, NJ, Humanities Press.

Niskanen, W. (1971), *Bureaucracy and Representative Government*, Chicago, Aldine-Atherton.

Nordlinger, E. (1981), *On the Autonomy of Democratic State*, Cambridge, Mass., Harvard University Press.

O'Connor, J. (1973), *The Fiscal Crisis of the State*, New York, St. Martin's Press.

Odiorne, G. (1979), *MBO II*, Belmont, CA, Fearon.

_____ (1965), *Management By Objectives*, New York, Pitman.

Offe, C. (1974), 'Structural Problems of the Capitalist States', in Von Beyme, K. (ed.), *German Political Studies*, 1, Beverly Hills, CA, Sage.

_____ (1972), 'Political Authority and Class Structures: An Analysis of Late Capitalist Societies', *International Journal of Sociology*, 2, pp. 73-108.

Olson, M. (1965), *The Logic of Collective Action: Public Goods and the Theory of Groups*, Cambridge, Mass., Harvard University Press.

Ostrom, V. (1974), *Crisis of American Public Administration* (rev. ed.), University, AL, University of Alabama Press.

Paik, Wan-Ki (1982), *Korean Public Administration Culture*, Seoul, Korea University Press.

Park, Dong-Suh (1991), *Public Administration in Korea*, Seoul, Bupmoonsa.

Parkinson, C. (1957), *Parkinson's Law*, Boston, Houghton Mifflin.

Perrow, C. (1979), *Complex Organizations* (2nd ed.), Glenview, IL, Scott, Foresman.

Peters, B. (1984), *The Politics of Bureaucracy* (2nd ed.), New York, Longman.

Pettigrew, A. (1979), 'On Studying Organizational Cultures', *Administrative Science Quarterly*, 24:4, pp. 570-581.

Pfeffer, J. (1981a), 'Management as Symbolic Action: The Creation and Maintenance of Organizational Paradigm', in Cummings, L. and Staw, B. (eds.), *Research in Organizational Behavior*, 1, Greenwich, CT, JAI Press, pp. 1-52.

_____ (1981b), *Power in Organizations*, Cambridge, MA, Ballinger.

Pindyck, R. and Rubinfeld, D. (1981), *Econometric Models and Economic Forecasts* (2nd ed.), New York, McGraw-Hill.

Pondy, L. and Mitroff, I. (1979), 'Beyond Open System Models of Organizations', in Cummings, L. and Staw, B. (eds.), *Research in Organizational Behavior*, 1, Greenwich, CT, JAI Press, pp. 3-39.

Poulantzas, N. (1978), *State, Power, Socialism* (tr. P. Camiller), London, New Left Books.

_____ (1975), *Political Power and Social Classes*, London, New Left Books.

Pressman, J. and Wildavsky, A. (1973), *Implementation*, Berkeley, CA, University of California Press.

Presthus, R. (1975), *Public Administration* (6th ed.), New York, Ronald Press.

Preston, L. (1987), 'Freedom and Bureaucracy', *American Journal of Political Science*, 31:4, pp. 737-795.

Price, D. (1973), 'Relationship of Decision Styles and Self-Actualization', *Home Economics Research Journal*, 2:1, pp. 12-20.

Rachleff, P. (1982), 'Machine Technology and Workplace Control: The U.S. Post Office', *Radical America*, 16:1-2, pp. 79-90. (Also in Fischer, F. and Sirianni, C. (eds.), *Critical Studies in Organization and Bureaucracy*, Philadelphia, PA, Temple University Press, pp. 143-156.

Radin, B. (1977), *Implementation, Change, and the Federal Bureaucracy*, New York, Teachers College Press.

Riggs, F. (1970), 'Comparison of the Whole Political System', in Holt, R. and Turner, E. (eds.), *The Methodology of Comparative Research*, New York, Free Press, pp. 73-121.

_____ (1968), 'The Dialectics of Developmental Conflict', *Comparative Political Studies*, 1:2, pp. 197-226.

Riley, P. (1983), 'A Structurationist Account of Political Culture', *Administrative Science Quarterly*, 28:3, pp. 414-437.

Rinehart, J. and Bernick, E. (1975), 'Political Attitudes and Behavior Patterns of Federal Civil Servants', *Public Administration Review*, 35:6, pp. 603-611.

Ripley, R. (1982a), *Congress, the Bureaucracy, and Public Policy Implementation*, Homewood, IL, Dorsey Press.

_____ and Franklin, G. (1982b), *Bureaucracy and Public Policy Implementation*, Homewood, IL, Dorsey Press.

Rokeach, M. (1966-1967), 'Attitude Change and Behavioral Change', *Public Opinion Quarterly*, 30:4, pp. 529-550.

Ronan, W. (1970), 'Individual and Situational Variables Relating to Job Satisfaction', *Journal of Applied Psychology*, Monograph, 54:Part 2, pp. 1-31.

Rose, R. (1979), 'Ungovernability: Is There Fire Behind the Smoke?', *Political Studies*, 27, pp. 351-370.

Rourke, F. (ed.) (1978), *Bureaucratic Power in National Politics* (3rd ed.), Boston, Little, Brown.

_____ (1976), *Bureaucracy, Politics and Public Policy* (2nd ed.), Boston, Little, Brown.

Rustad, M. (1984), 'Female Tokenism in the Volunteer Army', in Fischer, F. and Sirianni, C. (eds.), *Critical Studies in Organization and Bureaucracy*, Philadelphia, PA, Temple University Press, pp. 269-286.

Sahlins, M. (1976), *Culture and Practical Reason*, Chicago, University of Chicago Press.

Sarbin, T. and Scheibe, K. (1980), 'The Transvaluation of Social Identity', in Bellone, C. (ed.), *Organization Theory and the New Public Administration*, Boston, Allyn and Bacon, pp. 219-245.

Scott, W. (1974), 'Organization Theory: A Reassessment', *Academy of Management Journal*, 17:2, pp. 242-254.

Searing, D. (1978), 'Measuring Politicians' Values: Administration and Assessment of Ranking Technique in the British House of Commons', *American Political Science Review*, 72, pp. 65-79.

Selznick, P. (1949), *TVA and the Grass-Roots*, Berkeley, CA, University of California Press.

Sharkansky, I. (1978), *Public Administration: Policy-Making in Government Agencies* (4th ed.), Chicago, Rand McNally.

Silverman, D. (1971), *The Theory of Organizations*, New York, Basic Books.

Simon, H. (1985), 'Human Nature in Politics: The Dialogue of Psychology with Political Science', *American Political Science Review*, 79:2, pp. 293-304.

_____ (1982), *Models of Bounded Rationality*, Cambridge, Mass., MIT Press.

_____ (1981), *The Science of the Artificial* (2nd ed.), Cambridge, Mass., MIT Press.

_____ (1976), *Administrative Behavior: A Study of Decision-Making Processes in Administrative Organization* (3rd ed.), New York, Free Press.

_____ (1973), 'Organization Man: Rational or Self-Actualizing?', *Public Administration Review*, 33:4, pp. 346-353.

_____ (1957), *Models of Man*, New York, Wiley and Sons.

_____ , Smithburg, D. and Thompson, V. (1956), *Public Administration*, New York, Knopf.

_____ (1955), 'A Behavioral Model of Rational Choice', *Quarterly Journal of Economics*, 69, pp. 99-118.

Skinner, B. (1975), 'Comments on Watt's 'B.F. Skinner and the Technological Control of Social Behavior'.', *American Political Science Review*, 69:1, pp. 228-229.

Smircich, L. (1983a), 'Concept of Culture and Organizational Analysis', *Administrative Science Quarterly*, 28:3, pp. 339-358.

_____ (1983b), 'Studying Organizations as Cultures', in Morgan, G. (ed.), *Beyond Method: Strategies for Social Research*, Beverly Hills, CA, Sage, pp. 160-172.

Spiro, M. (1984), 'Some Reflections on Cultural Determinism and Relativism with Special Reference to Emotion and Reason', in Shweder, R. and Levine, R. (eds.), *Culture Theory: Essays on Mind, Self, and Emotion*, Cambridge, Cambridge University Press, pp. 323-346.

Starbuck, W. (1983), 'Organization as Action Generators', *American Sociological Review*, 48:1, pp. 91-102.

Stillman, P. (1975), 'The Limits of Behaviorism: A Review of Essays on B.F. Skinner's Social and Political Thought', *American Political Science Review*, 69:1, pp. 202-213.

Stone, A. and Stone, D. (1975), 'Early Development of Education in Public Administration', in Mosher, F. (ed.), *American Public Administration: Past, Present, Future*, University, AL, University of Alabama Press, pp. 11-48.

Strauss, E. (1961), *The Ruling Servants*, London, Allen and Unwin.

Sullivan, J. and Feldman, S. (1979), 'Multiple Indicators: An Introduction', Sage University Paper Series on Quantitative Applications in the Social Sciences, 07-015, Beverly Hills, CA, Sage.

Swidler, A. (1986), 'Culture in Action: Symbols and Strategies', *American Sociological Review*, 51:2, pp. 273-286.

Szalay, L. and Kelly, R. (1982), 'Political Ideology and Subjective Culture: Conceptualization and Empirical Assessment', *American Political Science Review*, 76:3, pp. 585-602.

Taylor, F. (1947), *Scientific Management*, New York, Harper and Brothers.

Thayer, F. (1981), *The End to Hierarchy and Competition* (2nd ed.), New York, Franklin Watts.

_____ (1980), 'Organization Theory as Epistemology: Transcending Hierarchy and Objectivity', in Bellone, C. (ed.), *Organization Theory and the New Public Administration*, Boston, Allyn and Bacon, pp. 113-139.

Therborn, G. (1978), *What Does the Ruling Class Do When It Rules?* London, New Left Books.

_____ (1977), 'The Rule of Capital and the Rise of Democracy', *New Left Review*, 103, pp. 3-41.

Thompson, V. (1977), *Modern Organizations*, University, AL, University of Alabama Press.

Toffler, A. (1970), *Future Schock*, New York, Random House.

Turner, S. (1983), 'Studying Organizations Through Levi-Strauss's Structuralism', in Morgan, G. (ed.), *Beyond Method: Strategies for Social Research*, Beverly Hills, CA, Sage, pp. 189-201. (Originally appeared as 'Complex Organization as Savage Tribes', *Journal for the Theory of Social Behavior*, 17:1, pp. 99-104).

Urban, M. (1978), 'Bureaucracy, Contradiction, and Ideology in Two Societies', *Administration and Society*, 10:1, pp. 49-84.

Van Riper, P. (1958), *History of the United States Civil Service*, Evanston, IL, Pow, Peterson.

Vroom, V. (1964), *Work and Motivation*, New York, Wiley and Sons.

Waldo, D. (1984), *The Administrative State: A Study of the Political Theory of American Public Administration* (2nd ed.), New York, Holmes and Meier.

_____ (1971) (ed.), *Public Administration in a Time of Turbulence*, New York, Chandler.

_____ (1948), *The Administrative State: Study of the Political Theory of American Public Administration*, New York, Ronald Press.

Wamsley, G. (1976), 'On the Problems of Discovering What's Really New in Public Administration', *Administration and Society*, 8:3, pp. 385-400.

Watson, T. (1982), 'Group Ideologies and Organizational Change', *Journal of Management Studies*, 19:3, pp. 259-275.

Watts, M. (1975), 'B.F. Skinner and the Technological Control of Social Behavior', *American Political Science Review*, 69:1, pp. 214-227.

Weber, M. (1958), *The Protestant Ethics and the Spirit of Capitalism* (tr. T. Parsons), New York, Allen and Unwin.

White, L. (1948), *The Federalist*, New York, Macmillan.

White, O. and McSwain, C. (1982), 'Transformational Theory and Organizational Analysis', in Morgan, G. (ed.), *Beyond Method: Strategies for Social Research*, Beverly Hills, CA, Sage, pp. 292-305.

White, W. Jr. (1956), *The Organization Man*, Garden City, NY, Doubleday.

Whyte, W. and Blasi, J. (1982), 'Worker Ownership, Participation, and Control: Toward a Theoretical Model', *Policy Science*, 14, pp. 137-163. (Also in Fischer, F. and Sirianni, C. (eds.), *Critical Studies in Organization and*

Bureaucracy, Philadelphia, PA, Temple University Press, pp. 377-405.)

Wildavsky, A. (1973), 'Government and the People', *Commentary*, 56, pp. 25-32.

Wilkins, A. and Ouchi, W. (1983), 'Efficient Cultures: Exploring the Relationship Between Culture and Organizational Performance', *Administrative Science Quarterly*, 28:3, pp. 468-481.0

Willoughby, W. (1927), *Principles of Public Administration,* Baltimore, MD, Johns Hopkins Press.

Wilson, W. (1887), 'The Study of Public Administration', *Political Science Quarterly*, 2:2, pp. 197-220.

Witte, J. (1980), *Democracy, Authority, and Alienation in Work: Workers' Participation in an American Corporation*, Chicago, University of Chicago Press.

Wolfe, A. (1977), *The Limits of Legitimacy*, New York, Free Press.

Wuthnow, R. (1985), 'State Structure and Ideological Outcomes', *American Sociological Review*, 50:6, pp. 799-821.

_____ , Hunter, J., Bergesen, A. and Kurzweil, E. (1984), *Cultural Analysis: The Work of Peter L. Berger, Mary Douglas, Michel Foucault, and Jurgen Habermas*, London, Routledge and Kegan Paul.

Wynia, B. (1974), 'Federal Bureaucrats' Attitudes Toward a Democratic Ideology', *Public Administration Review*, 34:2, pp. 156-162.

Yu, Hoon (1991), *Introduction to Public Administration*, Seoul, Bupmoonsa.

Index

A

B

E

Q

R

S

W

Y

MAJOR CONCEPTS IN POLITICS AND POLITICAL THEORY

This series invites book manuscripts and proposals on major concepts in politics and political theory—justice, equality, virtue, rights, citizenship, power, sovereignty, property, liberty, etc.—in prominent traditions, periods, and thinkers.

Send manuscripts or proposals, with author's vitae to:

Garrett Ward Sheldon
General Editor
Clinch Valley College
of the University of Virginia
College Avenue
Wise, VA 24293